Bible 101

Bible 101

God's Story in Human History

by

Duane L. Christensen

BIBAL Press
Publishing Agency of BIBAL Corporation
Berkeley Institute of Biblical Archaeology and Literature

Bible 101: God's Story in Human History

Copyright © 1996 by Duane L. Christensen and BIBAL Press

Library of Congress Cataloging-in-Publication Data
Christensen, Duane L., 1938-
    Bible 101 : God's story in human history / by Duane L. Christensen.
       p.   cm.
    Includes bibliographical references and index.
    ISBN 0-941037-42-8 (pbk. : alk. paper)
    1. Bible—Introductions.   I. Title.
QA76.76.O63S55527   1997
220.6'1—dc20   96-38518
                                       CIP

Published by BIBAL Press
P.O. Box 821653
N. Richland Hills, TX 76182

Cover by KC Scott, Ashfield, MA

Printed in the U.S.A.

To my parents
John and Elsie Christensen
who introduced me early to the
Incarnate Word of God
and encouraged me
in my study of the
Canonical Word of God
through the years

Contents

CONTENTS

CONTENTS

Publication of this work has been made possible by the generous contributions of John and Elsie Christensen and other donors to The Christensen Fund, a charitable fund administered by BIBAL Corporation, which supports the publication of deserving works in the field of biblical literature.

Preface to the Instructor

This book is intended as a textbook for a course on "Biblical Introduction," whether that course is offered to undergraduates in colleges and universities or to learners in local church settings. What distinguishes this book from other textbooks about the Bible is the fact that it consciously attempts to encourage critical thinking, to show the logical connections between ideas, and to help students to think through these connections—in short, to *think biblically.*

- *Learning Objectives* at the beginning of each chapter help students focus on key ideas. These learning objectives are easily transformed into thought-provoking essay questions.
- The *Thinking Exercises* help to develop critical thinking and writing abilities while increasing student understanding of basic concepts and fundamental questions about the Bible.
- *Concept Checks* allow students to check their understanding of main points every few pages.
- *Concept Map Summaries* provide a quick review showing how concepts connect to one another.
- *Discussion Questions* encourage an approach to critical thinking based on dialogue between teacher and students.
- *Marginal Definitions* provide a running summary and glossary of terms.

I take this opportunity to acknowledge my debt to Richard Paul, one of the more prominent leaders of the critical thinking movement, and Don Millman, who has adapted Richard Paul's concepts in a textbook for the field of economics, *Economics: Making Good Choices* (South-Western College Publishing, 1995), for inspiring me to rethink the format of this textbook.

Though this book is intended for beginners, there is much here of interest to my colleagues in the world of academia as well. Many of the ideas presented here have appeared elsewhere in journal articles, other books, academic papers, and lectures in a variety of settings.

The initial draft of this book was used as the text in a course called "Bible 101," which was taught at the Vineyard Christian Fellowship in Concord, California, in the fall of 1994. I am grateful to Pastor Daniel Brill, members of that class, and others who have offered their suggestions and criticism, especially to my students in courses taught for Fuller Theological Seminary in the Bay Area who have struggled with these ideas for the past several years.

I acknowledge my gratitude to my brother Darwin for his role in establishing the Christensen Fund, which made the publication of this book possible. As the publishing agency of BIBAL

Corporation (the *Berkeley Institute of Biblical Archaeology & Literature*), BIBAL Press is under the able direction of Dr. William Scott, whose skill did much to enhance the quality of this book. One of the ways to promote new publications which Bill has come up with is that of establishing publication funds in the name of specific donors. Books which are published in this manner bear the fund's name, and a portion of sales revenue from these books is returned to the fund so that it continues to support the publication of new books indefinitely.

I also wish to express my gratitude to Moody Press for granting me the privilege of including an abridgment of chapters 12-20 of the book by Norman L. Geisler and William A. Nix, *From God to Us: How We Got Our Bible* (Moody Press, 1974). This material appears here in chapter 4, where it is arranged in somewhat different order, updated at numerous points, and reduced in length by about 50 percent (from 116 to 60 pages).

The basic approach to the study of the Bible in this book will be unfamiliar to many readers. It is not what I was taught in my graduate studies at Harvard University, nor does it represent what is going on in the work of my colleagues in the Graduate Theological Union in Berkeley, where I taught for fifteen years (1978-1993). It is what I learned in my own teaching and personal reflection as I have struggled with the biblical text in its original languages over the course of the past twenty years.

In more than fifteen years of teaching the Old Testament at the seminary level, my research and teaching has been focused primarily on the historical-critical method and the conclusions to which it leads. During the past ten years, however, I have become increasingly aware of the fact that no matter how insightful and interesting such scholarship may be, it does not relate in a significant way to the needs of most students. No matter how hard we try to make the study of the Old Testament practical and relevant, something crucial seems to be missing.

Ten years ago (1986), Jo Milgrom, a Jewish colleague in the Graduate Theological Union (GTU) in Berkeley, introduced me to the world of rabbinic midrash in terms of a method of Bible study that utilizes right-brain activity in the study of narrative material in the Bible.[1] Classroom experiences in what she has called "Handmade Midrash" have opened new worlds of possibilities in affective learning, and have introduced me to the concept of synectics, an educational theory which is rather closely related to the ancient practice of creative midrash. As William Gordon has put it,[2]

> In synectic theory, play with apparent irrelevancies is used extensively to generate
> energy for problem solving and to evoke new viewpoints with respect to problems.
> Play generates energy because it is a pleasure in itself, an intrinsic end.

The relationship between "play" and creative adult behavior is worth exploring in greater depth, particularly in relation to the teaching of the Bible. Students learn best when they are having fun, and when their whole being is engaged in the process of learning.[3]

In 1987, I taught a seminar with Arthur Stevens of the Church Divinity School of the Pacific in Berkeley under the title "Jonah: A Spiritual Journey," which turned out to be the beginning of a significant journey of my own—a journey into the literature on spiritual direction. With the assistance of Arthur Stevens as my spiritual director, and the leisure of a one-semester sabbatical leave, I found new appreciation for the work of Gregory of Nyssa, Nicholas of Cusa, Ignatius Loyola, and a host of others from the so-called precritical period of biblical scholarship. In particular, I was reintroduced to the fascinating world of the medieval mystics in relation to both the personal spiritual journey and the biblical text.

A program of reading, prayer, and reflection led me eventually to the work of C. G. Jung, as mirrored in the writings of John Sanford. In *The Man Who Wrestled With God* (1981) and *King Saul: A Study in Individuation* (1985), Sanford shows how Old Testament stories can be seen as archetypal formulation of "the most important and fundamental process which goes on in human life: the transformation of human beings from egocentric, unconscious persons, to persons of wholeness, breadth of vision, and spiritual awareness."[4] This process, called individuation in Jungian thought, is embodied in the Old Testament stories about the transformative journey of faith.

The writings of Fritz Kunkel, once again as explicated by John Sanford, helped me to see more clearly the use of the Old Testament in my own process of individuation which emerged out of a personal crisis that led in turn to a remarkable surge of psychic energy. For me it was a series of stories within the Former Prophets (1 Kings 13, 18-19, 22; 2 Kings 22-23) and the book of Jonah, which provided a mazeway out of that crisis on an inner journey.

To my surprise, I discovered that other colleagues are apparently on similar journeys. One of the more significant parallel journeys of faith in relation to the Old Testament was brought to my attention some years ago by Lawrence Boadt of Paulist Press, who introduced me to a remarkable book by Conrad L'Heureux, a Harvard classmate of mine, entitled *Life Journey and the Old Testament* (Paulist Press, 1986). In this book, L'Heureux attempts to combine the best of modern critical study of the Old Testament with experiential encounter with the biblical text in workshops shaped by concepts from Jungian psychology.

A major task of theological education at the turn of the twenty-first century is to synthesize the impulses coming from traditional study of the Bible in academia with the emerging fields of spirituality and religious psychology—in a manner that utilizes the best of what some have called "left-brain" and "right-brain" approaches to learning. This book is written in an attempt to respond to this challenge. The focus of this textbook is on the canonical process in ancient Israel and the early Christian Church. At the same time, we do not intend to lose sight of the very nature of the individuation process in Jungian thought. In short, our goal is to integrate the historical-critical method of study with a concern for assisting "fellow travelers on the life journey." We are attempting to do what John Sanford expressed so well in the foreword to Conrad L'Heureux's book; namely, to "do what my biblical professors had not attempted to do in their classes: relate biblical stories and themes to personal life without sacrificing the valuable perspective of historical criticism."[5]

The turning point in my personal academic journey was my commitment to write the commentary on Deuteronomy for the Word Biblical Commentary series some years ago. My experience in the Hebrew text of Deuteronomy, and more recently the book of Psalms, opened my eyes to what Leonard Thompson once described as "a more fantastic country" [*Introducing Biblical Literature* (Prentice Hall, 1978)]. I gradually became aware of the fact that the Bible is much more than I had been taught. Time after time, I walked out of my study in awe at what I was beginning to see. The Bible is a single book and not a mere collection of loosely arranged texts. It has discernible structure which highlights its theological meaning.

Attempts to explain the phenomena I have observed have led me into the field of depth psychology, particularly in terms of what Carl Jung has described as the collective unconscious. I believe that the Bible was shaped through generations of transmission in professional circles in antiquity where that text was heard more than it was read. The text of the Old Testament, in particular, was chanted, or sung to music—in the broadest sense of that word. In short, the text was performed in a context of worship within a community of faith. As the canonical text of sacred Scripture was composed for liturgical usage and performed by the Levites, through generations of time, the text itself was shaped within ancient Israel, diaspora Judaism, and subsequently within the context of the Second Temple in Jerusalem. The Christian community of faith took shape within this same context and carried that canonical process to a conclusion in what is commonly called the New Testament, or what I would prefer to see as the Second Testament.

In short, the familiar liturgical description of the Bible as the "Word of God" has taken on fresh meaning for me personally. In a very real sense, the Bible is indeed "God's Story in Human History."

Duane L. Christensen
Patten College
William Carey International University

A Note to the Student

We all know that some knowledge about the Bible is essential for responsible life within the structure of our religious institutions. We also know that the great literature of past generations is only partially understood without knowing the Bible. But even though we may already have a Bible of our own; and though we may even be reading it in a devotional way, many of us still do not feel that we "know" the Bible.

For us the Bible appears to be a miscellaneous collection which includes a complex "library" of individual books. We may find individual verses that speak to us at points of personal need; but we do not have a feel for what the Bible is as a whole. We are not able to *think biblically*—the way many of our ancestors did.

My goals in writing this textbook are to communicate to you the excitement of biblical thinking and to show you how to enter the world of the Bible in ways that will help you to make better sense out of the so-called real world as well, in light of the Bible.

There are a number of aids to learning in this text:

- On the first page of each chapter are the chapter *Learning Objectives*, which tell what you should be able to do after studying the chapter.
- *Definitions* in bold type are given in the margin of the page as a running summary of main concepts.
- The *Concept Checks* allow you to test your understanding of main points every few pages. Try to answer each of these questions, then check your answer against the ones given at the end of the book. If you cannot answer these Concept Checks correctly, reread the material until you can.
- The *Thinking Exercises* are designed to develop your critical thinking and writing abilities. *Doing* these thinking exercises will add much to make the Bible more interesting and to help you to learn to think biblically.
- The *Concept Map Summaries* provide a quick review that shows how major ideas in the chapter are connected to one another. Ideas *are connected* to other ideas, and understanding comes largely from constructing these connections in your mind.
- The *Discussion Questions* are intended to encourage thought and discussion. Many instructors want students to ask questions; but students often hesitate to raise issues for discussion. These discussion questions give you a list of interesting topics to ask and to talk about.

1 The Word of God in Canon and The Word of God Incarnate

Learning Objectives

After studying the chapter, you should be able to:

1. Write an essay on "The Word of God in Complementary Forms."

2. Identify each concept in the chapter. Concepts are shown in **bold** typeface when introduced. *Identify* means:

    a. *define the term*, using your own words as much as possible,

    b. *give a specific example* to illustrate the idea, and briefly *explain the importance* of the concept. (Showing how one idea is connected to others helps to explain the significance, the relevance, and the importance of the concept.)

A. The Bible as the Word of God

Some years ago, a first-year seminary student gave me an unpublished paper which he had found useful in a personal journey out of a narrow fundamentalism into a more "enlightened" and open evangelical position, particularly in regard to his attitude toward the Bible. I read the paper with keen interest and at first was more or less persuaded by the central thesis which was argued forcefully: "that nowhere does the Bible equate itself, Scripture, with the **Word of God**."[1] But the more I thought the matter through, the more uneasy I became. I could not get away from the opening words of the book of Deuteronomy, *'elleh haddebarim* ("these are the words"). Now I know that the text goes on to say "the words of Moses." But as Robert Polzin has shown, there are at least two distinct voices present in this text—the voice of Moses and the voice of **Yahweh**, the God of ancient Israel.[2] And it is Yahweh himself whom Moses is quoting. In fact, the familiar liturgical expression, "The Word of the Lord," though applied primarily to the reading from the

Word of God: By "The **Word of God**," we mean what the scholars call "**revelation**"—what God chooses to disclose about Himself.

Yahweh: The personal name of God in ancient Israel; sometimes called the "tetragrammaton" (four letters, written in capitals as YHWH). The name was not pronounced.

Torah: The first five books of the Bible, also known as the Law, the Pentateuch, and the five books of Moses.

Canon: The official authoritative collection of sacred documents for a given religious body.

Prophets: The second major section in the canon of the Hebrew Bible,consisting of the **Former Prophets** (historical books of Josh, Judg, Sam and Kings) and the **Latter Prophets** (the classical prophets: Isaiah, Jeremiah, Ezekiel and the Book of the Twelve [minor prophets]).

Redaction: The editorial process that produced documents which evolved over extensive periods of time in antiquity.

Logos: The Greek term for "word" which became a philosophical concept for the rational principle that governs and develops the universe. The Gospel of John presents Jesus as the *logos*.

Gospels in public worship, most certainly pertains to the **Torah** (the first five books of the Bible) as well, within both Jewish and Christian communities down through the ages.

For Christians, the center of the Old Testament **canon** of sacred Scripture shifted from the Torah to the second major division—the **Prophets**. And here perhaps the most characteristic phrase of all is the familiar "Thus says Yahweh" or "utterance of Yahweh." To say that the Bible nowhere claims to be the Word of God is simply not true. The core of the Old Testament is permeated by such an implicit and explicit claim. It may perhaps be true that the New Testament nowhere claims to be the Word of God as such, but the Old Testament certainly does; and it was, I believe, so considered by Jesus and his followers in the New Testament era.

The question as to exactly what was meant by the phrase "the Word of God" in the New Testament community is not an easy one to answer, because the Hebrew Bible has taken on a whole new meaning in Christ. Norbert Lohfink has gone so far as to suggest that when the Old Testament was taken up by the New Testament community as sacred Scripture, that event itself was an act of "authorship" for the Old Testament. In short, the ultimate **redaction** of the Old Testament was carried out by Jesus Christ and certain of his followers in the early Christian Church.[3] The so-called *logos* doctrine in John's gospel suggests that the true word of God is Jesus Christ (John 1:1-2):

> In the beginning was the Word,
>   and the Word was with God,
>   and the Word was God.
> He was in the beginning with God;
>   all things were made through him,
>   and without him was not anything made that was made.

But at the same time, it is not all that difficult to show that the New Testament writers continued to see the Old Testament canon as the authoritative "Word of God" in the traditional sense as well. And if the Bible is in some sense the revealed "Word of God," It stands to reason that it is also the proper starting point in the matter of doing "theology," i.e., the study of God and the relationship between God and the universe he has created.

At this point, a brief aside may be in order. Much has been said recently about the nature of the canon in the minds of the writers of the New Testament. Since actual quotation of the Old Testament within the New Testament can often be shown to be closer to the LXX (the Greek translation of the Hebrew Old Testament known as the **Septuagint**) than the MT (**Masoretic Text** of the Hebrew Bible), does that suggest that the LXX was in fact the canonical Old Testament? Hardly! Within the Jewish community, the Hebrew language was no longer the language of the people, even before the New Testament era—as it is not today among perhaps most Jews. The translation of the Hebrew Bible into Aramaic was thus necessary when the Aramaic language displaced Hebrew within the Jewish communities of the ancient world. The translation into Greek known as the Septuagint (LXX) was also necessary in an analogous manner, among Greek-speaking Jews. But, at the same time, it should be remembered that such translations, in the past and the present, never displace the ancient Hebrew scrolls as such. The ark of the scrolls in Jewish synagogues always contains Hebrew scrolls. This fact was driven home to me personally with some force several years ago in Massachusetts. I was with my family in Everett visiting relatives when a fire broke out which destroyed a large synagogue in nearby Chelsea. I arrived at the building just as two firemen emerged from the flaming structure with the only two objects that were saved. The first fireman got out on his own. The second was literally blown out of the building by an explosion behind him. The two large objects were now in the hands of what looked like a young rabbi about twenty feet from me—they were the sacred scrolls. A woman next to me said simply: "We have our scrolls; we can start again!" It is the Hebrew text of those handwritten ancient scrolls that remains to the present day the authoritative basis of faith for Jews and Christians alike.

The recent Jewish translations of the Old Testament into English, however excellent, necessary, and helpful they may be in both private and public use, will never displace the canonical Hebrew text as recorded in the sacred scrolls. It is that ancient Hebrew text that remains canonical. It should not surprise us that quotations in the Greek New Testament should frequently come from the Greek translation of the Old Testament known as the Septuagint. The New Testament writers wrote and spoke in Greek. The situation is a bit analogous to the use of quotations from the Revised Standard Version (RSV) or the New International Version (NIV) in my own writings. Such a practice on my

Septuagint: The Greek translation of the Hebrew Bible, which is the oldest and most important of the ancient versions. According to tradition, it was done by 70 (*septuaginta* in Latin) or 72 Jewish scholars in Alexandria (3rd century BCE) in 72 days [hence the abbreviation LXX = 70]. Originally the name applied to the Pentateuch only, but by the 2nd century CE, the name was used for the whole Greek Old Testament which was completed about the 2nd century BCE.

Masoretic Text: The name of the traditional Hebrew text of the OT which appears to have been standardized in the first century CE. Between the 7th and the 10th centuries CE, this text was provided with vowel signs, accents, and punctuation marks and was divided into sections. The Jewish scholars who did this work were called masoretes. Hence it is known as the Masoretic text (MT).

part is a recognition of a social reality and not a canonical decision. The Hebrew Bible remains canonical for me personally even though I seldom quote it, particularly when addressing people who do not know Hebrew.

First Testament: Old Testament

Second Testament: New Testament

> ### Concept Check # 1
>
> For some time now, the editors of the *Biblical Theology Bulletin* have insisted that writers of articles for that journal use the terms **First Testament** and **Second Testament** rather than Old Testament and New Testament. What do you think the primary reasons for this decision were? (Check your answer on p. 221.)

B. The Two Centers in the Canonical Process

Inerrancy: The teaching within Jewish, Christian (and Muslim) tradition that the Bible (and the Koran) is free from error, which is a logical consequence of the belief that the Bible (and the Koran) is the "Word of God."

Let us return to the central question at hand—the place of the Bible in theological education at all levels, within the world of academia and the local church. In my opinion, the Bible must be retained at the center of reflection on matters of curriculum within theological education, particularly in an evangelical institution. At the same time, I would be quick to qualify that statement. If the Bible is made the center, alone, the end result may become heresy, particularly when it results in the obscurantism of fundamentalism expressed in some erroneous doctrine of **inerrancy**, as is sometimes the case in a good many Baptist churches with which I am familiar in my own tradition. For me personally, there are two centers which must be held in balance. In short, my model for theological education is that of an ellipse, with two foci: *the Word of God incarnate and the Word of God in canon* —i.e., the Gospel of Jesus Christ, on the one hand, and canonical Scripture, on the other.[4]

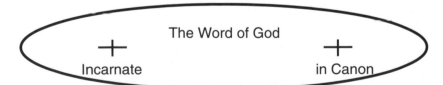

To select the first center at the expense of the second will produce theological liberalism; whereas selection of the second at the expense of the first all too often leads to reactionary fundamentalism. It was my teacher, Professor Leland Hine, who helped me see this fact years ago when he described what he called "a true conservative"—taken in either the political or theological sense of the word. The theological spectrum is a continuum from extreme liberalism on the left to fundamentalism on the right. A true conservative position, one that preserves the values of our heritage, is that position which stands between these two extremes and preserves the tension.

Liberal Left $\longleftrightarrow$ True Conservative $\longleftrightarrow$ Reactionary Right

Now how do we apply all this to the question of theological education? Robert Laurin, who introduced me to the academic study of the Old Testament, once published a curious statement that: "The period of separate disciplines in the theological curriculum is passing, and *the sooner the better* (emphasis mine)."[5] For a number of reasons I found that statement less than convincing. In fact, I wondered if perhaps Bob Laurin was not trying to convince himself of something which deep down he already knew was not really true at all. Sometimes we get so caught up in a dream, or perhaps in a fad of the moment, that we lose perspective. The psychologist Carl Jung once made the comment that true education can only start from naked reality, not from a delusive ideal. The integrity of the traditional academic disciplines, I believe, is an example of such a naked reality.

Concept Check # 2

Are the familiar academic disciplines of Old Testament, New Testament, the Biblical Languages (Greek and Hebrew), Biblical Theology, Systematic Theology, and Church History permanent fixtures so far as the formal curriculum of theological studies is concerned? (Check your answer on p. 221.)

C. Four Ways of Doing Theology

Theological education has been around a long time, and we can learn much by taking a closer look at the past. Utopian ideals have come and gone within the pages of that history. Though I do not profess to be an expert on the history of education, I have personal experience of some value, having taught the "History of Western Civilization" course for nine years at Bridgewater State College in Massachusetts. One section of that course was always the rise of the medieval universities in Europe which, incidentally, in many cases were primarily theological schools. At the time, I did not know why I could never satisfy myself with simply restating what the textbooks and what most of my colleagues said on the matter. For as long as I can remember, I have had a rebellious streak of sorts. I always found it difficult to simply believe what I was told, particularly in the absence of positive proof. I am beginning to understand much better why I responded in this way.

When I was fourteen years old, I was a newsboy; and I remember vividly a fateful Sunday morning. I had a fever and should not have been out early that morning delivering my newspapers. But I had a job to do and I was determined to do it. I started out and I kept going until I simply could not lift my feet off the sidewalk to take another step. I never finished the route. Finally my parents found me. It was a funny sight—a stubborn kid who wouldn't quit, even when he couldn't take another step. They rushed me to the hospital and thus began a fateful journey, one which only now is nearing completion. And even in its beginning, that journey was a bit ominous; for there was no room for me in the hospital ward to which I was assigned. A bed was quickly set up in the hallway. I was diagnosed as having rheumatic fever with a serious heart murmur caused by permanent damage to the mitral valve. I spent the next three months in bed, missing the second semester of my last year at Stewart Junior High School in Tacoma, Washington. And then for six years I was on a daily dosage of penicillin and restricted activity; all of which I accepted without complaint, or at least so I thought at the time.

And then gradually I learned that the whole thing was a mistake. I never had rheumatic fever at all. The heart murmur they found that Sunday morning was what would now be called a systemic heart murmur, which is common to perhaps one out of four teenagers, and has long since been outgrown. Apparently, the various parts of our bodies sometimes grow at different rates.

At the same time that I was discovering the misdiagnosis on the part of a heart specialist—a diagnosis which deeply affected my whole life—I was involved in an unfortunate incident in a Baptist church near Boston which culminated somehow in a heresy trial which cost me my job. It all got fused together in such a manner that I have subsequently had difficulty dealing with the autocratic exercise of power, or what appeared to me to be the abuse of power.

Well, be that as it may, I was never content in my teaching about the origins of modern universities with merely restating a consensus of opinion. Perhaps it was also the ethos of the time there in the early 1970s. We had at the college where I was teaching what some called a "free university"—an alternative curriculum which was part of the anti-war movement in that Vietnam era.

1. Al 'Azhar: the Free University

I began to wonder just how far back such a tradition might go. A free university has no tuition and offers no degrees. In some respects it is a bit like the Sunday School movement so familiar to most evangelical Christians. And so I began to explore the matter and found, to my surprise, that such an approach to education has an illustrious history which includes the University of Al 'Azhar in Cairo. In 1969 this university celebrated its 1000th anniversary of continuous existence. That makes it older by far than any of the more famous Western universities such as those in Paris, Oxford, and Cambridge. And Al 'Azhar was a theological school par excellence—organized for teaching the **Koran** and Islamic law.

Koran: The sacred text of Islam, believed to have been dictated to Muhammad by the angel Gabriel and regarded by Muslims as the foundation of law, religion, culture, and politics.

In 1976, I had the opportunity to go to Cairo and to visit Al 'Azhar. I shall never forget that experience. I was traveling alone. I knew where the university was, or at least I thought I did; and so I started out on foot from my hotel, only to get hopelessly lost. There's a peculiar custom in the Near East. To save face people usually give an answer to your questions even if they don't really know. And thus every inquiry I made as to the location of Al 'Azhar took me in fact farther and farther in the wrong direction. I finally hailed a taxi and eventually reached my destination, where I took off my shoes and entered a sacred place, for that ancient building is now a mosque. There were only a few people present in the building at the time, since the ancient university had been combined with the larger University of Cairo some years earlier. Nonetheless, I had little difficulty reconstructing in my mind remarkable scenes of past centuries as I walked about in that great hall. There was no curriculum resembling those to which we are accustomed. The curriculum was the Koran. The professors were those who had mastered the book, which Muslims claim to be the "Word of God." A person became a professor by simply standing up to lecture. If his (there were no women in that university) lectures attracted students, the student became a professor. If he was not successful, he returned to the status of a student to await another time.

A person who has seen the movie *Yentl*, or who has visited a yeshiva, knows a bit about the way of life in the so-called "free universities" of the East, which are structured around sacred texts. The curriculum is the text; and the faculty consists of those who have mastered that text. Such schools continue to be a valid model for theological education worthy of more careful attention on our part today, both in terms of our present institutions of graduate theological education, devoted to the training of professional ministers, and in the development of new programs of instruction within the context of local churches, committed to the task of training individual members for more effective ministry.

2. Medieval Christian Universities

Meanwhile, in Western Europe two different types of universities emerged in the Middle Ages, both of which had theology at the center of their concern as "queen of the sciences." The two kinds of universities are perhaps best exemplified by those in Bologna and Paris. For some reason, a number of these universities in Southern Europe, like that at Bologna, tended to become dominated by the students. The medieval universities were part of the guild movement of that era. Students organized guilds for their own protection against townspeople who sometimes demanded exorbitant sums for food and housing. Eventually these guilds went on to control the professors. In the earliest statutes of the University of Bologna (1317 CE), as Wallbank has noted:[6]

> We read that a professor requiring leave of absence for one day first had to obtain permission from his own students. He had to begin his lecture with the bell and end within one minute of the next bell. The material in the text had to be covered systematically, with all difficult passages fully explained.

For some, this particular model of higher education might appear to be a student's paradise.

In Northern Europe, a different situation was developing as illustrated by the University of Paris, the most influential intellectual center in medieval Europe, which grew out of the cathedral school of Notre Dame and specialized in liberal arts and theology. Charters for the university were issued by the French king as early as 1200 and by the pope in 1231, making the University of Paris an autonomous body controlled by the masters—the faculty.

3. Seminaries and Theological Schools

With the rise of the industrial revolution, a third type of educational institution began to appear, which flourished in the 19th and the 20th centuries as theological schools started breaking away from the now secular universities. A new center of political power became dominant in what we would now call the "administration," which generally includes a board of trustees. The heresy trial of W. Robertson Smith in Edinburgh and the Charles A. Briggs controversy in the United States at the turn of this century show clearly the emerging new factor—political power exercised within the churches by those in control of the purse strings of theological education. New historical forces were at work as denominational colleges, divinity schools, and seminaries took their place alongside the universities. Church and state were going their separate ways in the matter of education, particularly here in the United States. Theological education was returning to the churches where many would argue it rightfully belongs anyway.

In recent years, the tension has increased between theological education shaped primarily by forces within academia, whether secular or religious, and the felt needs of the churches. Manfred Brauch, who speaks as both a biblical scholar and seminary administrator, has expressed rather well the conviction of a growing number of educators on this issue:[7]

> In numerous seminaries and divinity schools around the country where theological education has increasingly become an academic preoccupation, there is a renewed recognition that theological education which is divorced from the life of the church is devoid of power . . . Theological education which is not focused toward the needs and ministry of the church has lost its reason for being and is devoid of glory.

4. A New Model for DoingTheological Education

What does all this mean for us today? I think it suggests the outline of a new model for theological education at the turn of the twenty-first century—one that takes the best elements of each of these historical precedents. What is needed today is a bit of Bologna and Paris within the emerging institutions of theological education! That is, we need a guild of students who are determined to exercise their own responsibility as they faithfully work out their respective callings under God to become effective ministers of our Lord within the churches. And we need a guild of professors as well—professional scholars and teachers who are faithfully fulfilling their separate callings to be specialized servants of our Lord and his Church within the various disciplines in what we call academia. Moreover, we need a strong and responsible administration carrying out its task, which is absolutely essential for the health of any theological institution, within academia or at the level of the local church. But, at the same time, we must not lose sight of Al 'Azhar. The spirit of the free university is one of trust—trust in God to work through people who are committed to the task of interpreting a sacred text, the "Word of God," which stands at the center of our concerns in theological education.

One example of the new model which we are seeking is taking shape at William Carey International University in Pasadena, California, under the leadership of Ralph Winter, namely, a university which is owned and operated by missionaries, for missionaries. In a booklet written in 1989 (and revised in May 1995), "Discipleship in Graduate Studies: Guidelines for the Ph.D. Mentor and Associate," Winter outlines what he has in mind. In many respects, the program includes elements of classical graduate education from the Middle Ages in the relationship established between the faculty mentor and the graduate associate. This new model has already led to a breakthrough in undergraduate studies as well in the development of the World Christian Foundations curriculum, which delivers a major part of an accredited baccalaureate degree through a field-based and mentored program. This new pattern makes the accumulated knowledge and understanding of the Christian movement available, with a mission perspective, to qualified, busy people—in the United States and around the world, wherever they are.

Thinking Exercise

On the Bible as the Word of God

The critical thinking goal for this exercise is to clarify the concept of the "Word of God" within the canonical process (the historical process in which the individual books of the Bible took their present shape as an authoritative, i.e., canonical, text of sacred Scripture within the context of ancient Israel, early Judaism, and the early Christian Church).

How To Do This Exercise

First, review the definitions of the "Word of God" and "canon," and think about canon in relation to religious authority. Write out your definitions below for items 1 and 2; and then state the answers you think are correct in 3a and 3b below. Indicate in a few words your line of reasoning. Finally, decide how to justify and explain your answers. Specific examples always help to clarify thinking.

1. The "Word of God" is

_____

_____

_____

_____

_____

2. Canon is

_____

_____

_____

_____

_____

3. a. The Bible is the "Word of God" because

_____

_____

_____

_____

_____

    b. For Christians Jesus Christ is the "Word of God" because

_____

_____

_____

_____

_____

4. I can justify and explain my answers as follows:

_____

_____

_____

_____

_____

Discussion Questions

1. There is more than one canon of sacred Scripture within the Christian religion, as we will see in chapter 2. Do you think that the canon is "closed" in the sense that other works cannot be added and accepted by the different communities of faith as the "Word of God"?

2. In addition to the First Testament (Old Testament) and the Second Testament (New Testament), another section is often included in printed editions of the Bible, namely the Apocrypha. Are these books also to be considered as the "Word of God"?

3. How realistic is the proposal for "A New Model of Theological Education," which combines the strengths of the three approaches to theological education in times past?

Concept Map: Summary of Chapter 1

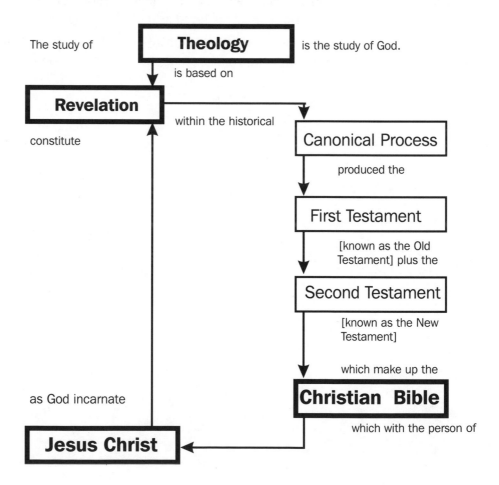

The study of **Theology** is the study of God.

is based on

Revelation within the historical

constitute

Canonical Process

produced the

First Testament

[known as the Old Testament] plus the

Second Testament

[known as the New Testament]

which make up the

Christian Bible

which with the person of

as God incarnate

Jesus Christ

2 The Canonical Process
The Word of God in Canon

Learning Objectives

After studying the chapter, you should be able to:

1. Write an essay on the "Canonical Process" which explains the relationship between the First Testament and the Second Testament in the Christian Bible.

2. Identify each concept and key word in the chapter. Concepts and key words are shown in **bold** typeface when introduced. *Identify* means:

    a. *define the term*, using your own words as much as possible,

    b. *give a specific example* to illustrate the idea, and briefly *explain its importance.*

A. The Structure of the Canon

In spite of the complex historical process, which spans more than a thousand years and includes a host of human "authors," the Bible displays a curious unity in its structure. This unity is best explained by embracing what countless ordinary, nameless Christians have claimed through the centuries, namely that the Bible has God as its "author" and that it is therefore for us "revelation," i.e., the *Word of God.* This is essentially what those church leaders who drafted "The Westminster Confession of Faith" had in mind when they insisted that:

> The authority of the holy Scripture, for which it ought to be believed and obeyed, dependeth not upon the testimony of any man or church, but wholly upon God (who is truth itself), the Author thereof; and therefore it is to be received, because it is the Word of God (1.4).

Students of the Bible today have access to newer tools and concepts by which to examine the historical process in order to determine, at least

Canonical process: The historical process in which the individual books of the Bible took their present shape as an authoritative (i.e., canonical) text of sacred Scripture within the context of ancient Israel, early Judaism, and the early Christian Church.

Moses: The founder of ancient Israel who led the people out of slavery in Egypt, in what is called the Exodus, and was their leader and lawgiver during their years of wandering in the wilderness.

First Temple: The temple in Jerusalem which was planned by David and built by his son Solomon (10th century BCE). It was destroyed by Nebuchadnezzar of Babylon in 587 BCE.

Joshua: The successor of Moses as leader of the people of ancient Israel, who led them into the Promised Land in what is called the Conquest (or Eisodus).

Talmud: The collection of Jewish law and tradition consisting of the Mishnah and the Gemara, which was produced in two separate editions: the Palestinian (ca. 400 CE) and the larger and more important Babylonian (ca. 500 CE).

in part, how the Bible emerged in time and space. The study of the canonical process which produced the Bible as we now know it is the concern of this chapter.

The word Bible came into English by way of French from the Latin *biblia* and the Greek *biblos*. It was originally the name given to the outer part of the papyrus reed in antiquity. By the second century of the common era (CE), Christians were using the term to describe their sacred text. The word canon (a rod, ruler) comes from the Hebrew word *kaneh*, which means a "measuring rod" (cf. Ezek 40:3). From ancient times, the word was used to indicate a standard or norm other than a literal rod or rules, as such. The New Testament employs the term in its figurative sense to indicate a rule for conduct (Gal 6:16). In early Christian usage the word canon came to mean the "rule of faith," or the normative writings of sacred Scripture.

One of the earliest concepts of a canon is simply that of writings which are considered sacred. The Torah of **Moses** was considered to be sacred in ancient Israel, and therefore canonical, as indicated by the holy place in which it was placed beside the ark of the covenant (Deut 31:24-26). Later, when King Solomon built the **First Temple** in Jerusalem, the Torah of Moses was preserved in it (2 Kgs 22:8).

The term canonicity speaks of the divine authority of Scripture. The authority of the Torah of Moses was impressed on **Joshua** (Josh 1:8). Each king of Israel was exhorted to "write for himself in a book a copy of this Torah . . . and he shall read in it all the days of his life, that he may learn to fear the Lord his God, by keeping all the words of this Torah" (Deut 17:18-19). As authoritative Scripture, the Hebrew Bible was considered canonical, or normative, for the people of ancient Israel—and both Jews and Christians after them.

In the teaching tradition of ancient Israel, there arose the concept that the written texts of the Hebrew Bible were so holy or sacred that those who used them had "defiled their hands." The **Talmud** declares that: "The Gospel and the books of the heretics do not make the hands unclean; the books of Ben Sira and whatever books have been written since his time are not canonical" (Tosefta Yadaim 3:5). In contrast, the books of the Hebrew Bible do make the hands unclean because they are sacred. These sacred texts require the user to undergo a special ceremonial cleansing.

In traditional usage, the Bible has been divided into two parts: the Old Testament and the New Testament. In some circles, scholars today prefer to use the terms First Testament and Second Testament to describe these two sections of the Bible. The reason for this preference is the fact that the English word "old" often carries a pejorative overtone, which suggests that it is superseded by what is "new," and that the "old" is thus inferior to the "new." As we will see, the First Testament was never superseded in early Christianity. Jesus was clear on this matter when he stated simply: "Think not that I have come to abolish the **law** and the **prophets**; I have come not to abolish them but to fulfill them" (Matt 5:17).

Law ... prophets: Jesus appears to be referring to the first two major parts of the canon of the First Testament: the law is the Torah and the prophets are what we have designated the Former Prophets plus the Latter Prophets.

> Concept Check # 3
>
> The authority of the Scriptures, in both Jewish and Christian tradition, is based on the belief that these texts are the "Word of God." Most official translations of the Bible in times past were given the title *Holy Bible*. Some recent publications omit the word "holy" in the title. Does this omission reflect a bias against seeing the Bible as the revealed "Word of God"? (Check your answer on p. 221.)

1. The Structure of the Hebrew Bible

The canonical process is complex and we are only beginning to see the details of how God accomplished this task in history. The outline of that process is more easily seen in the structure of the Hebrew Bible, as presented in the *Tanakh,* than it is in the more familiar order of the books of the Bible in Christian tradition, which is based on the topical arrangement in the ancient translation of the Hebrew Scriptures into Greek known as the Septuagint (LXX). The Hebrew Bible employs a fourfold division of its own, namely:

Tanakh: The Hebrew Bible, the First Testament, which is made up of the Torah plus the Prophets (Former & Latter) plus the Writings.

Books of the Hebrew Bible *(Tanakh)*

Torah—5 books of Moses	**Former Prophets**—4 books
Genesis	Joshua
Exodus	Judges
Leviticus	Samuel
Numbers	Kings
Deuteronomy	
Latter Prophets—4 books	**Writings**—13 books[1]
Isaiah	Psalms
Jeremiah	Proverbs
Ezekiel	Job
The Book of the Twelve	Five Festal Scrolls (Megilloth):
	Ruth
	Song of Songs
	Ecclesiastes
	Lamentations
	Esther
	Daniel
	Ezra
	Nehemiah
	1 & 2 Chronicles

Mishnah: The section of the Talmud which consists of the collection of oral laws edited ca. 200 CE by Rabbi Judah ha-Nasi.

The earliest witness to the division of the Hebrew Bible into the Torah, Prophets, and Writings is found in the prologue to the book of Sirach, or Ecclesiasticus, which was written in the second century BCE. The Jewish **Mishnah** (Teaching), the historian Josephus, and subsequent Jewish tradition have continued this threefold categorization of their Scriptures; though it should be noted that the category of the prophets was always recognized to be in two parts, namely the Former Prophets and the Latter Prophets. The Second Testament also makes allusion to a threefold division of the First Testament when Jesus said, "All things must be fulfilled, which were written in the law of Moses, and in the prophets, and in the psalms concerning me" (Luke 24:44). The reference to the psalms here probably stands for the whole of the Writings, in which the book of Psalms is the first item.

Concept Check # 4

The order of the individual books in the English Bible has been shaped in large measure by the ordering of those books in the ancient Greek translation of the Bible known as the Septuagint. Would it be useful to have an edition of the Christian Bible in which the books of the First Testament are arranged in the order of the Masoretic Text? (Check your answer on p. 221.)

2. The Structure of the Christian Bible

The Christian Bible is commonly divided into eight sections, four in the First Testament and four in the Second Testament:

Books of the First Testament

The Law (Pentateuch)—5 books
  Genesis
  Exodus
  Leviticus
  Numbers
  Deuteronomy

History—12 books
  Joshua
  Judges
  Ruth
  1 & 2 Samuel
  1 & 2 Kings
  1 & 2 Chronicles
  Ezra & Nehemiah
  Esther

Poetry—5 books
  Job
  Psalms
  Proverbs
  Ecclesiastes
  Song of Solomon

Prophets—17 books
A. Major Prophets
  Isaiah
  Jeremiah
  Lamentations
  Ezekiel
  Daniel

B. Minor Prophets
  Hosea
  Joel
  Amos
  Obadiah
  Jonah
  Micah
  Nahum
  Habakkuk
  Zephaniah
  Haggai
  Zechariah
  Malachi

Books of the Second Testament

Gospels—4 books
    Matthew
    Mark
    Luke
    John

History—1 book
    Acts of the Apostles

Epistles—21 books

Romans	Titus
1 & 2 Corinthians	Philemon
Galatians	Hebrews
Ephesians	James
Philippians	1 & 2 Peter
Colossians	1, 2 & 3 John
1 & 2 Thessalonians	Jude
1 & 2 Timothy	

Prophecy—1 book
    Revelation

Vulgate: The Latin translation of the Bible by St. Jerome at the end of the 4th century CE, in which the First Testament was translated directly from the original Hebrew texts used in Palestine at that time. It became the canonical text of the Roman Catholic Church until the twentieth century.

Christian Bibles, from the date of Jerome's Latin **Vulgate**, have followed the topical fourfold format of the Septuagint. Combining this division with the natural and widely accepted fourfold categorization of the Second Testament, the Christian Bible may be described in the following Christocentric structure:

First Testament:

Law	Foundation for Christ
History	Preparation for Christ
Poetry	Aspiration for Christ
Prophecy	Expectation for Christ

Second Testament:

Gospels	Manifestation of Christ
Acts	Propagation of Christ
Epistles	Interpretation & Application of Christ
Revelation	Consummation in Christ

Although there is no authoritative basis for seeing the Bible in this eightfold structure, the belief that the Scriptures are to be understood Christocentrically is firmly based on the teachings of Jesus. On four occasions in the Gospels (cf. also Heb 10:7), Jesus affirmed that he himself was the theme of the Hebrew Scriptures (see Matt 5:17; Luke 24:27, 44; and John 5:39). Further arguments for seeing Jesus Christ as the center of the canonical process will be presented in the next chapter of this book.

Concept Check # 5

When Christians in the early Church reflected on the nature of God's revelation in Jesus Christ, they thought in terms of the First Testament—the only Bible they knew. Is it possible that the structure of the Second Testament, which they produced, reflects what they already knew in the Hebrew Bible? (Check your answer on p. 221.)

B. The Torah and the Prophets

When Jesus made reference to "the law and the prophets" he was referring to the first two major parts of the canon of the First Testament. The word *Tanakh*, which is used to describe the Hebrew Bible, or the First Testament, in Jewish usage is an artificial term made up by supplying vowels to the linking together of three consonants: T = *Torah* (the Law); N = *Nevi'im* (the Prophets); and K = *Kethuvim* (the **Writings**).[2] This division of the so-called books of the First Testament into three major categories is a useful one, for Christians as well as for Jews. It is important to note, however, that the second category, the *Nevi'im* (the Prophets), is actually in two parts: the Former Prophets (Joshua, Judges, Samuel, and Kings); and the Latter Prophets (Isaiah, Jeremiah, Ezekiel, and the Book of the Twelve [minor prophets]). In short, the canon of the First Testament is fourfold in its structure:

Writings: The final section of the canon of sacred Scripture in Jewish tradition, which consists of Psalms, Proverbs, Job, the five Festal Scrolls, Daniel, Ezra-Nehemiah, and Chronicles.

Torah	Former Prophets
Latter Prophets	"Hagiographa" (Writings)

The four sections in this structure are arranged in a **chiasm** (or chiasmus), with the book of Deuteronomy functioning as a bridge connecting the four parts. In a chiasm there is a "crossing over" of

Chiasm: The principle of arranging items in a four-part structure, with two pairs arranged so that one pair frames the other: i.e., in an a-b-b'-a' pattern.

parallel terms within a rhetorical structure, as suggested by the form of the Greek letter *chi*, from which the letter X in the English alphabet is derived. A familiar example of such usage is the sentence used by President John F. Kennedy in his inauguration address: "Ask not what your country can do for you; but what you can do for your country." The pattern is frequently diagrammed as a-b-b-a.

The close relationship between the two central elements of this chiastic structure, the Former Prophets and the Latter Prophets, is obvious by the common name *Nevi'im* (the Prophets). The structural relationship between the Torah and the "**Hagiographa**" (the Writings) will be shown later in this chapter. It should be noted, however, that the fourth category, the "Hagiographa," remains somewhat "open" in the sense that additions were made in this section of the canon—which eventually became the Writings. In the earliest stages of the canonical process, it did not yet include Daniel, Ezra, Nehemiah, Chronicles, and the book of Esther.

The earliest version of the canon of the First Testament may be described in terms of a seventeen-book structure.[3] As Casper Labuschagne has noted, the numbers seventeen and twenty-six appear to be sacred numbers in ancient Israel and play a major role in shaping the received canonical tradition. The numbers are determined from the numerical value of the divine name YHWH in the Hebrew language: $Y = 10$; $H = 5$; and $W = 6$, in terms of the normal numerical values assigned to letters in the Hebrew alphabet. When these numbers are added, $Y (10) + H (5) + W (6) + H (5) = 26$. When the sum of the digits in these same numbers is added $(10 = 1 + 0) + 5 + 6 + 5 = 17$. In other words, the number seventeen is associated with God's personal name. Moreover, the number seventeen is also determined by the grouping of four structures of four books each, arranged around the book of Deuteronomy at the center:

Genesis	Exodus	Joshua	Judges
Leviticus	Numbers	Samuel	Kings
	Deuteronomy		
Isaiah	Jeremiah	Psalms	Proverbs
Ezekiel	The Twelve	Job	*Megilloth*

Hagiographa: The term is used here to refer to an early stage in the canonical process which produced the Writings: i.e., before the addition of Daniel, Ezra-Nehemiah, Chronicles, and Esther.

The term *Megilloth* here refers to the five **Festal Scrolls** of ancient Judaism: Ruth (Pentecost); Song of Songs (Passover); Ecclesiastes (Booths); Lamentations (9th of Ab, the destruction of the Temple); and Esther (Purim). In the earliest stages of the canonical process, Esther and possibly Ecclesiastes were not yet included among the *Megilloth* (Festal Scrolls).

The importance of the number seventeen within the canonical process in ancient Israel is also suggested by the recorded age of the patriarchs at the time of their death in the book of Genesis:

Ancestor	Age at Death	Sum of Digits
Abraham	$175 = 7 \times 5^2$	$7 + 5 + 5 = 17$
Isaac	$180 = 5 \times 6^2$	$5 + 6 + 6 = 17$
Jacob	$147 = 3 \times 7^2$	$3 + 7 + 7 = 17$

It was Nahum Sarna who noted that the ages of Abraham, Isaac, and Jacob at the time of their death in the Genesis narrative fit a numerical pattern; and Casper Labuschagne who subsequently pointed out that in all three cases the sum of the digits used in this formula add up to the number seventeen.[4] Labuschagne also suggested that the lifespan of Joseph (and Joshua as well) may be related to this numerical schema in that $110 = 5^2 + 6^2 + 7^2$. The significance of the number seventeen in the formation of the book of Psalms will be shown in the next section of this chapter.

> ### Concept Check # 6
>
> The subject of numerology in the Bible has been popular in both Jewish and Christian circles through the centuries, but it has also led to such excess in some circles that few biblical scholars of note have anything to say on the subject today. How important is it to observe the fascination for the number seventeen on the part of scribes in ancient Israel? (Check your answer on p. 221.)

The Torah is made up of the first five books of the Bible: Genesis, Exodus, Leviticus, Numbers, and Deuteronomy. These five books of Moses are more authoritative than any other parts of the Hebrew Bible; for, in most Jewish communities, this "Law of Moses" is read through in public worship on a regular basis, usually completed in a single year, and

Festal Scrolls or **Megilloth**: The five books which are associated with the five major festivals in Jewish tradition: Song of Songs, Ruth, Lamentations, Ecclesiastes, and Esther.

Primary History:
The Torah plus the
Former Prophets:
i.e., the section of
the Hebrew Bible
which extends from
Genesis through
2 Kings in the
masoretic tradition.

Josephus: The
Jewish politician,
military general, and
historian who lived
in the first century
CE and was
responsible for
writings which
constitute important
sources of
information for our
understanding of
biblical history and
of the political
history of Roman
Palestine.

sometimes on a triennial basis. The Samaritan community accepts only these five books of Moses as their sacred Scripture.

In recent years, numerous scholars have followed the lead of David Noel Freedman to describe the Torah (Pentateuch) and the Former Prophets (Joshua through Kings) as the "**Primary History**."[5] Scholars have long noted that the book of Deuteronomy serves as a bridge connecting the Pentateuch and the Former Prophets. This large block of material, i.e., Genesis through 2 Kings in the Hebrew Bible, which constitutes one half of the First Testament, is in fact a single literary unit as Freedman has observed.

The reference to the "prophets," along with the Torah of Moses, by Jesus and the early Christian community, speaks to another aspect of the meaning of the *canon* of sacred Scripture. According to **Josephus** (*Contra Apion* 1:8), only those books which were composed during the prophetic period from Moses to Artaxerxes could be canonical. As he put it, "From Artaxerxes until our time everything has been recorded, but has not been deemed worthy of like credit with what preceded, because the exact succession of the prophets ceased." During the period from Artaxerxes (fourth century BCE) to Josephus (first century CE) there was no prophetic succession. As the Talmud put it, "Up to this point (fourth century BCE) the prophets prophesied through the Holy Spirit; from this time onward incline thine ear and listen to the sayings of the wise" (Seder Olam Rabba 30). In order to be canonical, then, a text must come from the prophetic succession during the prophetic period.

In the early Christian community, the concept of prophetic authorship of sacred texts was extended. Inspired books come through Spirit-moved persons known as prophets (2 Pet 1:20-21). The Word of God is given to God's people through his prophets. Paul argued in Galatians that his book should be accepted because he was an apostle, "not from men nor through man, but through Jesus Christ and God the Father" (Gal 1:1). His book was to be accepted because it was from a God-appointed spokesman, or prophet. Books were to be rejected if they did not come from prophets of God, as is evident from Paul's warnings not to accept a book from someone falsely claiming to be an apostle (2 Thess 2:2) and from his warning about false prophets (2 Cor 11:13). John's warnings about false messiahs and trying the spirits fall into this same category (1 John 2:18-19 and 4:1-3). It was because of this prophetic principle that 2 Peter was disputed in some circles within the early

Church. Only when the Church Fathers were convinced that it was not a forgery, and that it really came from Peter the apostle as it claimed (2 Pet 1:1), was it finally accorded a permanent place in the Christian canon.

We should not imagine, however, a committee in ancient Israel or in the early Christian Church with a large pile of books and certain guiding principles before them when we speak of the process of canonization. No ecumenical committee was ever commissioned to canonize the Bible.

1. The Pentateuch: The First Step in the Canonical Process

The canonical process in ancient Israel began with reflection on the primary epic story of the "**Exodus**" from bondage in Egypt under the leadership of Moses. This was the central salvation event of the First Testament, from which all else developed. The "Exodus" ("going out") called for its counterpart in the "**Eisodus**" ("going in") namely the entrance into the Promised Land under the leadership of Joshua—the Conquest. The linking of these two events by Frank Cross in a single lexical item, the "Exodus-Conquest," in his discussion of what he has called the "Ritual Conquest" in ancient Israel, bears witness to the fact that these two events are so closely connected that they constitute a single category from the point of view of liturgical celebration.[6] The title *Book of the Wars of the Lord* in Num 21:14 refers to this same block of material. As I have argued elsewhere, this title seems to reflect how the people of ancient Israel referred to their epic story.[7] The *Book of the Wars of the Lord* was an epic poem, which contained the account of the deliverance of Israel from bondage in Egypt and their subsequent entrance into the Promised Land, against all odds from a human point of view. These "Mighty Acts" of the Divine Warrior displayed the grace of God, which was extended to his chosen people Israel. The "Wars of the Lord" were divided into two phases: namely, the Exodus under Moses and the Eisodus (the Conquest) under Joshua.

In each case the two halves of the primary epic story take on a threefold structure within the developing canonical process in ancient Israel by insertion of what scholars call "theophanic visitations," or encounters with God—first to Moses and subsequently to **Elijah** (the prophet like Moses; cf. Deut 18:15-18), on the same holy mountain. The

Exodus: The epic journey of the people of Israel out of slavery in Egypt under the leadership of Moses.

Eisodus: The epic journey of the people of Israel into the Promised Land under the leadership of Joshua.

Elijah: The historical Hebrew prophet of the 9th century BCE who plays a pivotal transitional role in the development of the prophetic tradition in ancient Israel.

Exodus involves a journey through the wilderness from *Yam Suf* (the "Sea of Reeds" or "Red Sea") to the Jordan River in three stages. The visitation with God on **Mount Sinai,** in which the presence of the Divine Warrior was revealed to Moses, was framed, on the one hand, by the wilderness journey from Egypt to Sinai; and, on the other, by the wilderness journey from Sinai to **Mount Nebo** and the transfer of leadership from Moses to Joshua.

Edward Newing has shown that the "Promised Presence," as depicted in Exod 33:1-17, is situated at the structural center of the Pentateuch.[8] Though his analysis is based on the final form of the biblical text, it seems to reflect the earliest stages of the actual canonical process, which eventually produced the Pentateuch as we now know it. The structure is threefold in nature. As Newing put it, "the journey from Egypt to Canaan is in three stages": (1) "From Slavery/Promise," to (2) the great theophany (divine visitation—the "Promised Presence") on the Mountain of God at Sinai/Horeb, and from there (3) "To Freedom/Fulfillment."

A	Land promised	Gen 12-50
B	Egypt judged	Exod 1:1 - 12:36
C	Exodus from Egypt	Exod 12:37 - 14:31
D	Song of Moses	Exod 15:1-21
E	Wilderness wandering	Exod 15:22 - 18:27
F	Covenant ratified and regulated	Exod 19-24
G	Sanctuary planned	Exod 25-31
H	Covenant broken	Exod 32
X	Theophany on Mount Sinai	Exod 33
H'	Covenant renewed	Exod 34
G'	Sanctuary built	Exod 35-40
F'	Covenant regulations	Lev 1:1 - Num 10:10
E'	Wilderness wandering	Num 10:11 - Deut 31:30
D'	Song of Moses; blessing & death of Moses	Deut 32-34
C'	Eisodus (Entry) into Canaan	Josh1-4
B'	Canaan judged	Josh 5-12
A'	Land promise fulfilled	Josh 13-24

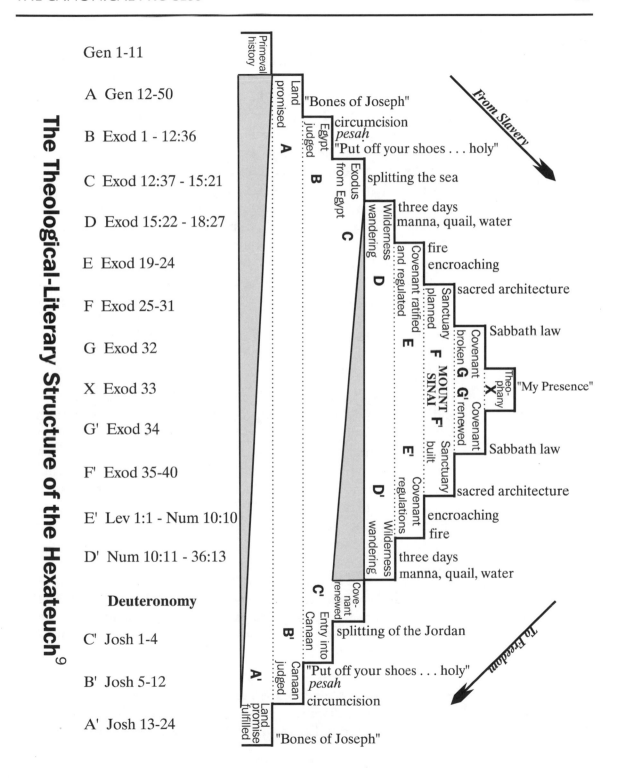

The Theological-Literary Structure of the Hexateuch[9]

Gen 1-11

A Gen 12-50

B Exod 1 - 12:36

C Exod 12:37 - 15:21

D Exod 15:22 - 18:27

E Exod 19-24

F Exod 25-31

G Exod 32

X Exod 33

G' Exod 34

F' Exod 35-40

E' Lev 1:1 - Num 10:10

D' Num 10:11 - 36:13

Deuteronomy

C' Josh 1-4

B' Josh 5-12

A' Josh 13-24

Primeval history

Land promised A

"Bones of Joseph"
circumcision
pesah
"Put off your shoes . . . holy"

Egypt judged B

Exodus from Egypt C

splitting the sea

Wilderness wandering D

three days
manna, quail, water
fire
encroaching

Covenant ratified and regulated E

sacred architecture

Sanctuary planned F

Sabbath law

Covenant broken G MOUNT SINAI G' Covenant renewed

Theo-phany X "My Presence"

Sanctuary built F'

Sabbath law

sacred architecture

Covenant regulations E'

encroaching
fire

Wilderness wandering D'

three days
manna, quail, water

Cove-nant renewed C'

Entry into Canaan

splitting of the Jordan

Canaan judged B'

"Put off your shoes . . . holy"
pesah
circumcision

Land promise fulfilled A'

"Bones of Joseph"

From Slavery

To Freedom

Hexateuch: The
first six books of the
Bible: the Torah plus
the book of Joshua.

Several points should be noted in this structure. As in all such concentric structures, the center (X) is crucial. Here it is the experience of Moses on Mount Sinai, which includes a reference to Joshua (Exod 33:11b). Not only is Exodus 33 the watershed of the wilderness narratives in Exodus through Numbers, it is the great divide of the **Hexateuch** (Genesis through Joshua). Sinai marks the end of slavery and the beginning of freedom. A number of specific repetitions in key words, phrases, and concepts mark off the symmetrical sections: the "bones of Joseph" (Gen 49:25; Josh 24:32; AA′); "put off your shoes . . . holy" (Exod 3:5; Josh 5:15; BB′); crossing the Red Sea and the Jordan River (Exod 14:9-15:21; Josh 3:4; CC′); the two "Songs of Moses" (Exod 15; Deut 32; DD′); the three days, manna, quail, and rock narratives (Exod 16-17; Num 11,20; EE′); the image of fire in the divine visitation (Exod 19:18; Lev 9:24) and approaching Sinai/Tabernacle incurs death (Exod 19:13; Num 1:51, FF′); law of the Sabbath precedes construction of the Tabernacle (Exod 31:12-17; Exod 35:1-3; GG′); the broken and renewed covenant on Mount Sinai (Exodus 32; Exod 34:10-28; HH′); and the divine visitation to Moses on the holy mountain at the center (Exod 33:1-11a; 33:12-34:9; X).

The reference to Joshua in Exod 33:11b, which states simply that he did not leave the tent of meeting outside the camp at Mount Sinai, even when Moses returned to the camp, appears to be deliberately placed in the actual center of the Pentateuch from a structural point of view. In one sense the reference forms the initial part of an envelope around the second half of the Pentateuch, which ends with the transfer of leadership from Moses to Joshua (Deut 31:7-23 and 34:9-12). Both texts make specific reference to the presence of these two leaders in the tent of meeting outside the camp and the fact that "Yahweh used to speak to Moses there face to face, as a man speaks to his friend" (Exod 33:11a; cf. Deut 34:10). The person of Joshua is also a connecting link between the Pentateuch and the Former Prophets, which begins with the emergence of Joshua as Moses' successor (Josh 1:1-9) and the leader of "Phase Two" in the epic story—the long anticipated entry into the Promised Land (the Eisodus).

Jezebel: A wicked
queen who was the
wife of King Ahab in
ancient Israel, and
the adversary of the
prophet Elijah.

In some respects, the brief and somewhat enigmatic reference to Joshua at the very center of the Pentateuch parallels the appearance of the wicked queen **Jezebel** at the structural center of the Former Prophets, which is discussed below. In both instances a more impressive and

obvious theological center of the larger concentric design of the literature as a whole, in which Moses and Elijah each experience decisive
theophanic visitations on the same holy mountain, tends to hide a brief
enigmatic comment at the actual center. As will be shown in detailed
examination of other segments of Scripture, in all three of the major
divisions of the traditional canon of the Old Testament, those who
compiled the canon in its present form apparently liked to put brief
enigmatic statements at the center of complex designs, the presence and
meaning of which could only be observed by the careful reader (or
hearer). More on this phenomenon later.

Concept Check # 7

It is often said that the exodus from Egypt is to the Old Testament
what the empty tomb is to the New Testament—namely the central
salvation event from which all else unfolds. From a theological perspective what is the most important consequence of the Exodus?
(Check your answer on p. 221.)

---

2. The Former Prophets: The Second Step in the Canonical Process

A somewhat parallel concentric structural design to what Newing
observed in his analysis of the Pentateuch can be seen in the Former
Prophets as well. Here the journey is from (1) the desert to the "Promised Land" symbolized as a mountain, to (2) the two central theophanies
(divine visitations) on Mount Carmel (1 Kings 18) and **Mount Horeb** (1
Kings 19), which depict the rule of God through both prophet and king;
and (3) the journey on to Mount Zion as the "City of God," particularly
as reflected in the climactic reforms of **Hezekiah** (2 Kings 18-20) and
Josiah (2 Kings 22-23).

The central stories within the primary structure of the Former
Prophets explore the role of the prophet in ancient Israel as follows:

A	Kingship and Prophecy: Prophet against Prophet	1 Kings 13
B	Elijah on Mount Carmel: Contest with Prophets of Baal	1 Kings 18
B′	Elijah on Mount Horeb: the Mosaic Prophet	1 Kings 19
A′	Kingship and Prophecy: Prophet against Prophet	1 Kings 22

Mount Horeb: Another name for Mount Sinai.

Hezekiah: One of the good kings in ancient Israel who was responsible for a religious reformation in the time of the prophet Isaiah (eighth century BCE).

Josiah: The king of Judah in the time of the prophet Jeremiah (late 7th century BCE), who was responsible for a great religious reformation which resulted in significant canonical activity centered in the book of Deuteronomy.

Baal: The great storm and fertility god of the Canaanites who was a rival to the Israelite god Yahweh in the time of the prophet Elijah.

Elijah is the focus of attention and is presented here as a Moses-figure who defeats the false prophets of the first kind as presented in Deut 18:9-14—namely, the Canaanite or pagan prophets who are an abomination. The second kind of false prophet, which is discussed in Deut 18:15-22, is the one who presumes to speak a word from Yahweh, the God of Israel.

The contest between Elijah and the prophets of **Baal** on Mount Carmel (1 Kings 18) is set against Elijah's theophanic experience on Mount Horeb (1 Kings 19). In this latter instance, Elijah's experience is patterned after that of Moses, who not only encountered God in the awesome "thunderstorm" on the holy mountain (Exod 19:16-24), but who also had the privilege of a glimpse of Yahweh's glory from a "cave" on that same holy mountain (Exod 33:17-23). But Elijah's experience is not, in fact, oriented toward the past. It foreshadows a new phase of prophetic activity within the canon of both the Former Prophets and the Latter Prophets in imagery which is particularly evident in the story of **Jonah**. Whereas Moses and Elijah ascended the mountain of God to experience a theophany, Jonah descended to "the roots of the mountains" where he also encountered Yahweh. The fact that details in the story of Elijah, as recorded in 1 Kings 19, are also reflected within the narrative of the book of Jonah has been noted by numerous scholars.[10] The *ruach qadim* ("sultry wind") of Jonah 4:8 is reminiscent of the *ruach gedolah wehazaq* ("great and mighty wind") of 1 Kgs 19:11. Note the other parallels: 1 Kgs 19:4-9 makes specific reference to a journey of one day (cf. Jonah 3:4); an experience beneath a strange tree (a "broom tree" in 1 Kgs 19:5; cf. the *qiqayon* [="vomiting Jon(ah)"] in Jonah 4:6-10), the death wish, reference to forty days, and the message from God (or an angel) addressed to the prophet twice.

Jonah: A prophet in Israel (8th century BCE), who is best known as the one who was swallowed by a great fish and survived three days in its belly and subsequently preached in the city of Nineveh. The story appears in the book of Jonah, which is the fifth book in the Book of the Twelve (minor prophets).

It is important to note the role of the wicked queen Jezebel, whose appearance connects the parallel stories of Elijah on Mount Carmel (1 Kings 18) and Mount Horeb (1 Kings 19). Like the reference to the transfer of leadership from Moses to Joshua at the center of the Pentateuch (Exod 34:11), we find here a remarkable leader in the person of Jezebel, the enemy of Elijah, and the subsequent transfer of her wicked influence to the southern kingdom of Judah through her daughter Athaliah (2 Kgs 9:37 and 11:16). The resulting structural pattern of "prophet" and "king" in the Former Prophets is a fascinating one:

A	Deborah and Barak	Judges 4-5
B	Jeroboam I and Prophetic Conflict	1 Kings 13
C	Elijah on Mount Carmel	1 Kings 18
X	Jezebel & Athaliah [1 Kgs 16:31 - 2 Kgs 9:37; 11:16]	
C'	Elijah on Mount Horeb	1 Kings 19
B'	Ahab and Prophetic Conflict	1 Kings 22
A'	Huldah and Josiah	2 Kings 22

In the opening story **Barak**, the son of Abinoam, foreshadows the idea of what constitutes a good king in the Former Prophets. Like **Saul** and **David**, Barak is primarily a war lord who is commissioned by the "prophet" to lead Israel in fighting Yahweh's wars. And, whatever his historical role may have been in ancient Israel, Barak as presented in this story is subject to the Word of God as delivered through the prophetess Deborah.

In similar fashion, Huldah plays a role of great importance in relation to King Josiah. It was to Huldah that Josiah sent Hilkiah, the high priest, to authenticate the "book of the Torah" which was found in the Temple (1 Kgs 22:13-14). And it was Huldah who pronounced a word of judgment, blessing, and instruction to both the people of Judah and their king (2 Kgs 22:16-20).

Besides Josiah, there are only two other kings who recognize the authority of the prophet in ancient Israel and thus are deemed to be good kings without qualification within the Former Prophets, namely: David, who recognized the authority of the prophet **Nathan**; and Hezekiah, who installed **Isaiah** as royal prophet in Judah after the fall of the northern kingdom of Israel to the Assyrians. It is curious to note that Isaiah's wife is also singled out as a "prophetess" in Isa 8:3. The only other time this term is used in the first two sections of the Hebrew canon (i.e., the Law and the Prophets) is to designate Miriam, the sister of Moses, as a "prophetess" in Exod 15:20.

The parallel stories on prophetic conflict in 1 Kings 13 and 22 present all three of the major themes of the Former Prophets:

1) the sin of King Jeroboam
2) the faithfulness of David and Josiah
3) the prophet like Moses

The story of the unnamed man of God who is slain by the lion of Judah is set over against the sin of **Jeroboam** at the very moment of the building

Barak: The military leader who, together with the prophetess Deborah, fought against the Canaanites (ca. 12th century BCE).

Saul: The first king in ancient Israel (11th century BCE) who fought against the Philistines.

David: The successor of King Saul, who established Jerusalem as the capital of the state of Israel and built an empire in which the people of Israel occupied the whole of the Promised Land for the first time.

Nathan: A prophet in Judah in the time of King David (ca. 1000 BCE).

Isaiah: A prophet in Jerusalem in the time of King Hezekiah (late 8th century BCE).

Jeroboam: The successor to Solomon and the first king of the northern state of Israel (as opposed to Judah), after the division of Israel into two separate political entities (late 10th century BCE).

Bethel: The religious center of the northern kingdom of Israel, and one of the two places in which King Jeroboam erected golden calves to replace the ark of the covenant as a primary religious symbol.

of the detested altar in **Bethel** (1 Kings 13). And Josiah is named explicitly, in what is perhaps the most glaring *vaticinum ex eventu* (prediction from or after the event) in the Bible (1 Kgs 13:2). The primary focus of the story, however, is on prophetic conflict, which takes on still deeper meaning when seen over against the story of Micaiah and Zedekiah in 1 Kings 22. Both stories deal with two prophets in conflict, each of whom presumes to speak the word of Yahweh (cf. Deut 18:20-22). In one case, the two prophets are anonymous; while, in the other, they are named. In one instance, the prophetic word is described as coming from a "messenger" (angel) of Yahweh (1 Kgs 13:18). On the other hand, Micaiah described a vision of the proceedings of the heavenly court with Yahweh himself presiding over the host of heaven (1 Kgs 22:19). The description of what Micaiah observed throws unexpected light on an ambiguous statement in the earlier story. In Micaiah's account, it was Yahweh who sent the "lying spirit" to entice Ahab to go up to his own death. In the previous story, the narrator added the simple statement, "He lied to him" (1 Kgs 13:18). Though the commentaries are almost unanimous in assuming that it was the old prophet from Bethel who deceived the man of God from Judah, it is certainly possible that the "angel" was the author of the lie; and that the old prophet lied unwittingly. Such an interpretation makes it much easier to understand his grief over the death of his "brother" (1 Kgs 13:30) and the curious instructions he gave to his sons (or followers): "When I die, bury me in a grave in which the man of God is buried; lay my bones beside his bones" (1 Kgs 13:31).

Concept Check # 8

A central concern in the Former Prophets is the relationship between the prophet and the king in ancient Israel. What is it that makes a king a good king in the Former Prophets? (Check your answer on p. 221.)

The Role of Women in the Former Prophets

The most interesting feature of the structuring device observed in this nesting of parallel stories within the Former Prophets is the actual center. It is the wicked Jezebel who forms the bridge between the two mountaintop experiences of Elijah. And the structure invites a comparison of Jezebel with Deborah and Huldah. In the account of Josephus, Jezebel's father, Ethbaal king of the Sidonians, was a priest in the Phoenician cult of Baal and **Astarte** (*Antiquities*, VIII, xiii, 2). Be that as it may, she certainly is responsible in the biblical story for advancing the cult of Baal in Israel; as her daughter Athaliah is subsequently in Judah (2 Kgs 2:18).

It is instructive to examine closely the description of the death of Jezebel and her daughter Athaliah. When Jehu came to Jezreel for Jezebel, she was in an upper room where "she painted her eyes, and adorned her head, and looked out of the window" (2 Kgs 9:30). What a splendid woman! Though she knew her death was imminent, she was going to make her exit in style. But of even greater interest to the careful reader is the actual wording here, which reminds one of the ending of the "Song of Deborah," where:

> Out of the window she peered;
> The mother of Sisera gazed through the lattice (Judg 5:28).

In Canaanite mythology the god Mot ("Death") entered Baal's palace through a window, which the latter had been urged not to construct. It would appear that the phrase, "Through the window (or lattice)," is a metaphor for the way in which death enters a building. The text in the "Song of Deborah" continues by quoting the mother of Sisera:

> Why is his chariot so long in coming?
> Why tarry the hoofbeat of his chariots? (Judg 5:28b)

The imagery here foreshadows the description of the death of Jezebel's daughter Athaliah who was taken out of the Temple "through the horses' entrance to the king's house" where she was brutally slain (2 Kgs 11:16).

But it is not just repetition of words or imagery as such, however, that ties together these four dominant women in the narrative account in the Former Prophets. The presentation of these four women also takes up the three central themes of the literary work as a whole, as already noted, while at the same time introducing something more.

A   Deborah: a "Prophetess" of Yahweh alongside Barak
B   Jezebel: a Royal Advocate of Baal in Israel
B′   Athaliah: a Royal Advocate of Baal in Judah
A′ Huldah: a "Prophetess" of Yahweh alongside Josiah

Astarte: A Canaanite goddess who was the consort of Baal and a popular deity among the common people in ancient Israel.

Huldah brings an added dimension to the theme of Josiah's faithfulness. In place of the sin of Jeroboam we have explicit pagan practice that centers in the worship of Baal. And though the two "prophetesses" here are not in conflict with each other, they are clearly set in sharp contrast to the two royal feminine personages to illustrate the inherent tension between "prophet" and "king" in ancient Israel.

But why did the author of the Former Prophets focus on these four dominant women in this structural schema? How are we to explain the fact that in the Former Prophets, which took final shape at the end of the national history of Israel, women are singled out to occupy major roles in both the royal and prophetic offices? The answer to these questions is perhaps to be found in placing the tradition of the Former Prophets within its proper social location in ancient Israel.

Though it may be going too far to see Huldah as Jeremiah's aunt, as Robert Wilson has suggested, it is clear that the circle of persons mentioned in 2 Kgs 23:3-14 includes members of the priesthood in **Anathoth**: namely, descendants of **Abiathar**, who were part of the central political establishment in Jerusalem under Josiah.[11] The "men of Anathoth" who subsequently plotted to kill Jeremiah are probably to be identified "as some of Jeremiah's priestly relatives who were still occupying positions in Jerusalem's religious establishment" after Jeremiah's removal from the royal court.[12]

The establishment of Levitical priests in Anathoth, a suburb of modern Jerusalem, was probably the social location which preserved the so-called Northern or Ephraimite tradition in ancient Israel. The prophet Jeremiah was born in Anathoth. Josiah's reform thus included a religious compromise which brought back the "Moses group" which stemmed ultimately from the ancient religious center of Shiloh—before the time of David. This ancient perspective was canonized in the Former Prophets alongside that of the royal **Zadokite** priesthood, which was long established in Jerusalem. It was this alternative view of Israel's ancient story that was in fact the more archaic. In fact, the description of Josiah's great Passover celebration is instructive: "For no such Passover had been kept since the days of the judges who judged Israel, or during the days of the kings of Israel or of the kings of Judah" (2 Kgs 23:22).

It was the institution of kingship in ancient Israel, at least from the point of view of the "men of Anathoth," which was ultimately responsible for all that was wrong in ancient Israel—including the subordination of

Anathoth: A town associated with the Levitical priests in ancient Israel, located about two miles NE of Jerusalem, and the birthplace of the prophet Jeremiah.

Abiathar: One of the two high priests in the time of David, whom King Solomon exiled to Anathoth.

Zadok(ite): Zadok was the other high priest whom David established in Jerusalem, and the single holder of that position after Abiathar was exiled by Solomon. His descendants, the Zadokites, continued as the established priesthood in Jerusalem until the time of Antiochus Epiphanes (mid-2nd century BCE).

women. The social stratification introduced by a new economic and political order, and the royal harem in particular, as introduced by Solomon, were responsible for subtle and far-reaching changes in status for women. The "Northern" (i.e., non-Jerusalem) perspective, as preserved among the "men of Anathoth," was more archaic in nature, rooted in agrarian values of a pre-monarchic era where the sexes were treated with relative equality. It was to this Moses-group in Anathoth that both Huldah and Jeremiah belonged. Among the agrarian values they brought to the canonical process in the time of Josiah was a high regard for the place of women in roles of leadership, both religious and political.

It should be noted that the treatment of women within the Former Prophets is simply part of a larger concern for the powerless in ancient Israel. The "men of Anathoth" were excluded from political power from the time of Solomon to Josiah and again after the fall of Jerusalem. The book of Deuteronomy represents their point of view in its concern for the widow, the orphan, and the alien within the social structure of ancient Israel. For the most part, women in general were among the powerless whose rights were protected by deuteronomic legislation. They also apparently provided an appropriate symbol around which to structure some of the central theological concerns of the Former Prophets.

> ### Concept Check # 9
>
> The plight of women in ancient Judaism is well known, as illustrated by the daily prayer among the Pharisees in the time of Jesus which included the sentence, "Thank God I was not born a woman." How do you explain the fact that women play such a dominant role in the literary structure of the Former Prophets? (Check your answer on p. 221.)

The Structure of the Former Prophets

The final arrangement of the canon of the Law and the Prophets in the First Testament still reflects an earlier "three plus one" structuring of the tradition within the developing canonical process. Wholeness in Jungian thought is normally expressed in fourfold structures. Within these structures the four elements in any given unit tend to be arranged in a chiasm; while at the same time, three of the four are generally set over against the fourth. In terms of the books in the Pentateuch and Former Prophets, the resultant structure is as follows:

Exodus	Leviticus	*Joshua*	Judges
Numbers	*Deuteronomy*	Samuel	Kings

Here the three "wilderness books" (Exodus, Leviticus, and Numbers) are supplemented by a "second recitation of the law" (Deuteronomy) on the part of Moses immediately before his death. This fourfold structure appears on first glance to be the story of Moses, beginning with his birth (Exodus 1-2) and ending with his death (Deuteronomy 34). A closer look at detail within Exodus and Deuteronomy reveals aspects of a concentric arrangement. There are two "Songs of Moses," Exodus 15 and Deuteronomy 32, which in turn frame two great covenant ceremonies under Moses' leadership—one at Mount Sinai (Exodus 19) and the other on the Plains of Moab (Deuteronomy 29-31), east of the Jordan River. The first of these covenant ceremonies is concluded by the giving of the "ten commandments" (Exodus 20) followed by the "Covenant Code" (Exodus 21-23); whereas the second is preceded by a second giving of the "ten commandments" (Deuteronomy 5) followed by the "Deuteronomic Code" (Deuteronomy 12-26).[13] And the books of Exodus and Deuteronomy seem to frame the two parallel wilderness books of Leviticus and Numbers. Newing has investigated the concentric design of this section of the Pentateuch in some detail and argues that the very center is to be found in Exodus 33, which he calls the "Promised Presence," where Moses gets a glimpse of the glory of Yahweh.[14]

According to A. H. van Zyl, the Former Prophets are also arranged in a concentric design.[15]

A	Conquest of the land under charismatic leadership	Deut & Josh
B	Possession of the land under charismatic leadership	Judg & 1 Sam
B'	Possession of the land under monarchic government	2 Sam & 1 Kgs
A'	Loss of the land under monarchic government	2 Kgs

Here the story moves from the conquest of the land under charismatic leadership (Joshua) to the loss of the land under monarchic government (2 Kings). In between we have the possession of the land under charismatic leadership (Judges and 1 Samuel) set over against the possession of the land under monarchic government (2 Samuel and 1 Kings).

The book of Deuteronomy functions as a literary bridge connecting the Torah (the five books of Moses) and the Former Prophets (Joshua through Kings), which most scholars refer to as the Deuteronomic (or Deuteronomistic) History. In short, Deuteronomy has a Janus-like quality in that it looks both backwards and forwards. Moses is at the end of his 120-year lifespan. On the one hand, he looks back and retells the story of deliverance from bondage and exile in Egypt including a second giving of the Torah which he received on Mount Sinai—this time from the plains of Moab. On the other hand, he looks forward as the people are now poised on the edge of the Promised Land; and Moses commissions Joshua to take them across the Jordan River to possess that land. The book of Deuteronomy may be outlined as follows:

A	The Outer Frame:	Part 1—A Look Backwards	Deut 1-3
B	The Inner Frame:	Part 1—The Great Peroration	Deut 4-11
X	The Central Core:	Covenant Stipulations	Deut 12-26
B′	The Inner Frame:	Part 2—The Covenant Ceremony	Deut 27-30
A′	The Outer Frame:	Part 2—A Look Forward	Deut 31-34

Joshua is introduced in Deut 1:38 as the person Moses is to encourage as the new leader of God's people. Joshua appears once again in Deut 3:21 as the one Yahweh has chosen. This transition in leadership from Moses to Joshua is the focus of attention in Deut 3:23-29; but Joshua does not appear again in the book of Deuteronomy until the beginning of the second half of the "Outer Frame" (Deuteronomy 31-34), when Moses stands at the end of his allotted 120 years (cf. Deut 31:1 and 34:7).

The book of Joshua begins with the death of Moses (Josh 1:1) and continues to the death of Joshua (Josh 24:29) at 110 years of age. The first half of the book tells the story of the "Eisodus" (entry into the Promised Land—chs. 1-12), which is climaxed with the simple statement that: "Now Joshua was old and advanced in years . . . and there remains yet very much land to be possessed" (Josh 13:1). The second half of the book is made up of boundary lists and the division of the land among the twelve tribes of Israel. This lengthy section plays a psychological function for the reader in that it slows down the action and serves to set the book of Joshua off from the three books that follow: Judges, Samuel, and Kings. At the same time, it is clear that the person of Joshua foreshadows that of King Josiah at the end of the Former Prophets (2 Kings 22-23), who presides over the fourth great **Passover**, which was unlike any such

Passover: The annual spring festival in ancient Israel and Judaism which celebrates the story of the Exodus in which the angel of death "passed over" the people of Israel and did not kill the first-born sons as he did with the Egyptians. The festival includes the "passing over" of the waters of the Red Sea when they left Egypt, which in turn is associated with the "passing over" of the River Jordan under Joshua when the people of Israel entered the Promised Land in the Eisodus.

Passover "since the days of the judges who judged Israel, or during all the days of the kings of Israel or of the kings of Judah" (2 Kgs 23:22).

The first great Passover was celebrated in Egypt when the "angel of death" passed over the houses where the blood of the sacrificial lamb was placed on the lintel and the two doorposts, as Yahweh had instructed (Exodus 11-12). The second great Passover was celebrated in the wilderness of Sinai "in the first month of the second year after they had come out of the land of Egypt" (Numbers 9). The third great Passover was celebrated in Gilgal near Jericho under Joshua, after the children of Israel had "passed over" the Jordan River; and, "on the morrow after the Passover . . . the manna ceased" (Joshua 5-12). King Josiah's Passover continued, and completed, this tradition.

On the surface, the book of Judges appears to be an almost miscellaneous collection of stories, without overall structure. However, a closer look reveals a fascinating concentric design:

A	Preview: the Nation Disintegrating	1:1-36
B	Judgement on Bethel	2:1-5
C	The Cycle of Idolatry, Oppression, and Deliverance	2:6 - 3:6
D	Three Judges from the South: Othniel, Ehud &Shamgar	3:7-31
E	Deborah/Barak vs. the Canaanites in the North	4:1 - 5:31
F	Gideon & His Son Abimelech in the Center/West	6:1 - 9:57
G	Tola in Ephraim (Center/West)	10:1-2
G ′	Jair in Gilead (Center/East)	10:3-6
F ′	Jephthah & His Daughter in the Center/East	10:7 - 12:7
E ′	Three Judges from the North: Ibzan, Elon &Abdon	12:8-15
D′	Samson vs. the Philistines in the South	13:1 - 16:31
C ′	A New Cycle of Idolatry, Oppression, and Deliverance	17:1-13
B′	Judgement on Dan	18:1-31
A′	Postview: the People Being Reunified	19:1-21:25

The center of this structure [FGG′F′] focuses attention on kingship. On the one hand, **Gideon** is presented as the first man in ancient Israel who is specifically invited to assume kingship: "Then the children of Israel said to Gideon, 'Rule over us, you and your son and your grandson also'" (Judg 8:22). But Gideon refused, saying: "I will not rule over you, and my son will not rule over you; Yahweh will rule over you" (Judg 8:23). Moreover, Gideon named his son **Abimelech**, which means "My father is king." Here Gideon is referring to God as his father.

A name like Abimelech, however, invites a different interpretation of its meaning. After Gideon's death, his son Abimelech slew his seventy

Gideon: One of the judges of Israel who delivered the people from the Midianites in the 11th century BCE. He was the first person whom the people of Israel asked to rule over them as king.

Abimelech: The son of Gideon who actually ruled as king in Israel for three years until his assassination, which occurred a century before the official inauguration of kingship under Saul.

brothers on a single stone and became, in fact, Israel's first king (Judg 9:1-6). It was as though Abimelech read his own name as "my father (Gideon) was king," even though Gideon had refused to accept that position. Abimelech ruled as king in Israel for three years, until he was assassinated by a certain woman who "threw an upper millstone upon Abimelech's head, and crushed his skull" (Judg 9:53).

The events of the stories of Gideon and **Jephthah** took place in the geographical center of the land of Israel. It is interesting to note, however, the direction of movement; which is from west to east, in a curious reversal of the "Eisodus" (entry into the land) under Joshua. The story of Jephthah begins in the "land of Tob" (*'erets tob*, Judg 11:3), which appears to be a word play on the "good land" (*'erets tobah*) in the "Song of the Good Land" (Deut 8:7-10). Though the "land of Tob" has not been located to the satisfaction of many scholars, it is certainly to be found east of the Jordan River in the land of Gilead, so far as the story of Jephthah is concerned. In short, the Promised Land is redefined in the Former Prophets to include the nations of the world among the people of God.[16]

The story of Gideon is the story of a man and his son; whereas the story of Jephthah is the story of a man and his daughter. The structural parallels take on deeper meaning as the biblical text is examined in detail. Abimelech, the son of Gideon, comes off as a self-centered person intent on grasping power. On the other hand, the unnamed daughter of Jephthah is the innocent victim of perhaps the most unjust deed perpetrated in all of Scripture, with the possible exception of another "only child," of a father much greater than Gideon, who died outside the city of Jerusalem more than a millennium later in time.

When the Ammonites made war on Israel, the elders of Gilead turned to Jephthah for help. Like King David after him, Jephthah had gathered around him a military band of "worthless fellows" who "went raiding with him" (Judg 11: 3; cf. 1 Sam 22:1-2). But there is much more here to suggest that the story of Jephthah is indeed exploring matters pertaining to kingship, from the time of David to that of Josiah—and beyond. At first, the elders of Gilead asked Jephthah to become both their "leader" (*qatsin,* Judg 11:6) and their "head" (*rosh,* Judg 11:8). As the story unfolds, Jephthah only agrees to be their "head" (vs. 9), even though the people "made him head and leader over them" (vs. 11). The distinction in meaning between these two words is significant; for

Jephthah: Another judge in ancient Israel who delivered Israel from the Ammonites in Transjordan. He is best known for the sacrifice of his daughter to fulfill a rash vow he made to Yahweh, the God of the Israelites, during a battle.

Jephthah goes on to perpetrate perhaps the most unjust deed recorded in the First Testament. To be "head" is to be military commander; whereas, to be "leader" is to dispense justice. The question is that of the relationship between justice and power in the hands of those who would be leaders, namely kings. Kingship is a necessary evil. As Mark Twain once put it, "Kings is mostly rapscallions"—and so they are. That is a central point so far as the book of Judges is concerned.

The stories that frame the central pair of stories about Gideon and Jephthah introduce the deuteronomic theology of kingship in relation to prophecy. The good king is the one who listens to the voice of the prophet whom God has raised up in that particular time. Earlier in the book of Judges, God raised up the prophetess **Deborah** when Israel faced a crisis at the hands of the Canaanites under their commander Sisera (Judges 4-5). In this story, Barak models the role of the good king, so far as military leadership is concerned, when he said to Deborah: "If you will go with me, I will go; but if you will not go with me, I will not go" (Judg 4:8). It is the prophet of God, and the prophet alone, who has the authority to declare God's "holy war" in ancient Israel. Moreover, a second woman prophet appears much later in the Deuteronomic History, alongside the good King Josiah, in the person of **Huldah** (2 Kgs 22:14-20; cf. 2 Kings 23). What makes Josiah a good king, so far as deuteronomic theology is concerned, is the simple fact that he recognized the authority of the prophet of God in ancient Israel. When the "Book of the Torah" was found in the Temple, it was brought to Josiah who instructed Hilkiah the priest to speak with the prophetess Huldah. It was Huldah who authenticated the document and who gave specific instructions to Josiah; and the king did what Huldah the prophetess instructed him to do. That's what made Josiah a good king, from the point of view of those who composed the Former Prophets; namely, he recognized the authority of God's chosen prophet.

It should be noted that the Deuteronomic History (the Former Prophets), like the Pentateuch, has a structural center, which consists of two parallel mountaintop experiences on the part of Elijah. In 1 Kings 18, Elijah calls down fire from heaven in the great contest with the prophets of Baal on Mount Carmel. In the next chapter, he flees from Jezebel and makes his way to Mount Horeb, the mountain of God's revelation earlier to Moses, where the prophet Elijah too gains a glimpse of the glory of Yahweh. But after each theophanic visitation, the narrator is careful to comment that God was not present in the wind, in the earthquake, nor in the fire. This time God communicates his glory through the awesome silence of his mysterious absence. Needless to say, the confluence of these two encounters with God on that same sacred mountain point beyond the present to another mountaintop experience in the distant future, where Moses and Elijah are joined by a prophet greater than either of them through whom the glory of God is revealed, in what the gospel writers call the transfiguration of Jesus.[17]

Concept Check # 10

The fact that the Former Prophets are also called the "Deuteronomic History" points to the close connection between this body of literature and the book of Deuteronomy. Describe the function of the book of Deuteronomy within the Primary History from a literary point of view. (Check your answer on p. 221.)

Thinking Exercise

On the Torah and the Former Prophets

What exactly is meant by the term "Primary History" as used by David Noel Freedman?

_____

The critical thinking goal for this exercise is to clarify the concept of the "Primary History" as an initial stage in the canonical process.

How To Do This Exercise

First, review the definitions of "Torah" and "Former Prophets." Then state the answers to questions 1 and 2. Read the stories in Exodus 33 and 1 Kings 19 before answering question 3.

1. The "Center" of the Pentateuch (Exod 33:1-17) presents:

_____

_____

_____

2. The "Center" of the Former Prophets (1 Kings 18-19) presents:

_____

_____

_____

3. What do these stories have in common?

_____

_____

_____

4. Can you think of another story in the Bible which includes Moses and Elijah on the same mountain? (See Luke 9:28-31.)

_____

_____

_____

3. The Latter Prophets: The Third Step in the Canonical Process

The Latter Prophets make up the third of the four major sections in the canon of the First Testament (i.e., the *Tanakh* = Torah + Former Prophets + Latter Prophets + Writings). Like the Torah and the Former Prophets, these books also display a chiastic structure, when examined in relation to each other:

Isaiah	Jeremiah
Ezekiel	"The Twelve" (Minor Prophets)

Though **Daniel** is often associated with the twelve minor prophets, that book stands among the Writings in the fourth part of the Hebrew canon and will be discussed in the next section of this book.

Isaiah and the Book of the Twelve

The close relation between Isaiah and the Book of the Twelve (the so-called "minor prophets") can be shown in a number of ways. In the first place, these books include the only explicit connection with the Former Prophets, in that Isaiah and Jonah are the only ones among the Latter Prophets who are mentioned by name in the Former Prophets. Neither **Jeremiah** nor **Ezekiel** are mentioned in 2 Kings. In the second place, both Isaiah and the Book of the Twelve cover the same time span—from ca. 750 to 500 BCE.

According to 2 Kgs 14:23-29, Jeroboam II "restored the border of Israel from Lebo-hamath as far as the Sea of the Arabah, according to the word of Yahweh, the God of Israel, which he spoke by his servant Jonah son of Amittai, the prophet, who was from Gath-hepher" (2 Kgs 14:25). The prophets **Hosea** and **Amos** are also placed in the time of Jeroboam II (see Hos 1:1 and Amos 1:1). It is interesting to note that Jonah's home town, Gath-hepher, is but a few miles from both Nazareth, where Jesus grew up, and the city of Sepphoris, which has been the focus of recent archaeological discoveries of note.

The prophet Isaiah appears in 2 Kings 19-20, where he was consulted by King Hezekiah at the time of the invasion of Judah by the Assyrian King Sennacherib. The text of 2 Kgs 18:13 – 20:19 (except for 2 Kgs 18:14-16) appears in Isaiah in 36:1 – 39:8 (except for 38:9-20) where it stands at the center of the book of Isaiah, as a bridge—connecting what

---

Daniel: A prophet who was exiled to Babylon, where he subsequently assumed a high position in the government of the Persian Empire (much like Joseph in Egypt). The book of Daniel is the only fully developed apocalyptic writing in the First Testament.

Jeremiah: A Hebrew prophet who ministered in Judah during the latter part of the 7th and the early 6th centuries BCE, primarily in Jerusalem. He died as an exile in Egypt.

Ezekiel: A Hebrew prophet who ministered in Babylon during the latter part of the 7th and the first half of the sixth centuries BCE, after being taken away from Jerusalem in exile.

Hosea: A Hebrew prophet of the 8th century BCE who ministered primarily in the northern kingdom (Israel) before and after its fall to the Assyrians. The book of Hosea is the first book in the Book of the Twelve.

Amos (see next page).

Amos: A Hebrew prophet of the 8th century BCE from Judah who ministered in the northern kingdom of Israel as well as in Judah before the fall of Samaria in 722/21 BCE. The book of Amos is the third book in the Book of the Twelve (minor prophets).

scholars have called Proto-Isaiah (chaps. 1-35) and Deutero-Isaiah (chaps. 40-66), or as John Watts recently put it:[18]

Part I: The Former Times: Judgement, Curse (Isaiah 1-39)

Part II: The Latter Times: Salvation, Blessing (Isaiah 40-66)

In his recent commentary on the book of Isaiah, John Watts divided the book into twelve "Acts of the Vision of Isaiah" as follows:[19]

Act I	Like a Booth in a Vineyard	chs. 1-6
Act II	The Gently Flowing Waters	chs. 7-14
Act III	Opportunity and Disappointment	chs. 15-22
Act IV	The Impact of Tyre's Fall	chs. 23-27
Act V	Requiem for the Kingdom of Judah	chs. 28-33
Act VI	From Curse to Blessing	chs. 34-39
Act VII	Good News for Jerusalem	40:1-44:23
Act VIII	Cyrus, the Lord's Anointed	44:24-48:22
Act IX	The Servant of Rulers	49:1-52:12
Act X	Restoration Pains in Jerusalem	52:13-57:21
Act XI	Zion's Light Shines	chs. 58-61
Act XII	For Zion's Sake: New Heavens & New Land	chs. 62-66

Watts argued that these twelve sections are arranged in chronological time frames, extending from 745 through 464 BCE, with the final section focusing on the eschatological "Age to Come" (Isaiah 63-66). This outline suggests a structural relation with the Book of the Twelve, in which Isaiah 36-39 (= 2 Kgs 18:13 – 20:19) functions as the structural center and a connecting link to the Former Prophets.

The Book of the Twelve appears to be arranged in a concentric structure, similar in ways to that of the book of Isaiah, as follows:

A   Hosea / Joel / Amos
B   Obadiah
C   Jonah—Micah
C'   Nahum—Habakkuk
B'   Zephaniah
A'   Haggai / Zechariah / Malachi

Once again, as is the case with Isaiah, the center of this structure is closely tied to the Former Prophets. Not only is Jonah mentioned by name in 2 Kgs 14:25, there are other links which connect the story of Jonah with that of Elijah in 1 Kings 19. Like Elijah, Jonah asked God that he might die (cf. 1 Kgs 19:4 and Jonah 4:3, 8). Both prophets sat down beneath a desert tree after a journey of one day (1 Kgs 19:4 and Jonah 3:4, 6) where they received an unexpected message from God; and both had lain down and had gone to sleep (cf. 1 Kgs 19:5 and Jonah 1:5) before receiving that message. Elijah was told a second time by the "angel of Yahweh" to journey forty days to meet God on the holy mountain (1 Kgs 19:8). Jonah met Yahweh at the "roots of the mountains" and, after his theophany, was told a second time to enter Nineveh, where his message was focused on forty days (Jonah 3:4). In short, Jonah is an anti-Elijah figure—he represents a reversal of the narrative journey of that great transitional prophetic figure in the Former Prophets.

The book of Jonah includes perhaps the most elaborate system of concentric structures to be found anywhere in the Bible. At the same time, the book also has curious ties to the book of Genesis (especially Genesis 1-11) in the Torah,[20] and to the book of Psalms,[21] which belongs to the Writings. In short, this literary masterpiece functions as a keystone in the literary structure of the First Testament. Concentric structures can be demonstrated for each of its four chapters, for each half of the book, and for the book as a whole:

Chapter 2

A	Yahweh appointed a Great Fish to swallow Jonah	2:1-2
B	Jonah's prayer from Sheol: a lament	2:3
C	Though driven from Yahweh's presence, Jonah continued to look to Yahweh's holy temple	2:4-5
D	Jonah's descent "to the roots of the mountains"	2:6-7b
D´	Jonah's ascent "from the pit"	2:7c
C´	Though his "soul-life had expired," Jonah continued to turn to Yahweh in his holy temple	2:8
B´	Jonah's prayer in Yahweh's "temple": a thanksgiving	2:9-10
A´	At Yahweh's word the fish vomited out Jonah	2:11

Chapter 4

A	A Great Evil came upon Jonah (his anger).	4:1-2b
B	Yahweh's compassion (reported by Jonah):	
	"You are a compassionate and gracious God"	4:2cd
C	Jonah's response: "I am better off dead!"	4:3
D	Yahweh's question: "Do you do well to be angry?"	4:4
E	Jonah built a booth to wait for God's "anger."	4:5
F	Yahweh/God appointed a *Qiqayon*,	
	which brought Great Joy.	4:6
F '	The God appointed a worm,	
	which destroyed the *Qiqayon*.	4:7
E '	God appointed the *ruach qadim*, which brought anguish.	4:8
D '	God's question: "Do you do well to be angry?"	4:9a
C '	Jonah's response: "I do well to be angry—unto death!"	4:9b
B'	Jonah's "compassion" (reported by Yahweh):	
	"You showed pity for the *Qiqayon*"	4:10
A'	Yahweh justifies his compassion for Nineveh.	4:11

Chapters 1-2

A	Yahweh told Jonah to enter the "House of the Fish."	1:1-2
B	Jonah fled from Yahweh (instead of "fearing" him).	1:3
C	Yahweh hurled a Great Wind to(ward) the sea,	
	and a Great Storm threatened to destroy the ship.	1:4
D	In fear the sailors prayed to their gods	1:5a
E	The sailors hurled the cargo into the sea;	
	Jonah went down inside the ship and fell asleep.	1:5b
F	The captain ordered Jonah to pray for salvation.	1:6
G	Jonah is found out by lot.	1:7
H	The sailors ask: "Who are you?"	1:8
I	Jonah's confession: "I am a Hebrew, I fear Yahweh."	1:9
I'	It is the men who feared—with a Great Fear.	1:10a
H '	The men asked: "What have you done?"	1:10b
G '	Jonah's flight is revealed.	1:10c
F '	The men asked Jonah what they must do.	1:11-12a
E '	Jonah told them to hurl him into the sea;	
	but the men rowed for shore.	1:12b-13
D '	The men prayed to Yahweh:	
	"Hold us not responsible for 'innocent' blood."	1:14-15a
C '	The men hurled Jonah to(ward) the sea,	
	which "ceased its raging."	1:15b
B'	The men feared Yahweh—with a Great Fear	1:16
A'	Yahweh appointed a Great Fish to house Jonah.	2:1-11

Chapters 3-4

A	Yahweh renewed Jonah's commission to enter Nineveh	3:1-2
B	Jonah's repentance: he proclaimed a message of "doom"	3:3-4
C	Nineveh's repentance	3:5-6a
D	The king's repentance	3:6b-7a
X	Decree of the king of Nineveh: "Turn from evil"	3:7b-8
D´	The king's hope (that God may repent)	3:9
C´	God's repentance	3:10
B´	Jonah's Great Evil—his anger (vs. Yahweh's compassion)	4:1-11
A´	Jonah's/Israel's response: oracle of salvation	implied

Jonah

A	Jonah's commission	1:1-2
B	Jonah vs. Yahweh: Jonah's flight & Yahweh's storm ("anger")	1:3-4
C	Dialogue between sailors and Jonah: "fear" motif	1:5-13
D	Sailors' prayer: "Hold us not responsible for this man's death."	1:14a
E	Yahweh's sovereign freedom: "What pleases you is what you have done."	1:14b
F	The sea ceased its raging ("anger").	1:15
G	The men feared Yahweh with a Great Fear.	1:16
H	Yahweh appointed Great Fish to change Jonah's mind.	2:1-2
I	Song of Jonah: a "proclamation" of deliverance	2:3-10
J	Jonah's deliverance	2:11
K	Jonah's commission renewed	3:1-2
K´	Jonah's response: an oracle of "doom" to Nineveh	3:3-4
J´	Nineveh's repentance	3:5-7a
I´	Decree of king: a proclamation to turn from evil	3:7b-9
H´	God changed his mind.	3:10
G´	A Great Evil came upon Jonah.	4:1a
F´	Jonah became angry.	4:1b
E´	Yahweh's sovereign freedom: "I knew you would repent from the evil."	4:2
D´	Jonah's prayer: "I am better off dead than alive."	4:3
C´	Dialogue between Yahweh/God and Jonah: "anger" motif	4:4-9
B´	Yahweh vs. Jonah: Yahweh justifies his compassion.	4:10-11
A´	Jonah's/Israel's response: an oracle of salvation	implied

The fact that Jonah and **Micah** constitute a single literary category is seen in the fact that the missing ending of the book of Jonah is supplied in the traditional practice within Judaism in which the book is read during the afternoon reading on **Yom Kippur** (the Day of Atonement). Without comment, the reading of the book of Jonah concludes with Mic 7:18-20.

Micah: A Hebrew prophet of the 8th century BCE who ministered primarily in the southern kingdom of Judah before and after the fall of Samaria in 722/21 BCE. The book of Micah is the sixth book in the Book of the Twelve.

Yom Kippur: The "Day of Atonement," a day of fasting, self-denial, and rest on which the sanctuary is cleansed of all impurities and the sins of the people are sent away on the scapegoat.

A somewhat similar connection between the books of **Nahum** and **Habakkuk** may be demonstrated. These two books are framed by theophanic hymns: the acrostic of Nah 1:2-10 and the psalm of Habakkuk 3. The concentric literary structure of Nahum-Habakkuk may be outlined as follows:

A	Hymn of theophany	Nahum 1
B	Taunt song against Nineveh	Nahum 2-3
X	The problem of theodicy	Habakkuk 1
B′	Taunt songs against the "wicked one"	Habakkuk 2
A′	Hymn of theophany	Habakkuk 3

The opening hymn of theophany (Nahum 1:2-10) is in the form of a **cipher** based on an acrostic of the first half of the alphabet (cf. Psalm 9),[22] which presents the two sides of God's character: he is slow to anger; but he will vent his wrath against those who defy him. The appearance of the Divine Warrior is presented in mythic imagery with the cosmos returning to chaos in the day of God's wrath. In the taunt song (Nah 2-3), sometimes described as an ode on the fall of Nineveh, the language is graphic, depicting in vivid form scenes of horror and vengeful rejoicing because Assyria is finally experiencing the atrocities she had inflicted on others.

The first chapter of Habakkuk discusses the central problem of just how long God will continue to look on while faithless and wicked people persecute those who are more righteous than they (Habakkuk 1). The text is in the form of a dialogue between the prophet and God in two cycles, which is concluded by the so-called "placarded revelation" in Hab 2:4—a text which plays a pivotal role in later history, on the lips of the apostle Paul (Rom 1:17 and Gal 3:11) and Martin Luther: "The just shall live by faith (and faith alone)." The book of Habakkuk continues with a meditation on the "Wicked Man" in the form of a taunt song in the form of a series of four "woes" (Hab 2:5-17) and a statement about idolatry (Hab 2:18-20), which sets the stage for the archaic hymn of theophany in Habakkuk 3. The Divine Warrior appears at the prophet's request in an awesome vision which causes the prophet to recoil in great distress.

Further evidence that these four books at the center of the Book of the Twelve constitute a literary unit is found in two observations about the books of Nahum and Jonah. In the first place, these two books both have the city of Nineveh as their subject. The book of Nahum is concerned with the destruction of that wicked city; whereas the book of

Jonah is concerned with its salvation. The second observation of note is the simple fact that these two books are the only ones in the Bible which end in a question.

Nahum is primarily a book about God's justice, not about human vengeance, hatred, and military conquest. The book is best read as a complement to the book of Jonah. The book of Jonah may be read as a midrashic reflection on Exod 34:6, and God's steadfast love (*chesed*); whereas the book of Nahum reflects Exod 34:7, and God's wrath. In short, Nahum focuses on the "dark side" of God, and Jonah portrays God's mercy and compassion toward the same wicked city. Both aspects are essential for an understanding of the divine nature.

The Book of the Twelve may be described as three groups of four books, with a central group, Jonah / Micah // Nahum / Habakkuk, framed by Hosea, Joel, and Amos + Obadiah, on the one hand, and Zephaniah + Haggai, Zechariah, and Malachi, on the other. The "**Day of Yahweh**" is a major structuring device for much of this material. The books of Hosea and Malachi form an envelope around the whole, with the focus on the covenant relationship with God in terms of love in the context of the analogy of marriage. The center of the Book of the Twelve, as reflected in the two pairs of books, Jonah / Micah // Nahum / Habakkuk, focuses attention on the nature of prophecy itself and the problem of theodicy, which will be explored in detail later in the final section of the canon, the Writings—particularly in the book of Job.

Day of Yahweh: A central feature in the message of the Hebrew prophets, which originally referred to the time when Yahweh would vindicate his people Israel by defeating their enemies. It came to mean an eschatological day of judgment for the people of Israel as well as foreign nations.

> ### Concept Check # 11
>
> The fact that the book of Isaiah includes specific reference to events which took place two centuries after his own time, including the name of the Persian king Cyrus, has led many scholars to divide the book of Isaiah into two or more books by different authors. Do the concepts presented here shed any light on this problem? (Check your answer on p. 221.)

Jeremiah and Ezekiel

The books of Jeremiah and Ezekiel form another structural pair, alongside that of Isaiah and the Book of the Twelve. In this case, the life and ministry of both prophets is narrowly focused in time: on the destruction of the Temple in Jerusalem in 587 BCE. Both prophets experienced the trauma of this event. Ezekiel viewed it from distant

Babylon where he was taken as a young man, against his will in the deportation of 597, and spent the major part of his long prophetic career in exile, after the destruction of Jerusalem in 587. Jeremiah spent the major part of his long prophetic career in Jerusalem, before the destruction of Jerusalem in 587. Some years later he was carried into exile to Egypt, where he subsequently died.

These two contemporary prophetic figures form a structural pair in contrast. The theology of Jeremiah represents that of the Levitical priesthood, as preserved in the town of Anathoth, a suburb of modern Jerusalem. This was the home of the high priest Abiathar, whom King Solomon exiled from Jerusalem. It was also a place of refuge for Levites from northern Israel after the fall of Samaria in 722 and the locus of the tradition of Deuteronomy and the deuteronomic corpus (i.e., the Former Prophets). Ezekiel, on the other hand, belongs among the Zadokites, who made up the royal establishment in Jerusalem from the time of Solomon to Josiah. In his vision of the future in Jerusalem, only Zadokite priests would minister in the holy city (see Ezek 40:46; 43:19; 44:15; and 48:11).

In short, Jeremiah and Ezekiel represent the two parallel trajectories of tradition in ancient Israel: the so-called deuteronomic tradition of northern Israel, on the one hand, and the Zadokite tradition of the royal establishment in the Temple of Jerusalem, on the other.

Though the prophet Jeremiah is not mentioned by name in the Former Prophets, the book of his prophecies does include a lengthy repetition of material from the concluding chapters of the Former Prophets (Jer 52 = 2 Kgs 24:18 – 25:30). The fact that Jeremiah is not mentioned even once in the book of 2 Kings has been noted by commentators as cause for astonishment. The reason for this omission must be deliberate on the part of those who edited the Prophets in their present two-part arrangement: the Former Prophets and the Latter Prophets. For some reason, they chose to separate the prophets of the first group from those of the second—except for Isaiah and Jonah.

Concept Check # 12

Jeremiah and Ezekiel were contemporary prophets each of whom witnessed the trauma of the destruction of Jerusalem by Nebuchadnezzar in 587 BCE. Is it possible that the central event around which their work was arranged was the destruction of Solomon's temple in Jerusalem? (Check your answer on p. 221.)

Conclusion

By way of summary, it should be noted that the Primary History is made up of two groups of four books, in which Deuteronomy is the connecting link. The focus of attention in the Primary History is on leadership in ancient Israel: namely, on the founding father Moses, in the Torah, and the subsequent succession of leaders in ancient Israel, which extends from Joshua through Jehoiachin, the last king of Judah who was released from prison in Babylon after the destruction of Jerusalem. In the period of the monarchy in ancient Israel, from the time of David to Josiah, leadership is shared by the king and the prophet. In fact, each king is judged by how true he is to the ancestral faith and whether or not he heeds the prophet.

The Primary History (Exodus through 2 Kings) is framed by stories of the "Ancestors" (Genesis 12-50) and the four books known as the Latter Prophets:

	Exodus	Leviticus	Joshua	Judges	
Ancestors					Prophets
	Numbers	Deuteronomy	Samuel	Kings	

Joseph Blenkinsopp has noted the structural parallel between Isaiah, Jeremiah, Ezekiel, and the Book of the Twelve on the one hand, and Abraham, Isaac, Jacob, and the twelve sons of Jacob/Israel, on the other.[23]

"Prophets"	=	Isaiah, Jeremiah, Ezekiel	+	Book of the 12
"Ancestors"	=	Abraham, Isaac, Jacob	+	Jacob's 12 sons

The designation of Abraham as a prophet in Gen 20:7 (cf. Ps 105:15 where Abraham, Isaac, and Jacob are called prophets), who is the recipient of God's covenant promise, now takes on deeper meaning. In the words of the great classical prophets of ancient Israel, the old epic story receives powerful new content.

The primary epic story of the Law and the Prophets in the First Testament may be outlined in linear form in terms of a journey out of bondage in Egypt, through the waters into the wilderness, on route to the Promised Land. And though these terms are rooted in past events, however elusive they may prove to be to the historian, in the hands of the great prophets of Israel each of these symbols is transformed and projected beyond history into an eschatological dimension. In fact, the creation stories of Genesis 1-11 anticipate a new *Opus Dei*,[24] the "City of God" which will be described as a "New Jerusalem." The people of God see themselves as once more in exile and bondage, awaiting a new deliverance which will carry them through the waters and the wilderness of a New Exodus to a New Conquest, which will eventually become the "Kingdom of God" (cf. Isaiah 11 where all these images appear). Is it any wonder that Luke describes the conversation between Moses, Elijah, and Jesus on the **Mount of Transfiguration** as focusing on "his Exodus," which was to be accomplished at Jerusalem (Luke 9:28-31)?

Mount of Transfiguration: The mountain where Jesus was transformed in the presence of certain of his disciples, and appeared with Moses and Elijah. Peter offered to build there three booths, one each for Jesus, Moses, and Elijah.

Thinking Exercise

On the Latter Prophets

The classical prophets in ancient Israel, whose books make up the Latter Prophets in the Hebrew Bible, lived in ancient Israel from ca. 750-500 BCE. This period saw the fall of the northern kingdom of Israel (722/21 BCE) and the city of Jerusalem and the southern kingdom of Judah (587/86 BCE).

The critical thinking goal for this exercise is to clarify the concept of the Latter Prophets within the canonical process.

How To Do This Exercise

Review the definitions of the individual prophets whose books make up the Latter Prophets. Note that the "outer pair" of books in the Latter Propets begins with a discussion of Jerusalem's devastation at the hands of Assyria in the eighth century BCE and the promise of future restoration of the "branch of the Lord" (Isaiah 1-4) and ends with an account of the rebuilding of the Temple in Jerusalem in the time of Haggai and Zechariah (ca. 520 BCE) followed by a description of the crowning of the messianic leader in Jerusalem "whose name is Branch" (Zech 6:9-14). Now, answer the following questions:

1. At the "center" of the book of Isaiah is a quotation from the Former Prophets (Isaiah 36-39 = 2 Kings 18-20); and the "center" of the Book of the Twelve begins with the book of Jonah, who is the only other person among the Latter Prophets mentioned by name in the Former Prophets (cf. 2 Kgs 14:23-29). Is there any significance in the fact that these are the only two places in which the Former Prophets and the Latter Prophets are explicitly connected?

_____

_____

_____

2. Though neither Jeremiah nor Ezekiel are mentioned by name in the Former Prophets, their respective books are connected by another quotation from the Former Prophets (Jeremiah 52 = 2 Kings 24-25). Since this quotation stands at the structural center of the Latter Prophets taken as a whole, what function do you think it plays in terms of literary design?

_____

_____

_____

_____

3. The two "central books" in the Latter Prophets are the books of Jeremiah and Ezekiel. What do these books have in common?

_____

_____

_____

_____

_____

_____

4. Besides the destruction of the Temple in Jerusalem, which took place during the lifetime of Jeremiah and Ezekiel, these two men also witnessed the end of the monarchy as such. How would you describe the relationship of Isaiah to the political establishment in Jerusalem in the eighth century BCE?

_____

_____

_____

_____

_____

_____

5. The critical events which occasioned the completion of the Book of the Twelve (minor prophets) focus on the rebuilding of the Temple in Jerusalem ca. 515 BCE, particularly in the books of Haggai and Zechariah, and the expectation of a coming messianic figure connected in some way with King David (cf. Zerubbabel as the scion of David in Haggai and Zechariah) and with both Moses and the prophet Elijah (cf. Mal 4:4-6). In what way does this description set the stage for the coming of Jesus Christ and the events of the Second Testament?

_____

_____

_____

_____

_____

_____

C. The Writings and the Completion of the First Testament

In the earliest stages of the canonical process in ancient Israel, the fourth major division of the seventeen books was made up of four parts, called the "Hagiographa," as follows:

Psalms   Job

Proverbs   *Megilloth*

The term *Megilloth* here refers to the collection of Festal Scrolls, which in the masoretic tradition eventually came to include the five books: Song of Songs, Ruth, Lamentations, Ecclesiastes, and Esther. The five-fold grouping corresponds to the five part division of the **Psalter**, which most scholars have assumed to be patterned after the five part division of the Torah. This is the first of several observations which suggest that the Hagiographa has a structural correspondence to the Torah in the chiastic structure of the four segments of the canon of the First Testament taken as a whole:

Torah   Former Prophets

Latter Prophets   Hagiographa (Writings)

Psalter: The book of Psalms in the Hebrew Bible, which is part of the Writings and the longest book in the Hebrew Bible (with 150 individual psalms).

1. Psalms and the Torah

The fact that the book of Psalms is structurally related to the Torah is most easily seen in terms of the system for the successive reading of the Torah which emerged in early Palestinian Judaism. In this Triennial Lectionary Cycle, which was generally replaced after the second century CE by the annual Babylonian cycle, the entire Pentateuch was read in a period of three years.[25] Assuming four sabbaths per lunar month and following Büchler's analysis of the use of the Torah in this three year cycle, Genesis would have been begun on the first Sabbath, Exodus on the forty-second, Leviticus on the seventy-third, Numbers on the ninetieth, and Deuteronomy on the one hundred and seventeenth. The similarity of such a scheme to the divisions of the books of Psalms is indeed striking. Except in the case of Deuteronomy, the Sabbath on which a new book in the Torah was begun is numerically equivalent to the opening psalm of each of the first four books (Psalms 1, 42, 73, and

90). Allowing four psalms per lunar month to parallel the four readings from the Torah per month would mean that the public reading of the first four books of the Psalter would have begun on the same Sabbaths as the corresponding books of the Pentateuch.

Norman Snaith has suggested that Psalm 119 should be seen as the psalm which originally opened the fifth book of psalms and which would have been read on the first of Elul in the third year of the triennial cycle—on the 117th Sabbath, at the time when the reading of Deuteronomy began.[26] He also argued, rather persuasively, that Psalms 108 and 117 were secondarily inserted between Psalms 90 and 119 in the masoretic tradition.

Various scholars have long noted numerous relationships between the order of the psalms and the reading of the Torah in the triennial cycle, as well as the interplay and the relationship with the festival calendar in the placement of numerous psalms. Moreover, this interplay of Psalms readings, Torah lections, and festival cycle can be seen in numerous instances in the rabbinic midrash on the book of Psalms (Midrash Tehillim). For example, the midrash to Psalms 17 and 18 contains homiletical material that is almost impossible to explain apart from the association of these psalms with the triennial cycle. Psalms 17 and 18 in a three year cycle would have been read early in the month of Ab. In the Jewish liturgical calendar, mourning over the destruction of the Temple by the Babylonians took place during the weeks extending from the seventeenth day of the fourth month (Tammuz) until the ninth of the following month (Ab). The Temple was burned at this time in Ab (2 Kgs 25:8; Jer 52:12), and a fast mourning its destruction developed at the time of the exile (Zech 7:1-5). In the midrash on Psalm 17, there is a long homily (17:4) which discusses the necessity to mourn for the Temple and the possible punishment for failure to mourn. In addition, the midrashic exposition (17:11) understands Ps 17:14 by interpreting it in terms of Nebuchadnezzar, his successors, and the Babylonian looting of the temple. The interpretation is then extended in the following section (17:12) and is related to Esau, because of the Edomites' participation in the Temple's destruction, and to Remus and Romulus as representatives of wicked Rome who, of course, burned the Temple in 70 CE. In similar fashion, the midrash on Psalm 18 contains long discourses on the destruction of Jerusalem and the city's fate. The midrashic discussion on 18:11 refers specifically to the burning of the Temple and its subsequent

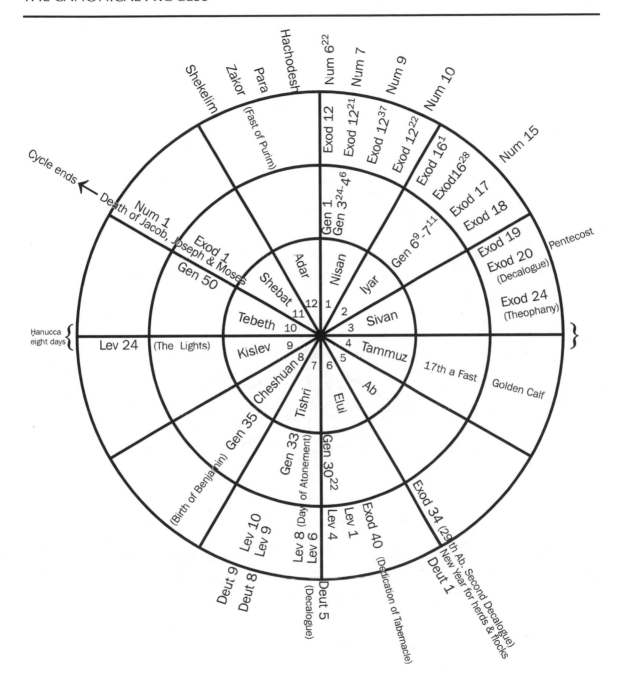

Triennial Cycle of Torah Readings[27]

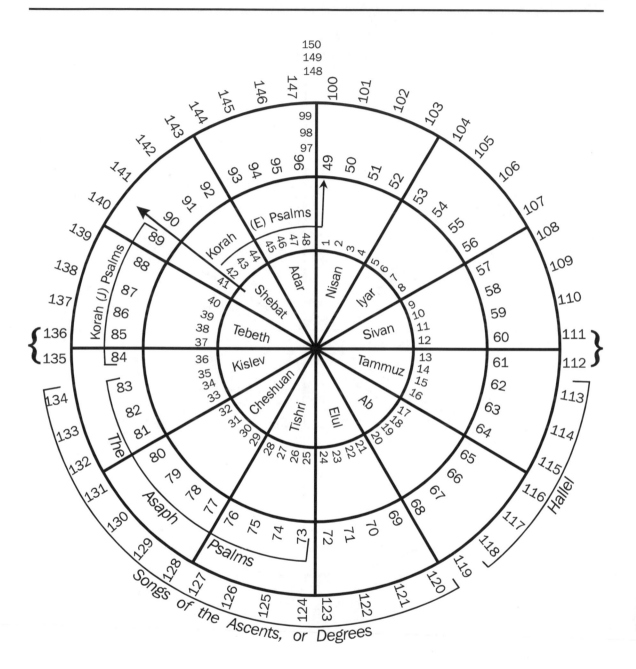

Triennial Cycle for Reading the Psalms[27]

fate. Numerous other close parallels between the content of individual psalms and the corresponding Torah reading of the triennial cycle have been noted.

A first glance at the Psalter suggests that, in addition to its structural ties to the Pentateuch, the number seventeen plays a significant role. Books III and IV of the Psalter each contain seventeen psalms. It is easy to see the possibility of a simpler version of the Psalter that lies immediately behind the present five-book canonical structure by positing Book II as a later insertion to complete the collection. There are three reasons why this particular book is to be taken as secondary: 1) as the so-called Elohistic psalter, it is different from the rest in its preference for the term *'Elohim* rather than the divine name *Yahweh;* 2) Book II ends with the statement: "The prayers of David the son of Jesse are ended" (Ps 72:20); and 3) when Book II is removed, all of the doublets noted by various scholars disappear (i.e., Psalms 14 = 53; 70 = 40:13-17; 108 = 57:7-11 and 60:5-12).

The reference in Ps 72:20 to the conclusion of the psalms of David may already have been the conclusion of Book II, before that particular collection was added to the present canonical arrangement of the Hebrew Bible. Of the thirty-one psalms in this collection, eighteen belong to David (i.e., Psalms 51-65 and 68-70). The headings of these psalms include some of the major moments in the narrative life of David: when Nathan confronted him over the affair with Bathsheba (Psalm 51); when Doeg the Edomite told Saul that David was residing in the house of Ahimelech (Psalm 52); when the Ziphites reported that David was hiding (Psalm 54); when the Philistines seized David in Gath (Psalm 56); when David hid from Saul in a cave (Psalm 57); when Saul sent men to watch his house and kill David (Psalm 59); when David struggled with Aram-naharaim and Aram-zobah, and Joab returned to smite twelve thousand Edomites (Psalm 60); and when David was in the wilderness of Judea (Psalm 63). The collection concludes with a series of songs of David (Psalms 64-70), a prayer of an old man for deliverance (Psalm 71), and the only psalm in the Psalter credited to David's son Solomon (Psalm 72). Though the collection begins with a series of psalms credited to the sons of Korah (Psalms 42-49) and one to Asaph (Psalm 50), it is dominated by the person of David from Psalm 51 on; and the collection

Ezra and
Nehemiah: Led the
revival of Judaism in
Palestine in the 4th
century BCE. Ezra
was a Jewish scribe
commissioned by
the Persian king to
be the religious
leader in Jerusalem.
Nehemiah was
appointed by the
Persians to be
governor.

Job: The book of
Job is an example of
wisdom literature in
the Hebrew Bible.
Job, a foreigner in
the time of
Abraham, is an
example of
undeserved suffering.

Abraham: A Hebrew
patriarch in the book
of Genesis. Known
earlier as Abram, he
is called "the father
of many nations"
(Gen 17:5) and the
friend of God
(2 Chr 20:7).

Isaac: The second
of the three major
patriarchs in the
book of Genesis, the
son of Abraham.

Jacob: The third of
the three major
patriarchs in the
book of Genesis, the
son of Isaac, whose
name was changed
to Israel.

fits nicely into the larger context as part of the sequel to the so-called Yahwistic collection of Davidic psalms in Book I (Psalms 2-32 and 34-41).

The earlier psalter, which was made up of Books I and III-V, appears to have been structured around the number seventeen; for it consists of 119 psalms, which is 17×7, in which two collections of seventeen psalms (Books III and IV) were framed by breaking apart what could be called the original "Davidic psalter" (Books I and V), which are made up of eighty-five psalms (=17×5), of which fifty-one (=17×3) belong to David, and thirty-four (=17×2) to other authors.

Thus it appears that there are three stages in the growth of the Psalter in ancient Israel, namely: 1) an original Davidic psalter, which is preexilic in date and preserved in Books I and V of the received masoretic canon; 2) a "deuteronomic" psalter, which was put together in the exile or early post-exilic period and features the number seventeen—made up by splitting the Davidic psalter into two parts after Psalm 41 and inserting two collections of seventeen psalms (Books III and IV); and finally: 3) the completed five-book Psalter as we now know it, which may well have been put together in the time of **Ezra** and **Nehemiah**, with the addition of another collection of thirty-one psalms (Book II) which may have originated in ancient sanctuaries other than Jerusalem such as that in Dan and Bethel.[28]

> ## Concept Check # 13
>
> What does the canonical process suggest in regard to the traditional belief, among both Jews and Christians, that David is the "author" of the Psalms? (Check your answer on p. 221.)

2. Job and the Torah

The relationship between the book of Job and Genesis is obvious to the observant reader. As I have argued elsewhere,[29] **Job** is presented as a "crypto-patriarch," a model of righteousness comparable to and complementary to Israel's ancestors as presented in the book of Genesis. The 140 years allotted to Job after his great testing (Job 42:16-17) is part of a larger structural pattern that associates that number with the Ancestors in Genesis. **Abraham** was 140 years old when his son **Isaac** married Rebekah. Isaac and Rebekah were married for 140 years. **Jacob** was 140 years old at the time of his wrestling bout with the angel at the Jabbok

River when his name was changed to Israel (Genesis 32). And, of course, Jacob's twin brother Esau/Edom was also 140 years old at the decisive reunion of the estranged brothers. Placing Job within this schema makes him the literary counterpart of Abraham, as suggested in the following diagram:

Job		Jacob (Israel)
	Isaac and Rebekah	
Abraham		Esau (Edom)

In short, from a canonical point of view, Job is the oldest of the Patriarchs who lives long enough to see his children's children to the fourth generation. His three daughters are named while his seven sons are left anonymous. Though the father of Abraham in the Genesis narrative is Terah (Gen 11:31), it is possible to see here a parallel to the statement of Jesus: "I tell you God is able from these stones to raise up children to Abraham" (Matt 3:9). God is also apparently able to provide a new father to Abraham, out of the dust of the past, in the person of the legendary figure of Job. This foreigner, whose name has been explained by W. F. Albright as meaning "Where is (my) Father?" [30] thus becomes the first of four great patriarchs in the lineage which produces the twelve sons (or tribes) of Jacob/Israel.

Orientation in time in modern western civilization is different than in the ancient Near East. We face the future whereas, as Isaac Kikawada has argued, people in that ancient world faced the past.[31] If one wished to know the future, one simply read the events of the past and projected them, as it were, behind him or her into the future. If the future in ancient Israel was projected as a "rerun" of the past, in reverse, which would begin with the appearance of a "new Moses," the picture might be as follows:

Joshua/Joseph $\rightarrow$ New Israel $\rightarrow$ Fathers $\rightarrow$ New Creation

Both **Joseph** and Joshua lived 110 years, which is the sum of the squares of the digits five through seven.[32] Israel is made up of twelve tribes, and the sum of the squares of the digits one through twelve is 650. The number associated with the Ancestors (including Job) is 140, which is the sum of the squares of the digits one through seven, and $110 + 650 + 140 = 900$, which is 30^2 or the square of the sum of the squares of the digits one through four. Within the narrative tradition in Genesis, Abraham was 160 years of age at the birth of his grandson, Jacob. Isaac

Joseph: One of the twelve sons of Jacob/Israel, who was sold into slavery in Egypt and rose to high position in that country through his ability to interpret dreams (see Gen 37:1-47:27).

was sixty years old when Jacob was born, and Jacob lived with Isaac for sixty-three years and with Laban for twenty years. Thus, Joseph's descent into Egypt at age seventeen took place in Isaac's 160th year; i.e., 60 + 63 + 20 + 17 = 160.

Moreover, the number of years between the birth of Shem and Terah is 320, which is two times 160. At any rate, it is interesting to note that $160 \times 900 = 144{,}000$. It is possible that this number, which becomes the community of the elect within subsequent **apocalyptic** speculation (cf. Rev 14:1), began in ancient Israel as simply the symbolic lapse of time from the promulgation of the Torah of Moses to the **eschaton**, conceived in terms of a grand reversal of past events in ancient Israel according to the following formula:

$$\text{Joshua/Joseph} \rightarrow \text{New Israel} \rightarrow \text{Fathers} \rightarrow \text{New Creation}$$

$$(110 \quad + \quad 650 \quad + \quad 140) \quad \times \quad 160 = 144{,}000$$

The advent of a new Moses figure would thus lead to the establishment of a future kingdom of Israel. This epoch would be succeeded by an ideal age, corresponding to that of the Ancestors in ancient tradition, which would culminate in a new creation where the people of God would eventually become what God intended them to be at the beginning of time. In short, it seems likely that the numbers in the biblical record are not to be taken as simply historical report. The mysterious numbers are theological statements that contain within them a look into the future as well as the distant past.

Concept Check # 14

What significance, if any, do you see in the fact that the home country of Job (i.e., the land of Uz) is outside the Promised Land? (Check your answer on p. 222.)

---

3. Proverbs and the Torah

Proverbs presents the fascinating figure of **Lady Wisdom**, which Michelangelo has included in the center scene of his masterpiece on the ceiling of the Sistine Chapel. There Lady Wisdom looks out over the shoulder of God who holds her in his left arm while extending his right hand toward that of the outstretched right hand of the reclining Adam at the moment of the bestowal of intellect to God's masterpiece. The eighth chapter of Proverbs identifies Wisdom as a feminine presence with God at creation. Further, Wisdom's presence at creation is inherent in the eloquent opening passage of John's gospel: "In the beginning was the Word, and the Word was with God, and the Word was God." The "Word" in the Greek text is *logos*, understood either as the Greek philosophical ideal of rationality or as divine wisdom. As F. L. Meshberger has shown,[33] the larger gestalt in which the figure of God and Lady Wisdom is placed by Michelangelo reflects a cross section of the human brain as observed by a careful student of anatomy.

It is no accident that the figure of Eve, in the adjacent panel, has the face of Lady Wisdom. That is but another way of expressing symbolically that Eve, like Adam, is an essential part of God's creation of human beings, and that she also reflects the image of God:

So God created *ha'adam* ("the man") in his own image,
In the image of God he created him;
Male and female he created them (Gen 1:27)

Michelangelo was as careful a student of the Bible as he was of human anatomy; and he was undoubtedly aware of the biblical tradition that includes Wisdom within the godhead. Meshberger's insight that Michelangelo showed God, encompassed within an image of the human brain, imparting intelligence to Adam reinforces our opinion that Lady Wisdom, not Eve, is the feminine figure at God's left in the center of the fresco at the center of the ceiling of the Sistine Chapel. In so doing, the artist has intuited the close connection between the book of Proverbs and the opening chapters of the book of Genesis.

Concept Check # 15

Is Lady Wisdom, as presented in the book of Proverbs, to be considered part of the godhead in the theology of ancient Israel? (Check your answer on p. 222.)

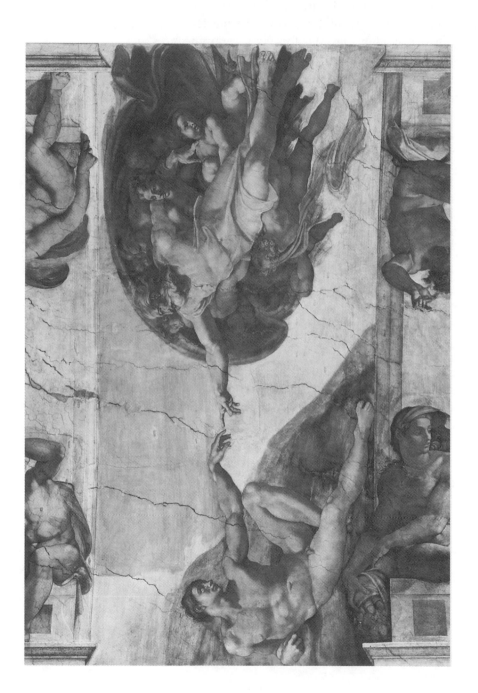

Michelangelo's "Creation of Adam"
The Central Panel in the Ceiling of the Sistine Chapel

4. The Festal Scrolls and the Completion of the First Testament

There are five Festal Scrolls ("Megilloth"), corresponding to the five parts of the book of Psalms and the five books of Moses in the Torah. The Festal Scrolls are the texts for the five great moments in the calendar year when the people of God gather to celebrate who they are and what God has done on their behalf in times past. The five-part book of Psalms, on the other hand, is the "hymnbook" for daily worship in ancient Israel.

In the canonical shaping of the Festal Scrolls, Lamentations was apparently the initial center around which the Song of Songs and Ruth were added as the festal scrolls for Passover and *Shavuoth* (the Feast of Weeks or Pentecost) respectively. Ecclesiastes was subsequently added as the scroll of *Succoth* (Feast of Booths) to form a four-part, chiastic pattern in which Ruth / Lamentations is associated with David; and Song of Songs / Ecclesiastes with Solomon as follows:

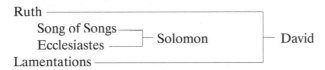

Ruth is the great-grandmother of David whereas Lamentations commemorates the destruction of the Davidic dynasty/temple in Jerusalem at the hands of Nebuchadnezzar of Babylon. On the other hand, the Song of Songs and Ecclesiastes is traditionally ascribed to Solomon.

It should be noted that Ruth, like Job, is a foreigner. In essence, Job and Ruth are to the Ancestors of earlier tradition what the nations are to Israel in the prophetic literature. Job was admitted into the ancestral structure of the Genesis account because he was righteous—"blameless and upright, one who feared God, and turned away from evil" (Job 1:1). Job and Ruth become part of the community of faith because of the quality of their lives. Thus, universalism need not have national roots, as the examples of Job and Ruth adequately show. But in the end, of necessity, universalism becomes national because those who swear allegiance to Yahweh, the God of Israel—as Ruth did—*are* Israel. They are the people of God from among the nations.

The expansion of the canon, which saw the completion of the Psalter, added other books to the collection of sacred Scripture producing a canon of twenty-two books. Josephus is the first clear witness to this next

Shavuoth
("Weeks"): The second of three pilgrimage feasts in Judaism, coming fifty days after Passover, called The Feast of the First Fruits of Wheat Harvest; associated with the giving of the Torah to Moses.

Succoth
("Booths"): The third major pilgrimage festival of Judaism. It is held in the fall and celebrates the the dedication of Solomon's Temple (1 Kings 8), the public reading of the Torah (every seven years, Deut 31:10-11), and the future ingathering of all nations to Jerusalem to worship God (Zech 14:16).

stage in the development of the canonical process, which reflects the received tradition within the Jewish community, at least within the masoretic tradition.[34] Note that a dual center emerges with the books of Daniel and Deuteronomy functioning as bridges, around which are arranged five "pairs of pairs" (four-part chiastic structures):

Genesis	Exodus		Joshua	Judges
		Deuteronomy		
Leviticus	Numbers		Samuel	Kings

	Isaiah	Jeremiah	
	Ezekiel	"The Twelve"	

Ezra	Nehemiah		Psalms	Job
		Daniel		
1 Chron.	2 Chronicles		Proverbs	*Megilloth*

Origen: A Christian theologian, teacher, and biblical scholar in Alexandria (ca. 185-254 CE).

The total number of twenty-two books in this canon was subsequently legitimated by the Christian scholar **Origen** (ca. 250 CE) in terms of the number of letters in the Hebrew alphabet.[35] This fact would suggest that this canon was theoretically closed (or complete), at least from a psychological point of view. It is the inclusion of Esther into this "closed" canon within Jewish tradition that ultimately "exploded" the canon in a transformation from twenty-two to the twenty-four-book structure of talmudic tradition. The inclusion of Esther resulted in the breaking up of the *Megilloth* as a canonical category within Jewish tradition, and the distribution of the Festal Scrolls so as to come up with twenty-four books. Ruth was attached to Judges in some instances, elsewhere to Psalms. Lamentations was attached to Jeremiah. The resultant loss of discernible canonical structure produced the fluidity of canonical reflection within both early Jewish and Christian communities. As Moses Stuart has noted, no two of these early lists are identical, even among those who insist on a total of twenty-two books.[36]

Within Christian tradition, it would appear that the addition of Esther resulted in a twenty-seven book canon of the First Testament, as well as in the Second Testament, as suggested in the curious argument of Epiphanius (ca. 368 CE) that the Hebrew alphabet does in fact have twenty-seven letters, since five of the letters appear in two forms.[37] It would appear that the structure of the canon of the First Testament influenced the subsequent structure of the Second Testament.

Thinking Exercise

On the Writings and Completion of the First Testament

Some scholars have argued that the heights of theological reflection in the First Testament are to be found within the final category of the canon, namely the Writings.

The critical thinking goal for this exercise is to clarify the concept of the Writings within the canonical process.

How To Do This Exercise

Review the definitions of the four major categories within the Writings: Psalms, Proverbs, Job, and the Festal Scrolls. Note that the outer pair of books, Psalms and the Festal Scrolls, are each in five parts like the Pentateuch. The inner pair of books, Proverbs and Job, represent the two major types of "wisdom" writing in the ancient Near East: aphoristic wisdom and the wisdom tale, in the form of an epic poem.

1. In their final canonical form, the Psalms include collections which apparently originated in centers other than that of ancient Jerusalem (such as Dan and Bethel). What is the significance of this fact?

_____

_____

_____

_____

_____

2. Scholars have shown that one section of the book of Proverbs (22:17 – 24:22) is adapted from the literature of ancient Egypt ("The Teaching of Amenemope"). What is the significance of this fact?

_____

_____

_____

_____

_____

3. The book of Job appears to be set in the time of the Ancestors of the book of Genesis; but there are no explicit ties to connect the events of the book to those of Genesis. How does this story about a Gentile effect your understanding of the canon of the Hebrew Bible?

_____

_____

_____

_____

4. Among the five books in the Festal Scrolls, the feminine figure plays a dominant role: i.e., Ruth, Esther, "daughter" Zion in the book of Lamentations, and the beloved in the Song of Songs. Do you think this fact has anything to do with the role of women in the structure of leadership in the Former Prophets (Deborah, Jezebel, Athaliah, and Huldah)?

_____

_____

_____

_____

5. What kind of theological statement do you see in the role of the foreigner and women within the Writings?

_____

_____

_____

_____

D. The Second Testament

Though the sacred Scripture of the early Christian community was the Hebrew Bible (the First Testament), it was clear at the outset that the received canonical text of sacred Scripture had taken on new meaning in the person of Jesus Christ. All of the Scriptures were read with fresh insight and with new interpretation on the part of these early believers who saw themselves as the true Israel, the people of God. As time passed, they began to see themselves in a more inclusive sense, particularly after the time of the so-called Jerusalem Council described in Acts 15, in which Gentiles were welcomed into the fellowship without the necessity of first converting to Judaism.

The early Christians were steeped in the Hebrew Bible. It is the only book they quote throughout the entire Second Testament, with perhaps a handful of exceptions. Almost all of the hundreds of citations and quotations in the Second Testament are taken right out of the Hebrew Bible, or from the Greek translation known as the Septuagint (LXX). In many ways, these people who wrote the Second Testament were much more conservative than the **Pharisees** or the **Sadducees.** They are the real biblicists of antiquity. For them the Hebrew Bible was the Word of God and the message of that book had taken on new form and meaning in the person of Jesus Christ who somehow embodied that very Word of God in his own person.

It should be remembered that the concept of the Bible as a single book in the modern sense had not yet arrived. The day of the great codices of sacred Scripture, in which the hundreds of manuscript pages were bound together by hand, to make the earliest form of a book as we know it today, was still far in the future. The text of the Bible was contained on scrolls, made of papyrus in the earliest period and subsequently of leather or parchment, when these texts achieved canonical status.[38] These ancient book-scrolls were bulky and difficult to handle. Moreover, they were extremely expensive, for the text itself was written by hand.

The curious symmetry of the Bible, which is discussed in detail later in this chapter, may have been shaped, at least in part, by the physical limitations in the size of these scrolls. The very concept of the Bible as a whole was a more dynamic concept than is familiar to us today. Individual Christians did not have their own copies of the entire Bible

Pharisees: A sect of especially observant and influential Jews in Palestine from the second century BCE to the first century CE who differ from the Sadducees in their strict observance of religious ritual, liberal interpretation of the Bible, adherence to oral laws and traditions, and belief in an afterlife and the coming of a Messiah.

Sadducees: A sect of Jews in Palestine from the second century BCE to the first century CE, consisting mainly of priests and aristocrats, who differ from the Pharisees chiefly in their literal interpretation of the Bible, rejection of oral laws and traditions, and denial of an afterlife and the coming of the Messiah.

to read at their leisure. They learned the Scriptures primarily by hearing the text read or sung in public worship; and the concept of the structure and content of the Bible as a whole was more open for them than it is for us today. New books were being written and new compilations of sacred texts were made, particularly in the form of translations of the Bible into vernacular language for the worshiping communities.

Concept Check # 16

Was the culture in Palestine at the time of Jesus a "literate" one in the modern sense? How much do you think individuals like the disciples Peter and John, or even the apostle Paul, actually read so far as the Scriptures of ancient Israel are concerned? (Check your answer on p. 222.)

The Structure of the Second Testament

For all practical purposes, the Bible of this Greek-speaking Christian community of faith soon became the Septuagint, which contained a number of additions to the familiar twenty-two-book canon of the Hebrew Bible. Within this tradition, the Second Testament emerged in the form of a twenty-seven-book canon, which may be structured as follows:

	Matthew	Mark		
			Acts	
	Luke	John		

Romans	1 Corinthians	Philippians	Colossians
2 Corinthians	Galatians	1 Thess.	2 Thessalonians

Ephesians

1 Timothy	2 Timothy	Hebrews	James
Titus	Philemon	1 Peter	2 Peter

	1 John	2 John	
			Revelation
	3 John	Jude	

The center of this structure appears, at first glance, to be a seventeen-book collection of epistles, most of which were associated with the apostle Paul, arranged around the letter to the Ephesians. But this conclusion is at odds with the obvious fact that the center of the Second Testament is the four Gospels, plus the book of Acts as a sort of "New Torah." Any observer of worship within the more liturgical church traditions knows that the congregation stands when the Gospels are read, and occasionally when the reading is taken from the book of Acts. The Gospels are the "canon within the canon." Everything else in the entire Bible is measured in terms of the gospel of Jesus Christ. How then are we to understand this phenomenon in terms of the structures observed here? This question will be explored in detail in the next chapter of this book, which focuses on the issue of "Jesus Christ as the Center of the Canonical Process."

The arrangement of the four Gospels illustrates the basic principle of unconscious canonical structuring. As noted by Carl Jung, wholeness tends to be found in four-part structures in which the four parts are arranged in a chiasm—while at the same time, three of the four parts are generally set over against the fourth in a "three plus one" pattern. Jung observed that Matthew, the gospel to the Jews, is set over against the Gospel of John, which is addressed to the Greeks. In between these two are the gospels of Mark and Luke, which form a pair: Mark as the gospel according to Peter, and Luke as the gospel according to Paul. The gospels of Matthew, Mark, and Luke stand together, in what scholars call the Synoptic Gospels, because they share much in common. On the other hand, Jung called the Gospel of John a "Gnostic Gospel" because it presents a different perspective on the life and person of Jesus from the Synoptics.

The centrality of Ephesians within the structure of the twenty-seven-book canon of the Second Testament can be argued in terms of its content. This particular letter of Paul to the Ephesians is written in powerful, poetic language, which is drawn, at least in part, from Christian hymns and liturgies. It celebrates the life of the Church as a unique community established by God through the work of Jesus Christ, who is its head and also the head of the whole created order. The Church was established in accordance with God's eternal purposes. In the Church, believers already live in union with God through Christ and the Holy Spirit in anticipation of full union in life to come.

The arrangement of the Second Testament in a twenty-seven-book canon, within popular Christian tradition, may have been patterned (consciously or unconsciously) on a twenty-seven-book canon of the First Testament. Within the Christian community, the addition of Esther to the canon of the First Testament somehow resulted in a twenty-seven-book canon of the First Testament, as well as the Second Testament. This number was subsequently legitimated by Epiphanius (ca. 368 CE) with the argument that the Hebrew alphabet does in fact have twenty-seven letters, since five of the twenty-two letters appear in two forms. The breakup of the earlier category of the *Megilloth* (Festal Scrolls), which was caused by the inclusion of Esther, produced a cluster of five books, which were distributed throughout the larger canonical collection in various ways.

If the structure of the two Testaments is in fact parallel, the actual content of the Christian First Testament may be reconstructed as follows:

Genesis	Exodus		
		Deuteronomy	
Leviticus	Numbers		

Joshua	Judges	Isaiah	Jeremiah
Samuel	Kings	Ezekiel	The Twelve
	Daniel		

Job	Psalms	Chronicles	Ezra
Proverbs	"Wisdom"	Nehemiah	Maccabees

Ruth	Song of Songs	
		Esther
Ecclesiastes	Lamentations	

From a structural point of view, this twenty-seven-book canon of the First Testament speaks to the open nature of the canonical process within certain communities in the early Church. The quaternary pattern, Psalms / Job // Proverbs / *Megilloth,* called for something to replace the *Megilloth* (Festal Scrolls) when that grouping became four (and later five) separate books. This open category, which is here called "Wisdom," attracted a wide range of possible candidates, including Ecclesiasticus (Sirach), Wisdom of Solomon, Tobit, Judith, various Testaments (of Adam, Job, the Patriarchs, etc.), the books of Enoch, and various other texts—all of which achieved some measure of canonicity in various Christian circles. The books of Ezra and Nehemiah were combined into a single category in many circles, as witnessed by the early canonical lists. The same was true of 1 and 2 Chronicles. 1 Maccabees appears to be a continuation of Chronicles, whereas 2 Maccabees appears to be an abridgement of a five-volume history, now lost (cf. 2 Macc 2:23-28).

What is perhaps more interesting in this structure is the observation that the book of Daniel emerged as the center of the First Testament when read through Christian eyes. The book of Daniel, with its apocalyptic imagery, anticipates the book of Revelation at the end of the Second Testament. The interest in each case focuses on the last days, which are the culmination of God's story in human history.

Concept Check # 17

How does the book of Daniel make an appropriate center for the First Testament from a Christian perspective? (Check your answer on p. 222.)

Thinking Exercise

On the Structure of the Second Testament

The critical thinking goal of this exercise is to clarify the relationship between the structure of the two testaments within the canonical process.

How To Do This Exercise

One of the factors which led to the official decision of the early Church councils in regards to the twenty-seven books to be included in the canon of the Second Testament was to provide an answer to the position taken by the heretic Marcion of Pontus (ca. 160 CE) who included only the letters of Paul and the Gospel of Luke and rejected the whole of the First Testament. Compare Marcion's canon with the structures presented here. Then answer the following questions:

1. What light does the structure of the canon of the First Testament throw on the nature of Marcion's choice?

_____

_____

2. Besides his awareness of the centrality of Paul in the emergence of early Christianity, Marcion was motivated by a strong anti-Jewish bias. Does the observance of a similar structure for the two testaments have anything to say regarding such an attitude?

_____

_____

_____

3. Within some of the more conservative Protestant church bodies there has been strong fascination for the books of Daniel and Revelation, sometimes to the exclusion of other books in the Bible. How do you explain the centrality of these two books in terms of the structures suggested here?

_____

_____

_____

E. The Pentateuchal Principle within the Canonical Process

David Noel Freedman has drawn attention to the "Symmetry of the New Testament" in terms of approximate word counts.[39] He noted that the **Synoptic Gospels** plus the book of Acts contain approximately 72,000 words, which constitutes 49 percent of the total of the Second Testament (147,000 words)—much the same as the total length of the Primary History (Torah plus Former Prophets) in the First Testament, which includes approximately 150,000 words, also constitutes 49 percent of the length of the First Testament (306,000 words). Freedman also noted that Luke-Acts, with its 40,000 words, is the same length as the total of the fourteen epistles traditionally assigned to Paul.

The symmetry of the Bible as a whole in terms of approximate word counts is even more striking than Freedman has observed, particularly when combined with the observation of what is here called the "Pentateuchal Principle" within the canonical process. Wholeness in Jungian thought is found in the number four and in four-part structures. But completion in terms of the canonical process is found in the number five, as suggested by the word "quintessential" in the English language. The quintessence is the most perfect embodiment of something. In ancient and medieval philosophy the fifth essence or element, ether, was supposed to be the constituent matter of the heavenly bodies, the others being air, fire, earth, and water. Be that as it may, the canonical process reaches completion in five-part structures, in which the central section is often much briefer and, in many cases, somewhat enigmatic in nature.

The curious thing is that this five-part structuring principle seems to operate at all levels of the canonical process. In other words, the structure of Genesis 1-11 (the introduction to the Bible) is the same as the structure of the book of Genesis, which in turn is the same as the structure of the Pentateuch, which is the same as the structure of the First Testament as a whole, which in turn is the same as the structure of the Bible itself. In all cases, the structure is a five-part concentric design with a somewhat enigmatic central element which is generally shorter in length than the other four parts. The structure of Genesis 1-11, as the introduction to the Bible as a whole, is in five parts as follows:

Synoptic Gospels: The Gospels of Matthew, Mark, and Luke in the Second Testament which reflect a similar perspective, a common view, in contrast to the Gospel of John.

A	Creation (ending with the three sons of Adam)	Gen 1-4
B	Enoch	Gen 5
X	The Sons of God & the Daughters of *ha'adam*	Gen 6:1-4
B′	Noah	Gen 6:5-9:28
A′	Dispersion (beginning with the three sons of Noah)	Gen 10-11

Noah: The ninth descendant from Adam, whose birth is the first recorded after Adam's death. Noah and his family are the sole human survivors of the Flood, which God used to punish human sin (Gen 6-9).

Enoch: The grandson of Adam who lived 365 years, walked with God, and "God took him" (i.e., like the prophet Elijah later, he did not die).

The Creation account, with the three sons of Adam (Cain, Abel, and Seth), ends in death, division, and separate genealogies. The Dispersion after the great flood begins with the presentation of the three sons of **Noah** (Shem, Ham, and Japheth), in which the genealogies of these sons constitute the very structure of the Table of Nations in Genesis 10. As my student Dan Olson has noted,[40] the centrality of the enigmatic story of the "Sons of God and Daughters of Men" episode in Genesis 6:1-4 is paralleled in the *Book of Enoch,* in which the centrality of this same episode is so self-evident as to require little commentary. As Olson has shown, "Virtually all of the material in 1 Enoch is related to one or another of two parallel themes: (1) the fall of the evil Watchers (a term referring to the so-called "sons of God" in Gen 6:1-4), their misuse of wisdom, and their doom, and (2) the ascension of righteous **Enoch**, his acquisition of wisdom, and the glorious future of all the righteous. Olson found a third theme in the Enoch materials which focuses on Noah, who is like Enoch—an example of righteousness. The three themes of 1 Enoch are therefore the three themes of Genesis 1-11, bracketed by Creation and Dispersion, each of which is demarcated by the stories of three sons. The pairing of Enoch and Noah is justifiable in Genesis 1-11, despite the extremely brief notice given to Enoch in Genesis 5, by the fact that *only these two men* are said to have "walked with God" (Gen 5:22, 24 and Gen 6:9), a phrase which is much too powerful and suggestive to pass over lightly.

Another argument for seeing Enoch as the focus of attention in the period from Adam through Noah is found in a close reading of the text in the genealogical "list of the descendants of Adam" (Genesis 5). For our purposes here, Eliezer Shulman's chart of the lives of the ancestors from Adam through Abraham is instructive (see p. 77).[41]

Among the pre-Flood ancestors, Enoch stands out because of the relatively few years of his life. There are ten ancestors in the list from Adam through Noah, and ten from Shem through Abraham. The seventh ancestor from Abraham is Enoch; and the seventh ancestor counting back from Abraham is Eber, the eponymous ancestor of the Hebrew people. When one counts the ancestors from Adam through

Noah's three sons, they number thirteen—with Enoch in the center. While Enoch is the seventh ancestor in the list from Creation; Eber is the seventh after Enoch.

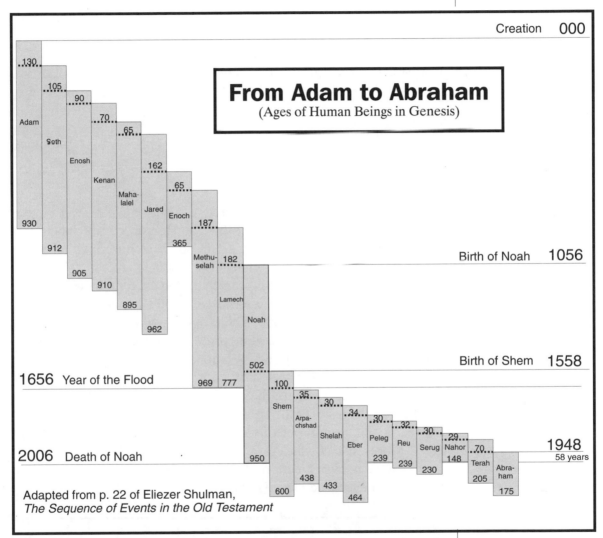

From Adam to Abraham
(Ages of Human Beings in Genesis)

Adapted from p. 22 of Eliezer Shulman,
The Sequence of Events in the Old Testament

In Genesis 1-11 the brief story of Enoch stands over against the elaborate story of Noah and the Great Flood, in which these two figures frame the enigmatic center: the curious story of the "sons of God and the daughters of *Adam*" (Gen 6:1-4). As I have shown in an earlier study,[42] this brief passage is written in poetic form. Two carefully balanced stanzas frame an enigmatic statement on the lips of Yahweh:

When *ha'adam* began to increase on the face of the earth,
    and daughters were bred for them,
The "sons of the god(s)" saw the daughters of *ha'adam*—
How beautiful they were!
And they took themselves women from any they chose.

And Yahweh said:
"My spirit shall not remain in *ha'adam* forever,
    {because of their going astray / in that}
He is flesh; and his days shall be 120 years."

The giants—they were in the land in those days,
    and also afterwards,
When the "sons of the god(s)" came in to the daughters of *ha'adam;*
And they bred for them—
These were the heroes of old, men of renown.

At the center of this structure stands a single enigmatic word in the Hebrew text: *beshaggam*. The fact that the Hebrew consonants in this word appear with a different vowel in some manuscripts led to an important discovery: namely, that both readings are intended to be heard here, at the level of a literary pun. On the one hand, we have reached a turning point in the narrative. God's patience has run out "because of their going astray." The Great Flood is a necessary consequence for human sin. At the same time, another message is carried in this same word, which may be rendered as a connecting phrase "*in that* he is flesh, and his days shall be 120 years." But the question then almost leaps off the page: of whom is the writer speaking? None of the ancestors to follow on the pages of the book of Genesis is limited to a life span of 120 years. And the only person in the entire Hebrew Bible to die at that age is Moses, a fact which is highlighted in the framing of the final section of the book of Deuteronomy (chapters 31-34), at the conclusion of the Pentateuch (see Deut 31:2 and 34:7).

Concept Check # 18

What practical reasons have been suggested for arranging the content of a document in five parts, within a concentric structural design? (Check your answer on p. 222.)

Like Genesis 1-11, the structure of the book of Genesis as a whole is also in five parts, as Isaac Kikawada has shown:[43]

A	Primal History	Gen 1-11
B	Abram/Abraham	Gen 12-25
X	Isaac	Gen 18-35
B′	Jacob/Israel	Gen 25-35
A′	Joseph Story	Gen 37-50

Once again the center of this structure is much briefer and more difficult to isolate and describe than either the Abraham cycle or the Jacob cycle which frame the somewhat elusive presentation of Isaac, who is so passive and his story so brief that one is hesitant to designate it either as an "epic" or a "cycle" in the way those terms are applied to the Abraham and Jacob accounts. Nonetheless, the centrality of Isaac has not escaped notice even in antiquity. Almost two thousand years ago, Philo of Alexandria saw Isaac as the central figure in the book of Genesis; and the influence of the *Akedah* (the story of the "binding of Isaac" in Genesis 22) on the New Testament is as undeniable as it is unspoken.[44]

Akedah: The "binding" of Isaac (Gen 22:1-19); the mysterious story of the testing of Abraham who was commanded by God to offer his son Isaac as a burnt offering on Mount Moriah (later identified as the Temple Mount in Jerusalem).

Both Duane Garrett and Gary Rendsburg have located the center of Genesis in the Jacob cycle.[45] Rendsburg analyzed this cycle and posited its center in the Haran episode (Genesis 29-32). This center is bracketed by two paired episodes in his analysis: the dream of the heavenly ladder at Bethel (Gen 28:10-22) and the wrestling match at Peniel (Gen 32:1-32). These mysterious passages also play an important role among those who produced the subsequent Enoch tradition, but in subtle and mysterious ways, as Dan Olson has noted.

It makes a profound difference whether one takes Isaac or Jacob as the true center of Genesis. Jacob struggles with God and attempts to see God, like Moses after him (Exod 33:18). In so doing, Jacob becomes Israel. Popular etymologies of the word "Israel" in antiquity include both "he who struggles with God" and "a man seeing God."[46] Jacob is wounded by his adversary in this encounter, which speaks to the profound "mystery of Israel." Christians through the ages, however, have been profoundly drawn to Isaac and the *Akedah* as an astounding foreshadowing of the mystery of Jesus Christ. By choosing the Jacob episode over that of Isaac in the *Akedah*, the *Book of Enoch* remains a distinctly Jewish document.

> ### Concept Check # 19
>
> How does the figure of Isaac in Genesis 22 (the *Akedah*) prefigure the redemptive work of Jesus in the gospel narratives? (Check your answer on p. 222.)

The same "pentateuchal" structure applies, of course, to the Pentateuch itself, which is in five parts:

A   Genesis
B   Exodus
X   Leviticus
B′   Numbers
A′ Deuteronomy

The book of Leviticus is the center, which is once again briefer and somewhat more elusive or enigmatic in its meaning than the two so-called "wilderness books" of Exodus and Numbers on either side of it. The book of Numbers picks up the narrative story where the closing verses of Exodus left it—with the Tent of Meeting which contained the very presence of God. Though the book of Leviticus also begins with reference to God speaking to Moses from the Tent of Meeting, it quickly moves on to specific detail about the laws pertaining to the burnt offering and other concerns of a legal nature. The book of Numbers, on the other hand, takes up the narrative journey from the numbering of the people in the wilderness to the conflicts and struggles in the wilderness in the circuitous journey of the people of Israel toward the Promised Land.

An analysis of Leviticus itself reveals that its central passage is the Day of Atonement ritual as described in chapter 16.

A	The Sacrificial System	Leviticus 1-10
B	The Purity System	Leviticus 11-15
X	The Day of Atonement (*Yom Kippur*)	Leviticus 16
B′	Holiness in "Daily Life"	Leviticus 17-22
A′	Festivals and Other "Moments"	Leviticus 23-27

Azazel: A demonic figure to whom the sin-laden scapegoat was sent on the Day of Atonement (see Lev 16:8-26).

Once again we find support among the Enochic theologians in antiquity in regard to taking the Day of Atonement (*Yom Kippur*) as the center of Leviticus, for the mysterious figure of **Azazel** (Lev 16:8, 10, 26) looms large in 1 Enoch. Azazel (= Asael) is one of the two leaders of the fallen

Watchers (Enoch 6: cf. Enoch 86) where he is chiefly responsible for teaching many of the forbidden arts to human beings (Enoch 8:1-2). He is singled out as the rebel angel who bears the greatest guilt among the fallen Watchers in a passage which alludes to Leviticus 16: "And the whole earth has been corrupted through the works that were taught by Azazel: to him ascribe all sin" (Enoch 10:8). He is bound and cast into a pit in the wilderness (Enoch 10:4-6). Azazel appears again as chief of the fallen Watchers, who are guilty of "becoming subject to Satan and leading astray those who dwell on the earth" (Enoch 54:6). The Messiah, variously known as "the Elect One," the "Son of Man," and the "Righteous One," will be the one who pronounces final judgment on Azazel: "Ye mighty kings who dwell on the earth, ye shall have to behold mine Elect One, how he sits on the throne of glory and judges Azazel, and all his associates, and all his hosts in the name of the Lord of Spirits" (Enoch 55:4). As the figurehead of all the forces of evil at work in the world, Azazel is undeniably a crucial element in the Enochic mythology, something of a foil to the righteous Messiah and to Enoch himself, who is actually to be identified with the "son of man" in Enoch 71:14.

Concept Check # 20

How did the early Christian community read the account of "The Day of Atonement" in Leviticus 16? (Check your answer on p. 222.)

The next step in the "Pentateuchal Structure" is that of the entire First Testament itself, with the book of Daniel in the central position:

A   Torah (Pentateuch)
B   Former Prophets (Joshua through Kings)
X   Daniel
B'   Latter Prophets (Isaiah, Jeremiah, Ezekiel, & the Twelve)
A'   Writings (Chronicles, Psalms, Job, Proverbs, Festal Scrolls, Ezra-Nehemiah)

The centrality of Daniel is in part based on its chameleon-like ability to join itself to different subgroupings in the First Testament in that it functions as a bridge between the prophetic literature, the wisdom literature, and narrative history. This conclusion is also suggested by the symmetry of word counts noted by David Noel Freedman, who dismissed Daniel as "late" and therefore irrelevant because it does not fit his scheme well. By putting Daniel at the center, we once again find the familiar short and enigmatic core, with a remarkable symmetry in word count as follows:

A	Torah	80,000	
B	Former Prophets	70,000	150,000
X	Daniel	6,000	
B′	Latter Prophets	72,000	
A′	Writings	78,000	150,000

Though the book of Daniel is here much shorter than the other four items in the "Pentateuchal Structure," it is still so large and complex in itself that one is compelled to search for a "center within the center." For the ancient Enochic thinkers, this center was the "son of man" vision of Daniel 7.[47] Nonetheless, a strong case can be made for the desecration of the vessels of the temple on the part of Belshazzar in Dan 5:1-4 as the structural center:

A	Nebuchadnezzar's initial desecration of the Temple	1:1-2
B	Daniel and his three friends faithfully observe the Torah	1:3-21
C	Nebuchadnezzar's dream—the statue and the four kingdoms	2:1-48
D	Daniel's three friends in the fiery furnace	3:1-30
E	Nebuchadnezzar's dream of the tree and his madness	4:1-37
X	Belshazzar desecrates the vessels of the Temple	5:1-4
E′	The handwriting on the wall and Belshazzar's death	5:5-30
D′	Daniel in the lion's den	6:1-28
C′	Daniel's dream of the four beasts	7:1-28
B′	Daniel's visions	8:1-12:4
A′	The final desecration of the Temple	12:5-13

One of the beauties of symmetric analyses of texts is that plumbing the text for psychologically "felt" patterns does not make it necessary to insist on any one model to the exclusion of all others. A work as artistically rich and subtle as the book of Daniel displays more than one overall pattern, depending on the questions put to the text. If the Enochians found a different center here, there is still no reason to conclude that one position is right and the other wrong. They are simply different ways of looking at the same text.

Another way of looking at the structure of Daniel is to observe the presence of two parallel "pentateuchal" structures as follows:

A	Nebuchadnezzar's desecration of the Temple	1:1-2
B	Daniel & his three friends faithfully observe the Torah	1:3-21
X	Nebuchadnezzar's dream—the four kingdoms	2:1-48
B'	Daniel's three friends in the fiery furnace	3:1-30
A'	Nebuchadnezzar's dream of the tree & his madness	4:1-37

A	Belshazzar's desecration of the Temple vessels	5:1-30
B	Daniel's experience in the lion's den	6:1-28
X	Daniel's dream—the four kingdoms	7:1-28
B'	Daniel's visions of the future	8:1 - 12:4
A'	Final desecration of the Temple	12:5-13

These two parallel structures highlight the central theological messages of the book of Daniel and help to explain why this book is so important in Christian circles, ancient and modern. The four kingdoms in the dreams of Nebuchadnezzar and Daniel anticipate the "fifth monarchy," which the gospel writers in the Second Testament designate as the "Kingdom of God" or the "Kingdom of Heaven" on the lips of Jesus. Moreover, the death and resurrection of Jesus is subsequently understood as the great reversal of the final "desecration of the Temple." Note the words of Jesus as recorded by John: "Destroy this temple, and in three days I will raise it up" (John 2:19). The Jews responded: "This temple has been under construction for forty-six years, and will you raise it up in three days?" (John 2:20). The Jews took Jesus' words literally, applying them to Herod's Temple; whereas Jesus spoke metaphorically: "he was speaking of the temple of his body" (John 2:21).

The most interesting observation on the symmetry of word counts, along the lines of what Freedman has seen, is that of the "Pentateuchal Structure" of the Bible as a whole:

A	Primary History	150,000	
B	Latter Prophets	72,000	222,000 words
X	Daniel	6,000	
B'	Writings (without Esther)	75,000	
A'	Second Testament	147,000	222,000 words

In this structure, Daniel remains at the center of the Bible and forms a bridge between the Prophets and the Writings. In the book of Daniel, we encounter the full blast of the apocalyptic age. The endtime has come with a crisis of unimaginable proportions; for the very root and foundation of human existence are being shaken to the core. The Second Testament forms an inclusion with the Primary History (Genesis through 2 Kings). The narrative story line of the Primary History carries the epic account from creation to the release of King Jehoiachin from prison in Babylonia, ca. 560 BCE. The Second Testament picks up the story with the birth of Jesus and continues the epic account to the very end of days depicted earlier in the apocalyptic visions of the book of Daniel.

Concept Check # 21

How does the presentation of the "four kingdoms" in the Book of Daniel set the stage for Jesus' teaching about the "Kingdom of God" in the Gospels? (Check your answer on p. 223.)

Jerome: A Christian biblical scholar (ca. 340-420 CE) responsible for the Latin translation of the Bible (Latin Vulgate) which became the official Bible of the Roman Catholic Church.

The book of Esther apparently did not achieve full canonicity until the time of **Jerome** (ca. 380 CE), as witnessed by its omission in the canonical lists of Melito (third century CE), Athanasius (ca. 326 CE), Gregory of Nazianzus (ca. 370 CE), and the anonymous writer of the *Synopsis* Scripturae Sacrae (contemporary with Athanasius); and by the fact that there is no agreement within the other early lists as to where Esther belongs when it is included. It was the delayed inclusion of Esther in the canon that broke up the category of the Festal Scrolls, which resulted in the distribution of these books within the canon and effectively replaced the concept of a twenty-two-book canon of the First Testament with the twenty-four-book canon of Talmudic tradition. Without Esther, the word counts of the Writings plus the Second Testament equal 222,000 words, which is virtually identical to that of the Primary History plus the Latter Prophets.

David Noel Freedman has posited a somewhat different picture of the formation of the Second Testament in terms of symmetry of word counts. He sees the equivalent of the Primary History of the Hebrew Bible in the New Testament combination of the three Synoptic Gospels (Matthew, Mark, and Luke) and the book of Acts. The first three gospels share a good deal of common material and have significant literary connections with each other. Though there is strong minority opinion to the contrary, it is commonly agreed in the mainstream of biblical scholarship that the gospels of Matthew and Luke are dependent upon Mark for a substantial part of their contents. Moreover, these three gospels share substantial other materials which many scholars conclude are derived from a hypothetical source (so-called Q for German "Quelle"). The result, for Freedman, is a block of narrative material that consists of the Synoptic Gospels along with the continuation of the Gospel of Luke in the book of Acts. This material constitutes what he calls the "Primary History" of the New Testament. While the Gospel of John is normally placed between Luke and Acts, no one doubts that Acts is in fact the continuation of Luke, as the author of Luke-Acts points out explicitly in the opening verses of the book of Acts.

This combination of the Gospels and Acts, like the Primary History in the First Testament, constitutes almost exactly half of the total number of words in the larger work. In both cases, the Primary History consists of 49 percent of the total length of each Testament. In the "Primary History" of the Second Testament, the natural literary division comes after Matthew and Mark, with the second unit, Luke-Acts, constituting the largest continuous narrative in the entire work. The numbers in terms of word counts are as follows:

Matthew—Mark	32,000 words
Luke—Acts	40,000 words

For the rest of the Second Testament, Freedman finds the next corpus in the Pauline Epistles, including both the so-called authentic epistles, universally attributed to the apostle himself, and those traditionally assigned to Paul, even if the authorship is disputed, such as the book of Hebrews. Altogether Freedman sees fourteen epistles traditionally assigned to Paul, with a word count of approximately 40,000. This symmetry corresponds to that between the Former Prophets and the Latter Prophets of the Hebrew Bible.

Freedman sees the remaining books of the Second Testament as corresponding to what he calls the "catch-all Writings" of the Hebrew Bible. This section is dominated by writings attributed to the apostle John, including his gospel, his three epistles, and the book of Revelation. Like the Chronicler's work in the Writings of the Hebrew Bible, the Gospel of John reaches back to the very beginning of Genesis, and presents itself as a parallel to that of the Primary History. If, in addition, the Gospel of John is linked with the book of Revelation at the end of the Second Testament, we see a pattern of envelope construction much like that of the Chronicler's work in the Writings of the Hebrew Bible. In that instance, the Writings begin with Chronicles and end with Ezra-Nehemiah (taken as a single book). These two books form an envelope around the rest of the Writings. In like manner, John's gospel and the book of Revelation form an envelope around what Freedman calls the General or Catholic Epistles (including those of John), and in some respects around the whole of the Second Testament extending from creation to the *eschaton* itself.

The numbers for the Johannine corpus are as follows:

The Gospel of John	17,000 words
The Book of Revelation	10,000 words

What remains are the so-called General or Catholic Epistles, including those attributed to James the brother of Jesus, Peter, John, and Jude (a brother of James). There are seven epistles in all, and the word counts are as follows:

James	1,857	words
1 Peter	1,790	
2 Peter	1,180	
1 John	2,250	
2 John	264	
3 John	235	
Jude	489	
Total	8,065	words

The total number of words in the Johannine corpus and the General or Catholic Epistles is thus about 35,000. Together with the Pauline Epistles, the remaining material in the Second Testament totals 75,000 words, compared to 72,000 words in what Freedman has called the "Primary History" (Matthew-Mark plus Luke-Acts). The total word count for the Second Testament is thus 147,000, which is roughly equivalent to the 150,000 words found in the Primary History of the First Testament.

Freedman argues that just as the Torah was pulled out of the Primary History in the First Testament, so the Gospels were pulled out of the "Primary History" of the Second Testament. But the Gospels are intended for a very different purpose. By putting the Gospel of John between Luke and Acts, the message is clear: the four Gospels are first. The intention is to stress the importance of the life, death, and resurrection of Jesus. He is the central figure of the Second Testament. Luke's objective in the composition of Luke-Acts is slightly different. He intended to show how the Christian movement started in Jerusalem and ended in Rome.

A less convincing aspect of Freedman's arguments is the exclusion of Second Peter, and Second and Third John so as to end up with a canon of twenty-four books which total 144,000 words. He notes that the number of the saved of the twelve tribes in the book of Revelation is 144,000 and suggests that there is a correlation between the number of words in the Second Testament and this sacred number in the book of Revelation. In Matthew and Mark, 32,000; in Luke and Acts, 40,000, for a total of 72,000; then 40,000 in the Pauline corpus, 32,000 in the Johannine corpus and the other apostolic writings, again for a total of 72,000 words; and a grand total of 144,000 words. The reason for this symmetry, in Freedman's opinion, is to establish the Second Testament as authoritative Scripture, just like the First Testament. Using the First Testament as the model, the early Christian community arranged the materials in an order that achieves the same kind of symmetry. Freedman sees this as a conscious effort to establish the authority of the Second Testament which took place sometime about the middle of the second century CE.

Thinking Exercise

On the Second Testament

The critical thinking goal for this exercise is to clarify the relationship between the two testaments in light of the Pentateuchal Principle of the canonical process.

How To Do This Exercise

Review the diagrams of the several five-part ("pentateuchal") structures within the canon of the Christian Bible in this section. Then answer the following questions:

1. In light of the proposed five-part structure of Genesis 1-11, and the function of the enigmatic story in Gen 6:1-4 in particular, what is the central message of these opening chapters of the Bible?

_____

_____

_____

2. In light of the proposed five-part structure of the book of Genesis as a whole, what is the central message of that book?

_____

_____

_____

_____

3. What do you make of the fact that in the proposed five-part structures of both the First Testament and the Christian Bible as a whole, the book of Daniel occupies central position?

_____

_____

_____

_____

Discussion Questions

1. Do you think the Bible is the "Word of God"? Justify your answer with specific arguments.

2. Even though Jerome translated the First Testament from the original Hebrew text rather than from the Greek Septuagint, the Latin Vulgate retains the order of the books in the Septuagint rather than that of the subsequent masoretic tradition. What significance, if any, do you see in this observation?

3. What is the significance of the fact that the theological center of the Pentateuch (in Exodus 33) and the Former Prophets (1 Kings 19) takes place on the same mountain involving Moses and Elijah respectively?

4. Who was responsible for the symmetry in word count within the Christian Bible?

Concept Map: Summary of Chapter 2

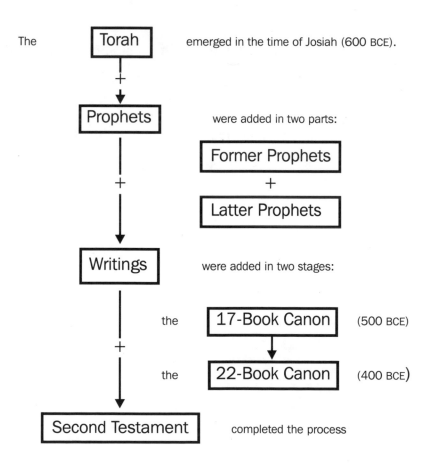

The **Canonical Process** took place in four stages:

The Torah emerged in the time of Josiah (600 BCE).

+

Prophets were added in two parts:

Former Prophets

+

Latter Prophets

Writings were added in two stages:

the 17-Book Canon (500 BCE)

+

the 22-Book Canon (400 BCE)

Second Testament completed the process

to form the **Christian Bible**

3 Jesus Christ as Center of the Canonical Process

Learning Objectives

After studying this chapter, you should be able to:

1. Write an essay on "The New Torah" in the Christian Bible.

2. Identify each concept and key word in the chapter. Concepts and key words are shown in **bold** typeface when introduced. *Identify* means:

    a. *define the term*, using your own words as much as possible,

    b. *give a specific example* to illustrate the concept, and briefly *explain its importance*.

A. A New Center in the Christian Bible

There is a simpler way of seeing the structure of the two Testaments, which is based on the twenty-two-book canon of the First Testament as described by Josephus, namely: five books of Moses, plus 13 "prophets" and four "hagiographa"; that is $5 + 17 = 22$. This structure was not invented by Josephus, but was already ancient for him and probably served as a pattern for the formation of the Second Testament in the emerging canon of the Christian Bible, as shown on the following page.

From a structural point of view, the four Gospels plus Acts stand in the center of this canon, as a kind of "New Torah." The resultant canonical structure is:

$$(5 + 17) + 5 + (17 + 5) = 22 + 5 + 22 = 49 \text{ books } (=7^2)$$

Since this "New Torah" (the Gospels plus Acts) constitutes the fulfillment of the First Testament, it stands between the two halves of the Christian Bible, belonging to both—each of which is made up of twenty-seven books. In one sense, then, one can argue that Jesus, together with the coming of the Holy Spirit in the book of Acts, is the center of the Bible in its present canonical form. This conclusion is similar to Norbert Lohfink's in his discussion of "The Inerrancy of Scripture," when he commented that, "the sole inspired 'author' of the Old Testament was Jesus, and certain figures of the primitive Church."[1]

		Exodus	Leviticus	
	Genesis			
		Numbers	Deuteronomy	
Joshua	Judges		Isaiah	Jeremiah
Samuel	Kings		Ezekiel	The Twelve
		Daniel		
Psalms	Job		Chronicles	Ezra
Proverbs	*Megilloth*		Nehemiah	Maccabees
	Matthew	Mark		
			Acts of the Apostles	
	Luke	John		
Romans	1 Corinthians		Philippians	Colossians
2 Cor.	Galatians		1 Thess.	2 Thessalonians
		Ephesians		
1 Timothy	2 Timothy		Hebrews	James
Titus	Philemon		1 Peter	2 Peter
	1 John	2 John		
			Revelation	
	3 John	Jude		

Another observation is in order: The Gospels and Acts are as much a part of the First Testament as they are of the Second. They stand between the testaments and belong to both. The Gospels plus Acts constitute a "New Torah," which completes the First Testament by fulfilling the canonical structures which shape that body of literature. In the remainder of this chapter, we will examine three different ways of viewing Gospels-Acts as the completion of the First Testament.

Concept Check # 22

Does the symmetry of the Bible, as described here, have implications regarding the authorship of the Bible? (Check your answer on p. 223.)

Thinking Exercise

On Jesus as the New Torah

The critical thinking goal for this exercise is to clarify how Jesus Christ became the center of the canonical process in ancient Israel by examining his relationship to the Torah.

How To Do This Exercise

Review the concept of the Torah as the five books of Moses (the Pentateuch) in chapter 2. The Torah became the "canon within the canon" in ancient Israel and subsequent Judaism in the sense that it was the most authoritative part of the Bible. As such, it was read on a regular cycle in public worship and study. Along with the readings from the Torah, readings from the Prophets and the Psalms were also included in the services of the synagogues. Read Luke 4:14-21 for a description of what took place in such a setting. Jesus unrolled the scroll of the prophet Isaiah on a Sabbath day in Nazareth and read the text aloud. He then sat down and taught the people what the text meant. Now answer the following:

1. Describe how the Bible was used in the synagogues of ancient Israel.

_____

_____

_____

_____

_____

2. In liturgical tradition within the Christian Church, the people stand during the public reading from the Gospels and often the book of Acts. Compare this tradition to that of the reading from the Torah and the Prophets in the synagogues as presented in Luke 4:14-21.

_____

_____

_____

_____

_____

3. Describe the function of the Gospels and Acts in the diagram of the Christian Bible on p. 92.

_____

_____

_____

_____

_____

4. What do you think Jesus meant when he declared: "I have not come to abolish the Torah and the Prophets; I have come to fulfill them" (Matt 5:17)?

_____

_____

_____

_____

_____

B. Jesus and the Completion of the Primary History

The Primary History in the First Testament may be diagrammed as follows:

A   Creation [Genesis 1-11]
B   Ancestors [Genesis 12-36]   Torah
C   Joseph [Genesis 37-50]

X   **Moses** → **David** ⟶ **Hezekiah** ⟶ **Josiah** ⟶ **Messiah**
                    Nathan   Isaiah   Huldah   Elijah
C′   Joshua
B′   Judges   Former Prophets
A′ Kingship [1 Samuel – 2 Kings]

In this diagram, "Creation" stands for Genesis 1-11, which is set over against the period of kingship as recorded in the books of Samuel and Kings. The God who created the world and all that is in it is the same one who ordained a new day in Israel in the shared authority of king and prophet.

What makes a good king in the context of the Primary History has nothing to do with morality as such. The good king is the one who chooses to listen to the prophet God has raised up in his day. With this criterion in mind, the only "good kings" in the story in an unqualified sense are **David**, Hezekiah, and Josiah; for they are the ones who share their authority with Nathan, Isaiah, and Huldah respectively. This model looks into the distant future in anticipation of a new day—in which a new king will appear as the **Messiah** ("anointed one") who will be accompanied by the prophet Elijah. It is this expectation that forms the setting of the Second Testament.

From the outset, the people wondered if Jesus was the long-awaited Messiah and what his relationship was to John the Baptist, whom many believed to be the prophet of the last days. As things turned out, Jesus was the Messiah, the son of David, but not in the manner expected. He did not share his authority with John the Baptist, nor with any other prophetic figure. He is the prophet as well as the long-awaited "king of the Jews;" but his kingdom was unlike any other the world has seen. Jesus is more like Moses than David. He is prophet, priest, and king—and much more; for he is the Word of God in human flesh. In him

David: The most powerful king of biblical Israel (ca. 1000 to 970 BCE) who established Jerusalem as the capital and is reputed to have written many of the psalms in the Psalter.

Messiah: "Anointed one," in the political sphere the word refers to the kings who would continue the Davidic dynasty in Israel; in Christian usage it became a title that refers only to Jesus (Messiah = Christ).

all the symbols of God's presence coalesce. He is the ancient Rock (1 Cor 10:4; cf. Deut 32:30-31); and even the Temple in Jerusalem is identified with his own body (cf. John 2:19). In fact, early Christians had little difficulty translating the ineffable name of Yahweh with the Greek word *kurios*, which they also used of Jesus; for he is identified with Yahweh. As Jesus put it in John's gospel, "I and the Father are one!" (John 10:30).

The term "Ancestors" in the diagram above refers to Genesis 12-36, and the stories about Abraham, Isaac, Jacob, and Jacob's twelve sons (the tribal Fathers). This material is set over against the stories of the Judges. In both cases, the stories are a bit like a picaresque novel, in that each of the individual episodes stands by itself. For example, one does not need to know any of the other stories of Abraham in order to read the *Akedah* ("binding" of Isaac) in Genesis 22. In the same manner, one does not need to know the story of Gideon in order to understand the story of Samson. Each individual episode is complete in itself; and each adds something of its own to the presentation of the larger whole. To understand the person of Abraham in the book of Genesis one must put together all the information presented in each of the several episodes.

The picture is different when it comes to the stories of Joseph (Genesis 37-50) and the story of Joshua (Joshua 1-11). Here we have a different type of literature—one that is much more like the novella in English literature; for the stories are longer and more complex than those of the Ancestors and the Judges of ancient Israel. One cannot omit any part of the Joseph story without doing major damage to the whole. At the very outset, essential details of what will follow are prefigured in the specific content of dreams and in literary puns and symbols. The same is true for the story of the sending of the spies and the subsequent conquest of Jericho in Joshua 1-6. The stories of Joseph and Joshua serve as a frame to highlight the person of Moses, as presented in the large block of material in Exodus through Deuteronomy.

A strong case can be made for seeing the major theme of the Torah and of the Former Prophets in the First Testament as that of leadership.[2] Moses is the paradigm of leadership in the Torah. He is prophet, priest, war lord, and even *de facto* king—long before kingship is established in ancient Israel. Joshua continues this model of leadership when the people of Israel enter the Promised Land; and he is followed in turn by the period of the Judges, which extends from the death of Joshua to the death of Samuel. As we noted earlier in this book, the ideal of kingship in the Former Prophets is presented in terms of a balance of power between the king and the prophet in ancient Israel. What makes a good king, at least within the Former Prophets, is the king who listens to the "Word of God" as expressed through the charismatic prophet of Yahweh in ancient Israel.

Concept Check # 23

If leadership for the people of God is a central theme in the Torah and the Prophets, in terms of the relationship between prophet and king, what are the implications for leadership today in the Christian Church? (Check your answer on p. 223.)

C. Jesus and the Latter Prophets

The transition in leadership from the time of the Judges to the early monarchy in ancient Israel is worked out through Samuel, the last of the judges and the first of the line of prophets in what is sometimes called the "Samuel compromise," in which leadership is shared by the king and the prophet. This phenomenon of shared authority is a dominant theme in the structuring of the Latter Prophets, along with the building, destruction, and rebuilding of the Temple in Jerusalem, as shown in the following diagram:

David/Nathan

Temple Built

Hezekiah/Isaiah
Josiah/Jeremiah

Temple Destroyed

Jehoiachin/Ezekiel
Zerubbabel/"The Twelve"

Temple Rebuilt

Messiah/Elijah

The Latter Prophets, as a canonical category, are shaped around the Temple in Jerusalem, which David anticipated and Solomon built in the latter part of the tenth century BCE. When that Temple was destroyed in 587 BCE by King Nebuchadnezzar of Babylon, both Jeremiah and Ezekiel experienced the trauma directly. Ezekiel was carried into captivity in 597 BCE and witnessed the destruction of the Temple in Jerusalem ten years later, from his place of exile in Babylon. Jeremiah lived through the destruction of the Temple in Jerusalem and then spent his final years in involuntary exile in Egypt. Ezekiel's prophecy is written from the perspective of the Zadokite priesthood in Jerusalem; whereas Jeremiah's work is written from the point of view of the rival deuteronomic school, which King Josiah had brought into the royal court from the nearby Levitical town of Anathoth.

The two central prophetic books of Jeremiah and Ezekiel, which frame the actual destruction of the Temple in Jerusalem, are in turn framed by the books of the prophet Isaiah and "The Twelve" minor prophets. The prophet Isaiah is linked with king Hezekiah in the second half of the eighth century BCE. Isaiah and Hezekiah spearheaded the first great religious reformation in ancient Israel, a time of significant canonical activity in Jerusalem. As Prov 25:1 bears witness, "the men of Hezekiah king of Judah" added certain proverbs to the existing collection of the proverbs of Solomon. They also played a major role in shaping the deuteronomic tradition, as Moshe Weinfeld has shown.[3]

The book of "The Twelve" emerged in the exile and focuses its attention on the rebuilding of the Temple in Jerusalem under Zerubbabel, the scion of David. The books of Haggai and Zechariah, in particular, are devoted to this vision, which results in the dedication of the Second Temple in Jerusalem in 515 BCE and the projection of a larger hope for a more splendid restoration in the distant future (Zechariah 9-14). The book of Malachi concludes the book of "The Twelve" minor prophets with at vision of the coming Messiah, who will be preceded by the return of the prophet Elijah (Mal 4:5-6). It is this vision which sets the stage for the appearance of John the Baptist and Jesus, and the formation of the Second Testament.

Concept Check # 24

As the apostle Paul put it, Jesus was sent by God "when the fullness of time was come" (Gal 4:4). Does this chapter shed any light on this statement? (Check your answer on p. 223.)

Thinking Exercise

On Jesus as the Fulfillment of the Prophets

The critical thinking goal of this exercise is to clarify further how Jesus Christ became the center of the canonical process in ancient Israel by examining his relationship to the Former and Latter Prophets.

How To Do This Exercise

The king and prophet in ancient Israel share complementary roles. Together they rule the people of God. Consequently a "good king" in the context of the Former Prophets is one who listens to the word of God as delivered by the prophet. Review the diagram on p. 97, which pairs the kings David, Hezekiah, Josiah, Jehoiachin, Zerubbabel, and the coming Messiah with their respective prophets on a time line in relation to the Temple in Jerusalem. Then answer the following:

1. What is meant by the term "Samuel Compromise" as used in this section?

_____

_____

_____

_____

_____

2. Read Mal 4:4-6. How can Elijah here be described as a prophet who is coming in the future? With whom is this coming prophet to be associated?

_____

_____

_____

_____

_____

3. Was Jesus considered a "king," a "prophet," or both by the writers of the Second Testament?

_____

_____

_____

_____

_____

4. Read John 2:19-22. Discuss what Jesus meant when he prophesied about the destruction and rebuilding of the Temple.

_____

_____

_____

_____

_____

D. Jesus and the Epic Story of the People of God

There are still other ways to show the centrality of Jesus Christ within the canonical process in ancient Israel. The primary narrative structure of the national epic in the formative era, before the monarchy emerged under David and Solomon, may be diagrammed as follows:

$$\text{BONDAGE} \longrightarrow \text{WATERS} \longrightarrow \text{MOUNTAIN OF GOD}$$
$$\text{Egypt} \qquad\qquad \text{Re(e)d Sea} \qquad \text{Sinai/Horeb}$$

The people of God were delivered from slavery in Egypt under Moses, who led them through the waters of *Yam Suf* (the Red Sea or "Sea of Reeds") to the holy mountain where God revealed his presence and his will in the Ten Commandments which were written on tablets of stone.

The ancient epic story was extended in the generation after the Exodus under Moses, as the people of God moved from their wilderness home at Kadesh-barnea in the Negev of southern Judah to the transfer of leadership from Moses to Joshua on the plains of Moab. The story of deliverance from slavery in Egypt under Moses was augmented with the story of the Eisodus (the Conquest) into the Promised Land under Joshua, which was understood in terms of what the people of Israel called the "wars of Yahweh."

The so-called *Book of the Wars of Yahweh,* which is cited only once in the Bible (Num 21:14), was apparently an epic account of God's "Holy War" directed against the enemies of Israel in the time of Moses and Joshua. Though many scholars have assumed it to be a lost anthology of ancient war poems dealing with the conflict between the invading Israelites and the original inhabitants of Canaan, it is more likely that this "book" was an epic poem that was eminently familiar to all—much as the *Iliad* and the *Odyssey* of Homer were well known in ancient Greece long before that epic material was written down in the form of books as we know them today.

The brief quotation from the *Book of the Wars of Yahweh* in Num 21:14 was cited by the narrator primarily because it placed the boundary of Moab at the Arnon River. Though the Hebrew text is difficult, it may be rendered as follows:[4]

The Benefactor (i.e., Yahweh) has come in a whirlwind;
Yes, He has come to the wadis of the Arnon.
He marched through the wadis;
He marched, he turned aside—to the seat of Ar;
He leaned toward the border of Moab.

Because of archaic features, the text was subsequently misread with resultant confusion in the ancient versions and experienced some textual corruption in the received masoretic tradition. The picture presented is that of the Divine Warrior poised on the edge of the Promised Land, before the most celebrated battles of the Exodus-Conquest. He has come in the whirlwind with his hosts to the sources of the Arnon River in Transjordan. He marches through the wadis, turning aside to settle affairs with the two Amorite kings, Sihon and Og, and then across the Jordan to the battlecamp at Gilgal and the conquest of Canaan. This epic story may be diagrammed as follows:

LAND ⟶ BONDAGE ⟶ WATERS ⟶ BATTLE CAMP
[Promised   (Jordan River)   Land Regained]

With the advent of the monarchy in the time of David and Solomon, the ancient epic narrative was extended and given a new ending, which focused on the kingdom of David as God's new creation. The new pattern was achieved by simply moving from the mountain of God's revelation at Sinai to the new mountain of God's abiding presence in Jerusalem on **Mount Zion,** as follows:

CREATION/LAND → BONDAGE → WATERS/MOUNTAIN → TEMPLE/NEW CREATION
                                  [Mount Sinai]   [Mount Zion]

This diagram summarizes the content of the Primary History in the First Testament. At the same time, it anticipates a second transformation of the ancient epic story which culminates in the formation of the Second Testament with its focus on the person of Jesus Christ.

In John's gospel, Jesus made the statement: "Destroy this temple, and in three days I will raise it up" (John 2:19). Those who heard him at the time thought that he was referring to the Temple in Jerusalem, which had taken forty-six years to build (John 2:20); but, after the resurrection of Jesus, "his disciples remembered that he had said this" (John 2:22), and now they understood. In some mysterious way, Jesus himself was

Mount Zion: Refers to three different aspects of the city of Jerusalem: the ancient "city of David"; the Temple Mount complex immediately to the north (where the Dome of the Rock is located); and the hill immediately south of the southwestern corner of the present "old city." Used metaphorically, the term designates the place of God's dwelling (i.e., the "heavenly Jerusalem").

the Temple in Jerusalem; and the ancient epic story now had a new and deeper meaning.

The epic pattern for this interpretation of the New Israel, as the people of God in Jesus Christ may be diagrammed as follows:

CREATION/LAND → KINGDOM → BONDAGE/WATERS/WILDERNESS → KINGDOM OF GOD
(Exile/New Exodus) (Israel)   (Present Church Age)   (New Jerusalem)

This transformation of the ancient epic narrative was achieved by elaborating the kingdom of David into a messianic kingdom with the anticipation of a new theophany in which the mountain of God's revelation and abiding presence in ancient Israel is extended in an eschatological vision.

The Gospel of Luke is a good illustration of how this transformation became the structuring principle for an altogether new reading of the ancient epic narrative. At the center of Luke's gospel stands his account of the transfiguration of Jesus. After making his enigmatic statement that "there are some standing here who will not taste death before they see the kingdom of God" (Luke 9:27), Luke goes on to describe a mysterious experience on a certain mountain where Moses and Elijah appeared with Jesus, and the three of them discussed "his *Exodus*, which he was to accomplish at Jerusalem" (Luke 9:31). Greek Orthodox tradition, which places this event in the vicinity of Mount Sinai where both Moses (Exodus 33) and Elijah (1 Kings 19) had their great encounters with God in times past, is surely correct at least symbolically. Jesus Christ appears on the mountain of God, which combines the experiences of Moses and Elijah on Sinai with the anticipation of what God will achieve on Mount Golgotha not many days hence in Luke's narrative account.

Concept Check # 25

Perhaps the most intriguing suggestion for the location of the transfiguration of Jesus in church tradition is that of the Greek Orthodox Church, namely Mount Sinai—where Moses and Elijah had earlier encountered God. In light of parallels in Matt 17:1-9 and Mark 9:2 to Moses' ascent of Mount Sinai in Exodus 24 (cf. also 1 Kgs 19:8-18 and 2 Pet 1:16-18), what is the meaning of the Transfiguration? (Check your answer on p. 223.)

Thinking Exercise

On Jesus as the New Ending to the Epic Story

The critical thinking goal of this exercise is to clarify further how Jesus Christ became the center of the canonical process in ancient Israel by examining his relationship to the basic epic story.

How To Do This Exercise

Review the four diagrams in this section which concern the epic story of the people of God in the Bible. Then answer the following:

1. The first diagram depicts the journey from slavery in Egypt to the experience at Mount Sinai where God revealed the Ten Commandments to Moses. Discuss the importance of these events.

_____

_____

_____

_____

_____

2. The second diagram extends this basic salvation experience by framing it with stories about the land promised to the Ancestors, on the one hand, which is subsequently regained under Moses and Joshua. Explain how all this is related to what the scholars call the Hexateuch?

_____

_____

_____

_____

_____

3. The third diagram extends the basic story by framing it with stories about creation, on the one hand, and the vision of a new day, on the other, in which the Temple in Jerusalem is the center of the world. Explain how this is related to the First Testament as a whole.

_____

_____

_____

_____

_____

4. The fourth diagram extends the basic story still further with a vision of the distant future, which is described as the "New Jerusalem." Explain how this is related to the entire Christian Bible.

_____

_____

_____

_____

_____

Discussion Questions

1. How does Jesus complete and replace the Torah for Christians?

2. How is Jesus the fulfillment of the prophets for Christians?

3. Explain how the Second Testament provides a new ending to the epic story of the First Testament.

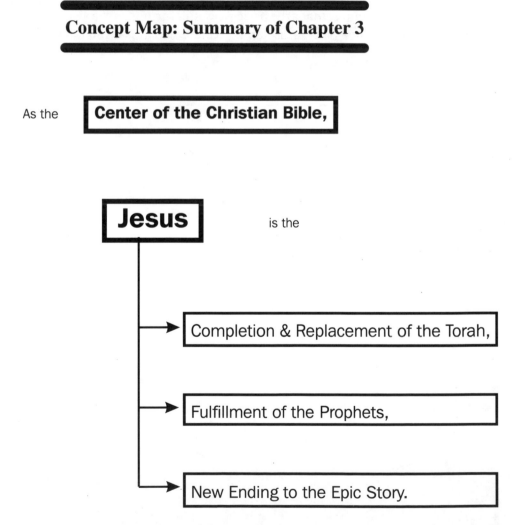

Concept Map: Summary of Chapter 3

As the **Center of the Christian Bible,**

Jesus   is the

Completion & Replacement of the Torah,

Fulfillment of the Prophets,

New Ending to the Epic Story.

4 How We Got Our Bible The Word of God in History

Learning Objectives

After studying this chapter, you should be able to:

1. Tell the story of how the Bible developed in space and time from recitation in ancient Israel and early Church history to written text and translations thereof.

2. Describe the major phases in the history of the English Bible.

3. Identify each concept and key word in the chapter. Concepts and key words are shown in **bold** typeface when introduced. *Identify* means:

    a. *define the term*, using your own words as much as possible,

    b. *give a specific example* to illustrate the idea, and briefly *explain its importance*.

In chapter 2 of this book we traced in broad outline the canonical process which produced the Bible as we now know it. That process was in large part an unconscious one, in which a living and changing community of faith shaped their sacred tradition into a coherent whole made up of five major parts, as follows:

Torah
[80,000 words]

Former Prophets
[70,000 words]

Second Testament
[147,000 words]

Latter Prophets
[72,000 words]

Writings (without Daniel)
[78,000 words]

The symmetry in this arrangement is striking, with the Torah and the Writings being approximately the same length (80,000 words), and the Former and Latter Prophets roughly the same length as well (70,000 words). Moreover, the Torah (Pentateuch) is made up of five books

Uncial codices:
Codices written in a formal style of handwritten letters adapted from the Greek capitals used in inscriptions, but more rounded rather than straight and angular.

Codex (pl. codices): A manuscript in the form of a leaf book rather than a scroll, with separate leaves sewn together. The idea apparently developed from parchment notebooks (*membranae*; cf. 2 Tim 4:13), an adaptation of the multileaved Greek and Roman tablets made of thin boards fastened together by a thong hinge. All extant MSS of the NT appear to be in this form.

Dead Sea Scrolls:
Leather, papyrus, and copper scrolls dating from ca. 100 BCE to 135 CE containing complete and partial texts of most of the books of the Hebrew Bible, which were discovered at or near Qumran on the west side of the Dead Sea in 1947 and the years following.

(Genesis, Exodus, Leviticus, Numbers, and Deuteronomy); while the Writings contain the five-book Psalter and the five Festal Scrolls (the *Megilloth* = Ruth, Song of Songs, Ecclesiastes, Lamentations, and Esther). It should also be noted that the remaining books in the Writings are frequently listed as five in number in the early canonical lists, namely: Job, Proverbs, Daniel, Ezra-Nehemiah, and Chronicles. Origen, the third century Church Father, is typical in his remarks on items 10 and 11 in his canonical list of twenty-two books: "Chronicles first and second, in one" and "Ezra first and second (i.e., Nehemiah) in one."[1] Meanwhile there are four books in the Former Prophets (Joshua, Judges, Samuel, and Kings) and four in the Latter Prophets (Isaiah, Jeremiah, Ezekiel, and The Twelve). This measured symmetry is surely not coincidental.

Though the process that produced the canon can be traced in broad outline, it is clear that it was largely an unconscious one; or, in concepts taken from Jungian psychology, the canon was the product of collective unconscious structuring within a community of faith over the course of many generations. At the outset, the books of the Hebrew Bible were written on scrolls which were used primarily for the recitation of the text in public worship. Even before the advent of Christianity, it was necessary to translate the biblical text into vernacular speech within certain Jewish communities outside Palestine—particularly into Greek (the Septuagint) and Aramaic.

By the fourth century of the Common Era, the Second Testament was assembled into a single work in the form of the great **uncial codices**. The fixing of the text of the Hebrew Bible within the context of a single **codex** seems to have taken place somewhat later than that of the Second Testament, in spite of the evidence for early recensional activity which has been demonstrated through study of the manuscript evidence preserved at Qumran in the **Dead Sea Scrolls**. The centrality of the use of the great Torah scrolls in Jewish public worship to the present day militated against the newer concept of arranging the entire biblical text into "book form" in a codex. It may well be that the earliest codices of the First Testament were actually done by Christians, in the Greek translation known as the Septuagint. The earliest known masoretic codex of the Hebrew Bible is the Cairo Codex (895 CE), which contains only the Former Prophets and the Latter Prophets. The codices on which modern printed editions of the Masoretic Text of the Hebrew Bible are based are from the tenth century. As far as we know, the actual pointing of the Hebrew text with **vowel points** and the complex **accentual system** were put into writing for the first time in the ninth and tenth centuries of the Common Era.

A. The Aural Tradition Behind the Bible

In the mainstream of critical study it has been assumed that the history of the biblical text includes a long period of oral transmission. For example, what Jesus actually said during the period of his teaching ministry in Palestine was remembered and passed down in oral form, by word of mouth, among his followers. Eventually those teachings were collected and edited by followers of Jesus to make up the Gospel tradition as we know it. The time period between the actual sayings of Jesus and the recording of these sayings in written form within the Gospel tradition took a generation or more. In the meantime, the content of the Gospels was passed on in oral form.

The term "oral" refers to the concept of the tradition being passed down by word of mouth. The term "aural" is used here to shift the emphasis to the ear. The text of the Bible was composed primarily for the ear and not the eye. The Bible, particularly in ancient Judaism, was composed to be heard in public recitation by professional cantors. It is probable that the text of the Gospels and much of the rest of the Second Testament was also composed primarily to be heard in public recitation.

Old Testament scholars have long assumed a complex history of what eventually became the Pentateuch. They assume that the books of Moses were not written by Moses himself. Rather they are the product of a complex editing process through the centuries, in which differing versions of what was remembered in separate communities of faith were combined at various points in time, beginning perhaps as early as the time of David and Solomon in ancient Israel.

Though a great deal of effort has been given by scholars to reconstruct the presumed history of the biblical text behind the received tradition, in both the First Testament and the Second Testament, very little attention has been given to the study of the accentual system of the Hebrew Bible and to reconstructing how the text was performed within the context of the **Second Temple** in ancient Judaism. The tradition of musical performance, or rhythmic recitation of the text, in the context of public worship, is worthy of careful attention and may prove to be the

Vowel points: A system of marks added to the consonantal text of the Hebrew Bible by medieval scribes known as the masoretes to indicate the vowel sounds.

Accentual system: A complex system of marks added above and below the consonantal text of the Hebrew Bible to indicate how the text was canted in public recitation. The system is essentially a form of musical notation.

Second Temple: The temple in Jerusalem, built in the time of the prophets Haggai and Zechariah and dedicated in 515 BCE, to replace the earlier Temple of Solomon which was destroyed by the Babylonian ruler Nebuchadnezzar in 587 BCE.

Masoretes: A family of Jewish scholars living in Tiberias on the Sea of Galilee who were responsible for providing the already standardized text of the Hebrew Bible with vowel signs and an elaborate accentual system between the seventh and tenth centuries CE known as the Masoretic Text.

key to understanding the symmetries in the structure of the canon of sacred Scripture. Much of the Bible as we know it was probably performed and sung in liturgical settings in ancient Israel, and thus the form of Scripture is essentially poetic. My own research in the book of Deuteronomy, in particular, suggests that the Hebrew text in its present form, as preserved by the **masoretes**, is a musical composition. The canting tradition of the synagogues preserves accurate memory of the original performance of the text during the period of the Second Temple in Jerusalem and perhaps earlier.

The Bible, as we have it, is not a collection of independent books, which scribes in antiquity gathered together into a library as such. It is a single book, by a single author—if we are to give credence to the common affirmation in public worship that it is the Word of God. We have already examined the canonical process that brought the book to us. Our task in this chapter is to explore the complex history of the written text of sacred Scripture through the centuries to the proliferation of modern translations and commentaries flooding the market at the end of the twentieth century.

As Bishop Robert Lowth noted two hundred years ago, the law codes throughout the Mediterranean world were sung at the festivals in antiquity.[2]

> It is evident that Greece for several successive ages was possessed of no records but the poetic, for the first who published a prose oration was Pherecydes, a man of the Isle of Syrus, and the contemporary with King Cyrus, who lived some ages posterior to that of Homer and Hesiod, somewhat after the time Cadmus the Milesian began to compose history. The laws themselves were metrical, and adapted to certain musical notes: such were the laws of Charondas, which were sung at the banquets of the Athenians: such were those which were delivered by the Cretans to the ingenuous youth to be learned by rote, with the accompaniments of musical melody, in order that by the enchantment of harmony, the sentiments might be forcibly impressed upon their memories. Hence certain poems were denominated *nomoi* which implied convivial or banqueting songs, as is remarked by Aristotle; who adds, that the same custom of chanting the laws to music, existed even in his own time among the Agathyrsi.

The law book we call the book of Deuteronomy was in the hands of the Levites (Deut 17:18), who were commanded by Moses to proclaim it at the Feast of Booths (Deut 31:9). Though we do not know the precise nature of this proclamation of the law, which was handed down within Levitical circles, it is likely that it was sung and that this greater "Song of Moses" (i.e., the entire book of Deuteronomy) was taught to the people of ancient Israel.

For centuries now, the mainstream of the scholarly community has virtually ignored the masoretic accentual system so far as detailed analysis and commentary on the text of the Hebrew Bible are concerned. Though there has been widespread agreement that the system is a form of musical notation of some sort, the consensus has been that, whatever the system represents, it is medieval in origin and imposed on the Hebrew text—perhaps as a form of chant to recite the text in a liturgical setting. After all, the so-called tropes of this masoretic system are still used to instruct those who cant the text within synagogal traditions.

Recently the French musicologist Suzanne Haïk-Vantoura has championed the idea that these cantillation signs represent an ancient tradition of musical interpretation, which predates the masoretes by a millennium or more.[3] Haïk-Vantoura argues convincingly that the masoretes did not invent the musical tradition reflected in their sophisticated system of notation. They merely fixed a once living tradition on paper so as to preserve it for all time. The source of their knowledge was apparently the "Elders of Bathyra," certain sages among the predecessors of the **Karaite** community during the first century CE.[4]

John Wheeler, who has studied Haïk-Vantoura's restitution of the musical meaning of the "accents" of the masoretic Hebrew Bible in detail, argues that the masoretic notation parallels a specific music "sign language" known as **chironomy**, which was used both to teach and conduct the liturgy. Some of the original hand signs, which are specifically mentioned in masoretic literature, dovetail neatly with the written signs, their ancient names, and their deciphered musical meaning. The chironomy which Wheeler has reconstructed is similar to the hand signs in the modern **Kodaly Method** which is used to teach musical literacy to children, as illustrated on the following page.[5]

Karaite: A Jewish sect in Persia founded in the 8th century CE by Anan ben David which rejected the Talmud and the teachings of the rabbis in favor of strict adherence to the Hebrew Bible as the single authoritative source of Jewish law and practice.

Chironomy: The "sheet music" of antiquity; music was transmitted to individual performers by means of an elaborate system of hand signs—somewhat like "signing for the deaf" today.

Kodaly Method: A method of music instruction developed by Zoltán Kodály, a noted Hungarian composer and educator, which emerged about 1940 and is now established internationally. The method uses a system of hand signs to instruct children with remarkable results.

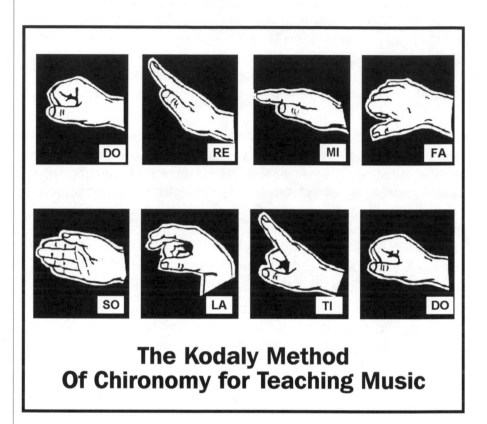

**The Kodaly Method
Of Chironomy for Teaching Music**

In Wheeler's estimation, the biblical musical system is based on a scale theory not far different from that of cuneiform texts in Babylonian (*ca.* 1800 BCE) and Ugaritic (ca. 1400 BCE). Like these systems, the "music of the Bible" is based on the major scale, with the primary "mode" being "dorian" (tonic on the third note of the scale).[6]

Concept Check # 26

What is the significance of the shift in focus from "oral" to "aural" in terms of understanding the nature of the biblical tradition in the earliest times? (Check your answer on p. 223.)

Chironomers at Work in Ancient Egypt
(from tomb paintings of the third and second millenium BCE)

B. The Earliest Textual Traditions[7]

When compared with the literary traditions of ancient Greece and Rome, the extent of preservation of ancient biblical manuscripts is striking. In contrast to more than 5,000 manuscripts of the Second Testament, only 643 copies of Homer's *Iliad* have survived from antiquity. Titus Livy's *History of Rome* survives in twenty manuscripts; and Caesar's *Gallic Wars* is preserved in nine or ten manuscripts. Thucydides' *History of the Peloponnesian Wars* survives in only eight manuscripts. There are no rivals from the world of antiquity to the manuscript evidence of the Bible, especially the Second Testament.

1. Manuscripts of the First Testament

Before the discovery of the **Cairo Geniza** texts in 1890, only 731 Hebrew manuscripts were known to be in existence. Rudolph Kittel's *Biblia Hebraica* (published from 1929 through 1937) was based on only four major Hebrew manuscripts, and primarily on just one of those, the Leningrad Codex, which was also selected as the basis of the current

Cairo Geniza: The storage place for sacred manuscripts and books which were worn out or otherwise no longer useable, found in a synagogue in Cairo in the latter part of the 19th century CE.

Aleppo Codex: The oldest copy of the Hebrew Bible (930 CE) in the tradition of the Ben Asher family of the masoretes at Tiberias.

Leningrad Codex: The oldest complete copy of the Hebrew Bible (1008 CE), in the tradition of the Ben Asher family of the masoretes at Tiberias.

standard critical edition of the Hebrew Bible, *Biblia Hebraica Stuttgartensia* (published from 1969 through 1976).

The *Cairo Codex* (895 CE) is the oldest known manuscript of the prophets, containing both the Former Prophets and the Latter Prophets. The *Leningrad Codex of the Prophets* (916 CE) contains only the Latter Prophets, and was written with the Babylonian system of accentuation. Though the ***Aleppo Codex*** (930 CE) of the entire First Testament is no longer complete, due to its partial destruction in a fire of modern times, it has been selected as the base text for a new critical edition of the Hebrew Bible, which is in the process of publication in Israel. The *British Museum Codex* (950 CE) is an incomplete manuscript of the Pentateuch, which contains Gen 39:20 through Deut 1:33. The ***Leningrad Codex*** (1008 CE) is the largest and the only complete manuscript of the entire First Testament and the base text for the current standard critical edition of the Hebrew Bible, *Biblia Hebraica Stuttgartensia*. It is available in a facsimile edition through the Ancient Biblical Manuscript Center in Claremont, California. The original manuscript was written on vellum, with three columns of twenty-seven lines each per sheet. The vowel points and accents appear as published in *Biblia Hebraica Stuttgartensia*, though the so-called *setuma* and *petucha* paragraph markers of the published tradition differ substantially. The *Reuchlin Codex* (1105 CE) of the Prophets is a recensional text which attests to the fidelity of the Leningrad text of the masoretic tradition.

The Cairo Geniza fragments (500-800 CE), which include some 10,000 biblical manuscripts and fragments discovered in 1890, are now scattered throughout various libraries. The relatively scarce number of early First Testament manuscripts, apart from the *Cairo Geniza* texts, may be attributed to several factors. The ancient Israelites were subject to the ravages of deportation during the Babylonian Captivity and to foreign domination following their return to Palestine. In its history from ca. 1800 BCE to 1948 CE, Jerusalem was conquered forty-seven times. This single fact helps to explain why most masoretic texts discovered have been found outside Palestine proper. Another important factor centers around the sacred scribal laws demanding the burial of worn or flawed manuscripts in Jewish tradition. According to the Talmud, any manuscript that contained a mistake or error, and all those that were aged beyond use, were systematically and religiously destroyed. More-over, during the fifth and sixth centuries CE, when the masoretes are believed to have standardized the Hebrew text, it appears that they systematically and completely destroyed all the manuscripts which did not agree with their standardization of the sacred text. Archaeological evidence in terms of the absence of surviving early manuscripts supports this judgement. As a result, the printed text of the Hebrew Bible today is based on relatively few manuscripts, none of which antedates the tenth century CE.

Although there are relatively few early manuscripts of the Hebrew Bible, the quality of the extant manuscripts within the masoretic tradition is very good. This fact is to be attributed to several factors. Though we are now aware of the fact that there were at least three major competing textual traditions at an earlier period, all extant manuscripts, with the exception of some of the Dead Sea Scrolls, are descendants of one text type which was established about 100 CE. Unlike the Second Testament, which bases its textual fidelity on the multiplicity of manuscript evidence from antiquity, the First Testament text owes its accuracy to the fidelity of the scribes within the masoretic tradition who transmitted it. Moreover, scribal accuracy was achieved through the almost superstitious reverence for the biblical text. According to the Talmud, only certain kinds of animal skins could be used, the size of the columns was carefully regulated, and the ritual a scribe followed in copying a manuscript was carefully prescribed. If a manuscript was found to contain even one mistake, it was discarded and destroyed.

Another line of evidence for the integrity of the received masoretic tradition is found in the comparison of duplicate passages within the First Testament itself. For example, Psalm 14 occurs again in Psalm 53, much of Isaiah 36-39 is found also in 2 Kings 18-20, Isa 2:2-4 appears in Mic 4:1-3, and large portions of the text of Chronicles are found in Samuel and Kings. A careful examination of these passages shows that not only is there substantial textual agreement; there is, in some cases, almost exact identity. It may thus be concluded that the First Testament texts have not undergone radical revisions as some scholars have assumed.

Perhaps the most convincing support for the integrity of the masoretic text of the First Testament comes from study of the Greek translation known as the Septuagint (LXX). This work was done in Alexandria during the third and second centuries BCE. For the most part, it was a relatively careful book-by-book, chapter-by-chapter

Proto-Lucianic recension: A revision by unknown scholars, used by Lucian (ca. 240-312 CE), a theologian and biblical scholar in Syria, as the basis for his revision of the Greek text of the Hebrew Bible.

John the Baptist: The forerunner and baptiser of Jesus (see Matt 3).

Manual of Discipline: One of the manuscripts in the Dead Sea Scrolls found at Qumran which contains the rules of the monastic community which lived there.

Apocryphon: A religous writing of uncertain origin regarded by some as inspired, but rejected by most authorities.

War Scroll: Also known as the *War of the Sons of Light Against the Sons of Darkness*, this scroll is an eschatological composition which concerns the final battle between Israel and the nations.

rendition of the Masoretic Text. There are numerous places, however, which suggest that the translators were working with a rather different Hebrew text from that of the masoretes of later times. Through the years the LXX was corrected to conform to the Masoretic Text, particularly by Lucian and the so-called **proto-Lucianic recension**. In addition, there are passages and even books in the LXX which are not found in the Masoretic Text at all. Most Second Testament quotations were taken directly from the Septuagint.

Concept Check # 27

How do you account for the fact that the Bible is so much better represented in terms of surviving manuscripts than other classical literature from antiquity? (Check your answer on p. 223.)

---

2. The Dead Sea Scrolls

The greatest manuscript find of the twentieth century occurred in March 1947, when an Arab boy (Muhammed edh-Dhib) threw a rock into a cave some seven and a half miles south of Jericho on the western side of the Dead Sea. There he found pottery jars which contained several leather scrolls. Between that time and February 1956, eleven caves were located near the ancient settlement of Qumran, which contained scrolls and fragments. In spite of intense scholarly work and nine volumes in the official publication, *Discoveries in the Judean Desert* (1955-1994), much of this material still remains to be published and has been the source of considerable controversy in scholarly circles. A Jewish religious sect contemporary with **John the Baptist** and Jesus housed their library at Qumran. The thousands of fragments of manuscripts from these caves constitute the remains of some six hundred manuscripts.

Of particular interest to us are the remains of the Old Testament, in which every book except Esther has been found. Cave 1, which was discovered by Muhammed edh-Dhib, contained seven more or less complete scrolls including the earliest known complete book of the Hebrew Bible (Isaiah A), a **Manual of Discipline**, a commentary on Habakkuk, a Genesis **Apocryphon**, an incomplete text of Isaiah (Isaiah B), the so-called **War Scroll**, and about thirty thanksgiving hymns.

Fragments of about a hundred manuscripts were found in Cave 2, which was discovered by Bedouins who pilfered it. In Cave 3, two halves of a copper scroll were discovered which provided directions to presumed hidden treasures mostly in and around the area of Jerusalem.

Cave 4 was also ransacked by Bedouins before it was excavated in September 1952. Nonetheless, it proved to be the most productive of all the caves with literally thousands of fragments. The fragment of Samuel found there is thought to be the oldest known piece of Biblical Hebrew at that point in time, dating from the fourth century BCE. Cave 5 contained biblical and apocryphal books in advanced stages of deterioration. Cave 6 produced mostly papyrus fragments rather than leather. Caves 7-10 provided valuable archaeological information, but nothing of relevance to our interests. Cave 11, the last to be excavated in early 1956, produced a well-preserved manuscript of the psalms, including a copy of the apocryphal Psalm 151 which hitherto was known only in Greek translations. In addition, it contained an important fragment of Leviticus and an Aramaic Targum (paraphrase) of Job.

Subsequent discoveries in caves at nearby Murabba'at produced self-dated manuscripts including fragments from the scroll of the Minor Prophets (Joel through Haggai) which stands within the subsequent masoretic tradition.

Concept Check # 28

What is the major significance of the Dead Sea Scrolls so far as the text of the Bible is concerned? (Check your answer on p. 228.)

---

3. Manuscripts of the Second Testament

Whereas the First Testament has only a few complete manuscripts from antiquity, all of which are good, the Second Testament has many more copies which are of inferior quality. In the earliest period, manuscripts of the Second Testament were written in a formal printed style known as uncials (or majuscules). The letters are written in capitals with no breaks between words or sentences. This style persisted into the tenth century CE when the demand for manuscripts had become so great that a faster writing style was developed. This *cursive* style employed smaller, connected letters with breaks between words and sentences. The term

Minuscules:
Manuscripts written in a script of smaller letters than the uncials in a cursive hand, dating from about the ninth century on.

minuscule was applied to these manuscripts, which emerged after the sixth century and gradually displaced the uncial form, becoming the dominant form during the so-called golden age of manuscript copying, the eleventh through the fifteenth centuries.

In the earliest period, words were written in capital letters and run together with little punctuation. An amusing illustration of the problems in interpretation which this situation produced is the English example, DIDYOUEVERSEEABUNDANCEONTHETABLE, which could be read in two very different ways: "Did you ever see abundance on the table?" or "Did you ever see a bun dance on the table?" During the sixth century, scribes began to make general use of punctuation. By the eighth century they had come to utilize periods, commas, colons, breath, and accent marks. Somewhat later, interrogatives were introduced.

Council of Nicea:
The first major ecumenical council in the early Church which was convened in 325 CE to deal with the Arian heresy.

Prior to the **Council of Nicea** (325 CE), the Second Testament was divided into sections, called *kephalaia*, which differ from modern chapter divisions. Other systems were introduced during the fourth century in which divisions were longer than modern verses, but shorter than modern chapters. It was not until the thirteenth century that these divisions were modified, and then only gradually. The work of modification was done by Stephen Langton, a professor at the University of Paris and later Archbishop of Canterbury, although some scholars give the credit to Cardinal Hugo of St. Cher (d. 1263). The Wycliffe Bible (1382) followed this pattern and provided the basis for standardization of the system. Modern verses, first used by Robert Stephanus in his published version of the Greek New Testament in 1551, were introduced into the English Bible in 1557. The first English Bible to employ both the modern chapter and verse divisions was the Geneva Bible (1560).

Testimony to the fidelity of the Greek New Testament text comes from three sources: manuscript evidence, ancient translations, and patristic citations. The first of these sources is the most important and can itself be divided into three classes: the **papyri**, the uncials, and the minuscules.

Papyri: The oldest existing witnesses for the text of the Second Testament are written on papyrus, a form of paper manufactured from the stalks of the papyrus plant grown in Egypt.

The manuscript evidence known as papyri date from the second and third centuries, when Christianity was still illegal and its sacred texts were transcribed on the cheapest possible materials. Seventy-six such papyrus manuscripts of the Second Testament are known, which range in time from a mere generation after the apostolic period, and contain most of the Second Testament.

The John Rylands Fragment known as P52 (117-138 CE), the earliest known and attested fragment of the Second Testament, was written on both sides and contains portions of five verses from the Gospel of John (18:31-33, 37-38). P45, 46, and 47, the Chester Beatty Papyri (250 CE), consists of three codices containing most of the Second Testament. P45 contains thirty leaves of a papyrus codex which includes the Gospels and Acts. P46 contains most of Paul's epistles and the book of Hebrews, although portions of Romans, 1 Thessalonians, and all of 2 Thessalonians are missing. P47 contains portions of Revelation. The Bodmer Papyri, P66, 72, and 75 (175-225 CE) are next in importance. P66 (200 CE) contains portions of the Gospel of John. P72 (early third century CE) is the earliest known copy of Jude, 1 Peter, and 2 Peter, along with certain apocryphal works. P75 (175-225 CE) contains Luke and John in clear and carefully printed uncials.

On the whole, the most important manuscripts of the Second Testament are generally considered to be the great uncials written on vellum and parchment during the fourth through the ninth centuries. There are 297 such uncial manuscripts, the seven most important of which are as follows:

Codex Vaticanus (B) (325-50 CE), the oldest uncial on either parchment or vellum, and one of the most important witnesses to the text of the Second Testament, was first known to biblical scholars in 1475, when it was catalogued in the Vatican Library. It was first published in complete photographic facsimile in 1889-90 and contains most of the First Testament, as well as the Greek New Testament and the Apocrypha (with some omissions). The codex lacks Gen 1:1 - 46:28; 2 Kgs 2:5-7, 10-13; Pss 106:27 - 138:6 and Heb 9:14 through the end of the Second Testament. Mark 16:9-20 and John 7:58 - 8:11 were also intentionally omitted from the text, which was written in small and delicate uncials on fine vellum.

Codex Sinaiticus (ℵ) (4th century CE) is considered to be the most important single witness to the Greek text of the New Testament because of its antiquity, accuracy, and lack of omissions. The story of its discovery by the German Count Tischendorf in the monastery of St. Catherine at Mount Sinai in 1844 is one of the most fascinating stories in the history of the biblical text. Tischendorf discovered forty-three leaves of vellum, containing portions of the Septuagint (1 Chronicles, Jeremiah, Nehemiah, and Esther) in a basket of scraps which were used

Codex Vaticanus: The oldest and one of the most important uncial texts of the Septuagint and the Greek New Testament (mid-4th century CE).

Codex Sinaiticus: An important uncial text of parts of the Septuagint and the Greek New Testament (4th century CE), found by Tischendorf at the Monastery of St. Catherine in Sinai.

by the monks to light their fires. He secured the manuscript and took it to Leipzig in Germany, where it remains as the *Codex Frederico-Augustanus.* On a second visit in 1853, Tischendorf found nothing new; but in his third visit in 1859, under the direction of Czar Alexander II, just before he was scheduled to depart for home, the monastery steward showed him an almost complete copy of the Scriptures and certain other books. These texts were subsequently acquired for the Czar as a "conditional gift." Now known as *Codex Sinaiticus,* this manuscript contains more than half of the First Testament (LXX) and all of the Second Testament, with the exception of Mark 16:9-20 and John 7:58 - 8:11, all of the First Testament Apocrypha, the Epistle of Barnabus, and the Shepherd of Hermas. The material is vellum, made from antelope skins. The manuscript contains scribal "corrections" done at Caesarea in the sixth or seventh century. In 1933, the British government purchased *Codex Sinaiticus* for £100,000. It was published in 1938 in a volume entitled *Scribes and Correctors of Codex Sinaiticus.*

Codex Alexandrinus (A) (ca. 450 CE) is a well-preserved manuscript from Alexandria which was presented to the Patriarch of Alexandria in 1078 and subsequently taken to Constantinople in 1621, where it was received by Sir Thomas Roe, English embassador to Turkey, for presentation to King James I, who died before it actually reached England. It was presented to King Charles I in 1627, which means it was not available for use by the translators of the King James Bible in 1611. In 1757, King George II presented the codex to the National Library of the British Museum. It contains the entire First Testament (LXX), except for certain mutilated portions (Gen 14:14-17; 15:1-5, 16-19; 16:6-9; 1 Kingdoms [1 Sam] 12:18 - 14:9; Ps 49:19 - 79:10). The New Testament lacks only Matt 1:1 - 25:6; John 6:50 - 8:52; and 2 Cor 4:13 - 12:6. It also includes 1 and 2 Clement and the Psalms of Solomon, with some missing parts. The large square uncial letters are written on thin vellum with divided sections marked by large letters.

Ephraemi Rescriptus Codex (C) (345 CE), a manuscript which probably originated in Alexandria, was brought to Italy about 1500 by John Lascaris and later sold to Pietro Strozzi. Catherine de Medici acquired it in 1533. After her death, the manuscript was placed in the National Library at Paris. Most of the First Testament (LXX) is missing, except for portions of Job, Proverbs, Ecclesiastes, and Song of Solomon. It includes the Wisdom of Solomon and Ecclesiasticus. The Second Testa-

---

Codex Alexandrinus: A well-preserved uncial text of the Septuagint and the Greek New Testament (mid-5th century CE) from Alexandria in Egypt.

ment lacks 2 Thessalonians, 2 John, and parts of other books. The manuscript is a *palimpsest* (rubbed out, erased) *rescriptus* (rewritten), which originally contained the Old and New Testaments. These texts were erased to make room for sermons written by Ephraem, a fourth-century Syrian father. Tischendorf was able to decipher the almost invisible original writing. It is currently located in the National Library at Paris. The manuscript contains two sets of corrections which were done in sixth-century Palestine and ninth-century Constantinople.

Codex Bezae (D) (450-550 CE), also known as Codex Cantabrigiensis, is the oldest known bilingual manuscript of the Second Testament, written in Greek and Latin somewhere in southern Gaul (France) or northern Italy. It was discovered in 1562 by Theodore de Beze (Latin Beza), a French theologian at St. Irenaeus Monastery in Lyon, France. In 1581 Beza gave the manuscript to Cambridge University. It contains the four gospels, Acts, and 3 John 11-15 (the Latin text only).

Codex Claromontanus (D^2) (sixth century), which contains much of the Second Testament, seems to have originated in Italy or Sardinia and receives its name from a monastery at Clermont, France, where it was found by Beza. It was purchased for the National Library at Paris by King Louis XIV in 1656. The manuscript was fully edited by Tischendorf and contains all of Paul's epistles and Hebrews, although Rom 1:1-7, 27-30, and Heb 13:21-23 are missing in Latin. This bilingual text is artistically written on thin, high-quality vellum.

Codex Washingtonianus I (W) (fourth or early fifth century) was purchased in 1906 by Charles F. Freer of Detroit from a dealer in Cairo, Egypt, and subsequently edited by Professor H. A. Sanders of the University of Michigan (1910-18). The manuscript, currently located in the Smithsonian Institute (Washington, D.C.), contains the four gospels, portions of Paul's epistles (except Romans), Hebrews, Deuteronomy, Joshua, Luke, and Mark (which includes the long ending, 16:9-20; but with an additional insertion after verse 14).

The minuscule manuscripts are both later (ninth through fifteenth centuries) and generally inferior in quality to either the papyrus or uncial manuscripts. There are 4,643 minuscules (2,646 manuscripts and 1,997 lectionaries [early Church-service books]). Their main importance is in regard to the textual families they include, namely:

Alexandrian text type: A type of text of the Greek NT current in Egypt as early as the second century CE.

1) The **Alexandrian text type** is represented by manuscript 33, the so-called "queen of the cursives," which dates from the ninth or tenth century. It contains the entire Second Testament (except Revelation) and is located in the Bibliotheque Nationale in Paris.

2) The **Caesarean text type** includes manuscripts 1, 118, 131, and 209; all of which date from the twelfth to the fourteenth centuries. The Italian subfamily of this text type, which is represented by about a dozen manuscripts known as family 13, were copied between the eleventh and fifteenth centuries. They include manuscripts 13, 69, 124, 230, 346, 543, 788, 826, 828, 983, 1689, and 1709. Some of these manuscripts were formerly considered to be of the Syrian text type.

Caesarean text type: A text type of Greek MSS of the NT which lies between the Alexandrian and Western with affinities to both. It was used by Origen in Caesarea.

3) The remaining text type families are of lesser importance, adding little new evidence to the text of the Second Testament. They were copies from earlier uncial or minuscule manuscripts and bear witness to the continual line of transmission of the biblical text. Other classical works, such as Caesar's *Gallic Wars* and the *Works* of Tacitus, have breaks of nine hundred to a thousand years between the autographs and their manuscript copies.

Concept Check # 29

Why are the uncials considered the most important manuscripts of the Second Testament and what do you make of the fact that they contain little or no punctuation and nothing of the chapter and verse division with which we are so familiar? (Check your answer on p. 223.)

Ostraca: Broken pieces of pottery on which written messages were inscribed.

4. Other Witnesses to the Text of the Bible in Antiquity

The discovery of papyri, **ostraca**, and **inscriptions** in the past two centuries has transformed basic assumptions about the nature of the text of the Bible, and the Second Testament in particular. Before the publication of the works of Moulton and Milligan, *Vocabulary of the Greek New Testament. Illustrated from the Papyri and Other Non-Literary Sources* (1914), A. T. Robertson, *A Grammar of the Greek New Testament in Light of Historical Research* (1914), and Adolf Deissman, *Light From the Ancient East* (translated in English in 1923), the Second Testament was thought to be written in a special language which God had commu-

Inscriptions: Information which is cut, impressed, painted, or written on stone, brick, metal, or other hard surfaces.

cated directly to specially chosen human "authors" who simply tran-scribed it. At the turn of the twentieth century, it became clear that the Second Testament was written in what scholars call *koine* Greek, the common trade language of colloquial speech in the first century of the Roman world. The Second Testament was not written in some "perfect language," as some of the Church Fathers of antiquity had assumed. The obvious conclusion of all this regarding dating the Second Testament is clear: If the Greek of the Second Testament is the common language of the first century, then it must have been written in the first century.

The transmission of the biblical text can be traced with some certainty from the late second and early third centuries to modern times by means of the great uncial and minuscule manuscripts discussed above. Other witnesses are useful in matters of detail. One such example is the use of ostraca (broken pieces of pottery) for transmitting the Bible. A particularly interesting example is that of a seventh-century "poor man's Bible," which contains a copy of the Gospels recorded on twenty pieces of ostraca. Allen P. Wikgren has listed some 1,624 specimens of potsherds which contain records of historical interest in his work, *Greek Ostraca*.

The growing list of ancient inscriptions also bears witness to the importance of the biblical text. This evidence which is found in engrav-ings on walls, pillars, monuments, and coins is of relatively little impor-tance in terms of establishing the text of the Second Testament. In this regard, the lectionaries (church-service books) of antiquity are of greater importance; for they served as manuals for use by various Christian communities. Most of these lectionaries come from the sev-enth to the twelfth centuries, although a dozen leaves and fragments survive from the fourth to sixth centuries. Only five or six exemplars on papyrus have survived, and these utilize uncial script even after the minuscule type script had become dominant in the biblical manuscripts. Caspar Rene Gregory listed 1,545 Greek lectionaries in his *Canon and Text of the New Testament* (1912). The United Bible Societies edition of *The Greek New Testament* (1966) utilized about 2,000 in its critical apparatus. The great majority of these texts contain readings from the Gospels. The remainder contain portions of Acts, sometimes accompa-nied by passages from the Epistles. The lectionaries were often elabo-rately adorned, sometimes with musical notation.

Concept Check # 30

What is the most important single contribution to our knowledge of the biblical text which emerged from archaeological discovery of papyri, ostraca, and inscriptional witnesses to the text of the Second Testament? (Check your answer on p. 223.)

C. Early Editions, Versions, and Translations of the Bible[8]

The Second Testament was translated into Latin prior to 200 CE. This Old Latin version served as the Second Testament for the Bible of the early Western Church. By the end of the fourth century, a translation of the Second Testament into Syriac was in use as the Second Testament for the Bible of the Eastern Church. This text also represents a text originating in the second century. By that time, a number of translations and versions of the First Testament were already in use and widely known.

1. The Samaritan Pentateuch

Samaritan Pentateuch: The Samaritan version of the first five books of the Hebrew Bible, which constitute the entire canon for that community. It is written in archaic Hebrew script.

The **Samaritan Pentateuch** may be from as early as the time of Ezra and Nehemiah; and it is certainly not later than the second century BCE. Though it is not really a translation or version of the Bible as such, it is of value in matters of textual criticism. This work is actually a manuscript edition of the Pentateuch, written in a paleo-Hebrew script similar to that found on the Moabite Stone, the Siloam Inscription, the Lachish Letters, and some of the older biblical manuscripts at Qumran. The textual tradition of the Samaritan Pentateuch is independent of that of the Masoretic Text. Though the existence of this text was known to such early Church Fathers as Eusebius and Jerome, it was "rediscovered" by Christian scholars in 1616. It was first published in the *Paris Polyglot* (1645) and then in the *London Polyglot* (1657).

The roots of the Samaritan community go back to the time of Omri (880-874 BCE), who established Samaria as the capital of the northern kingdom of Israel, which was known as the kingdom of Samaria (1 Kgs 16:24). In 732 BCE, Assyria conquered Samaria under Tiglath-pileser III

(745-727), who established a policy of deportation of the native inhabitants and importation of other captive peoples into the area. This policy continued under Sargon II (721-705), who completed the conquest of the region by incorporating the province of Samarina (Samaria) into the Assyrian Empire. Intermarriage was imposed by Assyria on the populace to guarantee that no revolt would occur (2 Kgs 17:24-18:1). When the Jews returned from their own exile in Babylon some two hundred and fifty years later, the Samaritan colonists sought to join them. The Jews rebuffed the Samaritans, who in turn opposed Israel's restoration (see Ezra 4:2-6 and Neh 5:11 - 6:19). About 432 BCE, however, the grandson of the high priest Eliashib in Jerusalem married the daughter of Sanballat of Samaria. This couple was expelled from Judah and the event provided the occasion for the historical break between the Jews and the Samaritans (see Neh 13:23-31).

The Samaritans retained a copy of the Torah, which was subsequently placed in a temple they built on Mount Gerizim near Shechem (Nablus), where a rival priesthood was established and continues to the present day. The Samaritans rejected the rest of the canon of the First Testament and lived in isolation from the Jews, which resulted in a separate tradition for the five books of Moses known as the Samaritan Pentateuch.

The earliest manuscript of the Samaritan Pentateuch dates from the mid-eleventh century as a fragmentary portion of a fourteenth-century parchment known as the Abisha Scroll. The oldest Samaritan Pentateuch codex bears a note about its sale in 1149-50. The New York Public Library owns another copy dating from about 1232. Immediately after its discovery by the scholarly community in 1616, the Samaritan Pentateuch was acclaimed as superior to the Masoretic Text. Subsequent study, however, has demonstrated its inferior status. It contains approximately six thousand variants from the Masoretic Text, most of which are orthographic in nature and rather insignificant. Its most important difference is doctrinal—its claim that Mount Gerizim rather than Jerusalem is the center of worship.

Concept Check # 31

Though the textual tradition of the Samaritan Pentateuch is much older than the official masoretic tradition of the First Testament, it is considered inferior in quality. What does this imply about the nature of the biblical text? (Check your answer on p. 223.)

2. The Aramaic Targums

Targums: Name
given to the Aramaic
translations of the
Hebrew Bible.

Ancient Jewish scribes were making oral paraphrases of the Hebrew Bible into Aramaic as early as the time of Ezra (see Neh 8:1-8). These **Targums** were not intended to be translations as such, but rather aids in understanding the archaic language of the Torah. The person involved in the presentation of these paraphrases was called a *methurgeman* and played an important role in communicating the content of the ancient Hebrew scrolls in the everyday language of the Jewish people in that setting. Long before the Christian era, almost every book in the First Testament had its own oral paraphrase or interpretation (Targum). Gradually these Targums were committed to writing and an official text emerged.

The earliest Aramaic Targums were probably put in writing in Palestine during the second century CE, although there is some evidence of Aramaic Targums from the pre-Christian period. The official Targums contained only the Torah and the Prophets, although unofficial Targums of later times also included the Writings. A number of unofficial Aramaic Targums were found among the Dead Sea Scrolls at Qumran. In the third century CE, the official Palestinian Targums of the Torah and the Prophets were displaced by another family of paraphrases, the Babylonian Targums. A convenient edition of the Babylonian Targums was edited by Alexander Sperber under the title, *The Bible in Aramaic* (4 vols, 1959-73). A new edition is in progress, *The Aramaic Bible* (Michael Glazier, 1987-93 [13 of 20 volumes published]).

Targums are extant for all the books of the Hebrew Bible except for Ezra, Nehemiah, and Daniel. The most important texts are Targum Onkelos (the Pentateuch) and Targum Jonathan ben Uzziel (the Prophets). Though Onkelos was known in Babylonia in the Talmudic period, there is good reason to believe that it originated in Palestine in the first or early second century CE. Targum Jonathan also originated in Palestine dating from the fourth century. It is a freer rendering of the text than Onkelos. Both Targums were read in synagogues along with the regular readings from the Torah (*Parashoth*, pl.) and the Prophets (*Haphtaroth*, pl.). Since the Writings were not read in regular synagogue worship, no official Targums were made, although unofficial copies were used by individuals. During the seventh century another Targum on the Pentateuch appeared which is known as Pseudo-Jonathan. It is a mixture of Targum Onkelos and some materials from the Midrash. Still later, about

700 CE, Targum Jerusalem appeared, which now survives in fragments only. Though none of these Targums is of much importance on textual grounds, they do provide information on the manner in which the Scriptures were interpreted in Judaism.

> ## Concept Check # 32
> How do you account for the fact that official Targums appeared for the Pentateuch and the Prophets, but only some of the Writings in the First Testament? (Check your answer on p. 223.)

3. The Talmud and Midrash

The scribal tradition in Judaism from 100-500 CE is known as the Talmudic period. The Talmud ("instruction") is a body of Hebrew legal tradition based on the Torah and represents the opinions and decisions of prominent Jewish teachers from about 300 BCE to 500 CE. It is in two main divisions: the Mishnah and the **Gemara**. The Mishnah ("repetition" or "explanation") was completed about 200 CE as a digest of all the oral legislation from Moses to that point in time. It is highly regarded within Judaism as second in importance only to the Torah itself. The Gemara ("completion") is an Aramaic expanded commentary on the Mishnah, which exists in two traditions: the Palestinian Gemara (ca. 200 CE) and the larger, more authoritative Babylonian Gemara (ca. 500 CE).

The **Midrash** is actually a homiletical exposition of the Torah, written in Hebrew and Aramaic, which dates from 100 BCE to 300 CE. This body of literature was gathered into what is called the *Halakah* ("procedure"), an expansion of the Torah, and the *Haggadah* ("declaration" or "explanation"), which consists of commentaries on the entire Hebrew Bible. The Midrash differs from the Targums in that they are commentaries rather than paraphrases of the Torah. The Midrash contains some of the oldest extant preaching of the synagogue on the Hebrew Bible.

4. Greek Translations

In his conquest of the ancient world, Alexander the Great showed considerable favor to the Jews. Many of the centers of population he established to administer his empire were named Alexandria, and they

Gemara: The section of the Talmud consisting essentially of commentary on the Mishnah.

Midrash: An early Jewish interpretation of or commentary on a biblical text, which is sometimes creative in nature in the form of a story.

subsequently became centers of Jewish culture. Just as the Jews had abandoned their native Hebrew tongue for Aramaic in the Near East at an earlier period, they now abandoned Aramaic in favor of Greek—particularly in Alexandria, Egypt.

When Alexander's empire was divided after his death in 323 BCE, the Ptolemies gained control of Egypt, the Seleucids took charge in Asia Minor, and the Antigonids ruled Macedonia. During the reign of Ptolemy II Philadelphus in Egypt (285-246 BCE), the Jews in Alexandria shared in the great cultural and educational programs, including the founding of a museum and the translation of great literary works into Greek. Among the works selected for translation was the Hebrew Bible. This was indeed the first time that the First Testament was extensively translated into any language.

The Jewish leaders in Alexandria produced a standard Greek version of the First Testament which is commonly known as the Septuagint (LXX). According to legend (in the letter to Aristeas), the librarian at Alexandria persuaded Ptolemy to translate the Torah into Greek. Six translators from each of the twelve tribes of Israel were selected and their work was completed in only seventy-two days, hence the name Septuagint ("seventy"). Though the term originally was applied only to the Pentateuch, it subsequently came to designate the entire Greek translation of the First Testament, most of which was translated during the third and second centuries BCE. The larger task was completed by 150 BCE, since it is discussed in the letter of Aristeas to Philocrates (ca. 130-100 BCE).

The quality of the translation of LXX is not consistent throughout, ranging from a slavishly literal translation of the Pentateuch to rather free translations of the Writings. The purpose in view for the LXX was different from that of the Hebrew Bible, in that it was a scholarly work by scribes for general reading as opposed to a text specifically for public reading/recitation in the Second Temple or the synagogues. As a pioneer effort in translation of the First Testament that is generally faithful to the reading of the original Hebrew text, the LXX is obviously of enormous importance in matters of textual criticism so far as the text of the Hebrew Bible is concerned. Moreover, it provided an important precedent for subsequent translations of the whole Bible into various languages.

In the early centuries of Christianity, a reaction set in among the Jews against the Septuagint which had become the Christian Bible. Consequently, a number of new Greek translations began to appear, such as Aquila's version and that of Symmachus and eventually the first great work of textual criticism in the mid-third century, Origen's *Hexapla*. There appear to be two basic reasons for Jewish rejection of the LXX: 1) it had been adopted by Christians as their own Bible and was widely used by them in propagation and defense of their faith; and 2) a revised edition of the standard Hebrew text was established about 100 CE. The end result of this revision process was the establishment of the Masoretic Text.

Aquila's version (ca. 130-150 CE) was a new translation of the Hebrew Bible made for Greek-speaking Jews. Aquila is reputed to have been a relative of the Emperor Hadrian. While living in Jerusalem, Aquila converted to Christianity; but when he was subsequently rebuked by the elders of the Church for his ideas and conduct, he then rejected Christianity and returned to Judaism, studying under the renown Rabbi Akiba. Though much of this story may well be fiction, it is clear that Aquila was a Jewish proselyte from the area of the Black Sea who translated the Hebrew Bible into Greek during the first half of the second century. His version of the First Testament is an extremely rigid translation of the Hebrew text in which Greek words are used to render Hebrew thought patterns and sentence structure. Nonetheless, Aquila's translation soon became the official Greek version of the Hebrew Bible among non-Christian Jews. It survives only in fragments and quotations.

The **translation of Theodotion** (ca. 150-185) appears to be a revision of an earlier Greek version, possibly that of Aquila. Though the place and date of this work are disputed, Theodotion was a native of Ephesus who was either a Jewish proselyte or an Ebionite Christian. His revision is freer than Aquila's. His translation of Daniel soon replaced the LXX version among Christians. His rendition of Ezra-Nehemiah may also have replaced the LXX in some circles.

The **translation of Symmachus** (ca. 185-200) is also a revision. Symmachus seems to have followed Theodotion in time as well as theological commitment. Jerome describes him as an Ebionite Christian; but Epiphanius argues that he was a Samaritan convert to Judaism. His purpose was to make an idiomatic Greek translation, which thus stands at the opposite pole from that of Aquila. Symmachus was

Aquila's version: A slavishly literal translation of the Hebrew Bible into Greek which enjoyed popularity in Jewish circles (ca. 130-150 CE).

Theodotion's version: A somewhat less literal translation of the Hebrew Bible into Greek than that of Aquila, which was done during the reign of Marcus Aurelius (161-180 CE).

Symmachus's version: A translation of the Hebrew Bible into much more elegant Greek than either Aquila or Theodotion.

concerned with the sense of the text rather than the exactness of rendition in the target language. It should be noted, however, that he achieved such a high standard of accuracy in his work that it had a profound influence on later translators of the biblical text. Curiously, he had greater influence on the Latin Bible than on subsequent Greek translations because Jerome made such heavy use of his work in the preparation of the Latin Vulgate.

The translations of the Hebrew Bible into Greek produced four major textual traditions by the beginning of the third century: 1) the LXX; 2) Aquila's version; 3) the revision of Theodotion; and 4) the revision of Symmachus. This rather muddled situation opened the door for the first serious attempt at what is called text criticism, which was undertaken by Origen of Alexandria (185-254), who set out to establish an authoritative Greek text of the First Testament for the Christian world. For the most part, his work was essentially a recension rather than a version or a revision of the text, since he made systematic corrections and attempted to unify the Greek and Hebrew texts of the Bible. His primary objective was twofold: to demonstrate the superiority of the revisions of Aquila, Theodotion, and Symmachus over the corrupted LXX text of the First Testament; and to provide a means of comparing the correct Hebrew text with the divergent Greek translations. Origen considered the Hebrew Bible as essentially what some today would call an "inerrant transcript" of the revealed Word of God.

Origen's *Hexapla* was arranged in six parallel columns, each of which contained a particular version of the First Testament. The first column contained the Hebrew text with a Greek transliteration of the Hebrew text in column two. The literal translation of Aquila was placed in column three and the idiomatic revision of Symmachus in column four. Origen then placed his own revision of the LXX text in column five, and added Theodotion's revision in the last column. In his rendition of the Psalms, Origen added three further columns. This massive work has not survived the ravages of time, though Eusebius and Pamphilus did publish the fifth column (Origen's translation) with additions of their own. *Codex Sarravianus* (fourth or fifth century) contains portions of Genesis through Judges of Origen's *Hexapla*. There is also a Syriac translation of the work which dates to the seventh century, along with some later manuscript copies.

Origen's Hexapla: A systematic comparison of the Greek Septuagint with the Hebrew text in six parallel columns, which includes the versions of Aquila, Symmachus, and Theodotion.

Origen was primarily concerned with the task of bringing the LXX texts into greater conformity with the Hebrew text of the first column in his *Hexapla*. In the process he uncovered many corruptions, omissions, additions, and transpositions in the extant editions of the Greek translations of the Hebrew Bible. He developed an elaborate system of critical notation to describe the problems he had uncovered, which enables the reader to see which corruptions he has corrected, which omissions and additions he has made, and where words and phrases were transposed in the various Greek texts. Origen used an obelus (—), a horizontal stroke, to mark readings in the LXX which were not in the Hebrew text. An asterisk (⁜ or ※) was used to indicate readings in the Hebrew text which were omitted in the LXX but present in Theodotion's revision. He marked the end of these corrections with a metobelus (γ). Where short passages were transposed, Origen marked them with a combination asterisk-obelus sign (⁜ — or ※ —) at the beginning and a metobelus at the end. In cases of lengthy transpositions, he restored the Hebrew order.

Though Origen's work is of enormous significance, it should be noted that his basic objective was quite different from that of the modern textual critic. His purpose was to produce a Greek version of the First Testament which corresponds as closely as possible to the Hebrew text. The modern textual critic seeks to recover the original text of the LXX itself in an attempt to see what the Hebrew text was before the emergence of the received masoretic edition of the First Testament. The circulation of Origen's LXX without the diacritical markings essentially led to the dissemination of yet another corrupted Greek text of the First Testament. It is the loss of columns one and two of Origen's *Hexapla* which is sorely missed today; for that would provide us with a copy of the standard Hebrew text of the third century CE and the key to solving the dispute over Hebrew pronunciation.

Eusebius of Caesarea and his friend Pamphilus published their own editions of Origen's fifth column early in the fourth century, which became the standard edition of the LXX in many places. Two other scholars also made attempts to revise the Greek text of the Hebrew Bible independently from that of Origen. Hesychius, an Egyptian bishop (d. 311), made a recension which is preserved only in quotations on the part of his followers such as Cyril of Alexandria (d. 444). The recension of Lucian, a resident of Samosata and Antioch (d. 312), has been

Eusebius of Caesarea: A Christian theologian and historian (ca. 263-340 CE) who became the bishop of Caesarea (ca. 315-340).

Lucianic recension: Lucian (ca. 240-312 CE), a theologian and biblical scholar in Syria, revised the Greek text of the Hebrew Bible.

Kaige **recension:** A revision of the Greek translation of the Hebrew Bible which predates that of Aquila and Theodotion, which is labeled *Kaige* because it translates Hebrew *gam* ("also") by Greek *kaige*.

recovered through the works of Chrysostrom (d. 407) and Theodoret (d. 444). This **Lucianic recension** is of considerable importance in modern textual criticism, because it reflects an earlier so-called proto-Lucianic recension, which was made in pre-Christian times, presumably in Palestine. The Hebrew text it presupposes appears to be identical with certain of the Samuel scrolls from Qumran.

In 1952 a collection of manuscripts from Nahal Hever in the Judean wilderness, rather than from Qumran itself, surfaced which led to the discovery of yet another recension of the LXX known as the *Kaige* **recension**. The name comes from the rendition of the Hebrew *gam* ("also") by the idiomatic *kaige*. This recension is dated to the first half of the first century CE and has been identified with the tradition used by Theodotion in his revision. It is not a new translation as such but rather a revision of the Old Greek. It appears to be similar to the fifth column of Origen's *Hexapla* and is reflected in the biblical citations of Justin Martyr (d. 165). The *Kaige* recension lies behind certain readings in the Sahidic Coptic version and in the Greek *Codex Washingtonianus*.

The recensions of Origen, Lucian and Hesychius, along with the earlier translations of Aquila, Theodotion, and Symmachus, provided Christians in North Syria, Asia Minor, Greece, Egypt, and Palestine with the text of the First Testament in Greek. All of this took place before the time of Jerome who produced the Latin Vulgate. These early translations of the Hebrew Bible are of enormous value to the modern textual critic.

Concept Check # 33

Though, for practical reasons, the Bible of the early Christian Church was the Septuagint, it became clear as early as the time of Origen (ca. 200 CE) that the Greek translations of the First Testament were not trustworthy in matters of detail. What does this suggest about the nature of translation of the biblical text? (Check your answer on p. 223.)

---

5. Syriac Translations

The Syriac (a dialect of Aramaic, with a unique script) language, like that of the Koine in Greek and the Vulgate in Latin, was the common language of the market. Jesus spoke Aramaic, the language of this region, and it is reasonable to assume that Jews in nearby Syria also spoke it. When the Christians went into this area, and then on into Central Asia, India, and even China, the basic language of this entire branch of Christianity was Syriac (sometimes referred to as "Christian Aramaic"). The Bible translated into Syriac is known as the **Peshitta** ("simple"). The First Testament text of the Peshitta dates from the mid-second and early third centuries CE, although the name Peshitta itself dates from the ninth century. The First Testament was probably translated from the Hebrew; but it was revised to conform to the LXX.

Peshitta: The standard Syriac version of the Bible, which was completed by the 3rd century CE.

The standard edition of the Syriac New Testament, believed to be the work of Rabbula, Bishop of Edessa (411-435), is actually a revision of earlier Syriac versions which were brought into closer agreement with the Greek manuscripts then in use in Constantinople (Byzantium). Rabbula's edition of the Syriac New Testament, plus the Christian recension of the Syriac First Testament, has come to be known as the Peshitta. Following Rabbula's order that a copy of this text be placed in every church in his diocese, the Peshitta had a wide circulation in the fifth century and subsequently became the authorized version of two main branches of Syriac Christianity: the Nestorians and the Jacobites.

The **Syro-Hexaplar** text of the First Testament was a Syriac version of the fifth column of Origen's *Hexapla* (six-column Bible). Although it was translated about 616 by Paul, bishop of Tella, it never actually gained wide acceptance in the Syrian churches, perhaps because it was such an excessively literal rendering of the Greek text. The literal rendering of the Greek, however, makes the Syro-Hexaplar valuable in matters of textual criticism. Manuscript portions survive in Codex Mediolanensis which contains 2 Kings, Isaiah, The Twelve (minor prophets), Lamentations, and the poetic books (except for Psalms). The Pentateuch and historical books were still known as late as 1574; but have subsequently disappeared.

Syro-Hexaplar: A 7th century Syriac translation of Origen's revision of the Septuagint.

The *Diatessaron of Tatian* (ca. 170) has not survived. It is thus difficult to determine whether it was originally written in Syriac or, more likely, in Greek and then translated into Syriac. Tatian was an Assyrian Christian who was a follower of Justin Martyr in Rome. The *Diatessaron* ("through the four") was a "cut-and-paste" harmony of the Gospels, which is known through references. It was abolished by Rabbula and Theodoret, bishop of Cyrrhus, in 423 because Tatian had belonged to a heretical sect known as the Encratites. Nonetheless, Tatian's work was

Diatessaron of Tatian: A harmony of the Gospels which was regarded as an authoritative gospel text by the early Syriac-speaking Church.

so popular that Ephraem, a Syrian father, wrote a commentary on it before Theodoret had some two hundred copies of the text destroyed. Unfortunately, Ephraem's commentary on the *Diatessaron* has also been lost, though an Armenian translation survives along with two Arabic translations.

The *Diatessaron* was not the only form of the Gospels in use within the Syrian churches. Even before the time of Tatian, Hegesippus quoted from another Syriac version of the Bible commonly called the Old Syriac Manuscripts. This text of the gospels was typical of the Western text type and survives in two manuscripts: a parchment known as the Curetonian Syriac, and a palimpsest (parchment which has been erased to make room for a new text) known as the Sinaitic Syriac. These gospels are sometimes called "the Separated Ones," because they were not woven together into a single account like that of Tatian's *Diatessaron*. Both of these Old Syriac texts date from the late second or early third century.

Three other Syriac versions deserve comment. In 508, a new translation of the Second Testament into Syriac was completed, which included the books omitted in the Peshitta (2 Peter, 2 John, 3 John, Jude, and Revelation). This work was actually a revision of the entire Bible by Bishop Polycarp, under the direction of Zenaia (Philoxenus), a Jacobite bishop at Mabbug in eastern Syria. This so-called Philoxenian Syriac translation makes it clear that the Syrian church had not accepted the entire Second Testament canon until the sixth century. In 616, Thomas Harkel (Heraclea) republished the Philoxenian text, to which he added marginal notes. The First Testament portion of this Harklean version was done by Paul of Tella. The critical apparatus of the Harklean Book of Acts is perhaps the second most important witness to the Western text form, being surpassed in this respect only by Codex Bezae. A third Syriac version, known as the Palestinian Syriac, survives only in fragmentary form from lectionaries of the gospels dating from the eleventh and twelfth centuries.

A number of secondary translations emerged in eastern Christendom. When the Nestorians were condemned at the Council of Ephesus in 431, their founder Nestorius was confined to a monastery. The Persian Nestorians became a separate schismatic church which spread into Central and East Asia, where they translated the Bible from Syriac into several languages. What little remains of this work comes from the ninth, tenth, and later centuries. The devastating work of Tamerlane, "the Scourge of Asia," virtually exterminated the Nestorians in the fourteenth century.

After the rise of Islam in the seventh century, the Bible was translated into Arabic from Greek, Syriac, Coptic, Latin, and various combinations of these traditions. The earliest of these Arabic translations is dated to ca. 720 and appears to have been made from the Syriac. The only standardized translation of the First Testament into Arabic was done by the Jewish scholar Saadia Gaon (ca. 930). With the exception of the First Testament, Arabic translations are based on translations rather than original texts, and thus provide little assistance in matters of textual criticism.

George M. Lamsa published his translation of *The Holy Bible from Ancient Eastern Manuscripts* (1957), which remains a useful volume for English readers who want access to the Syriac Peshitta.

Concept Check # 34

The Orthodox Church in Syria developed its own canon of sacred Scripture and its own official version of the biblical text. What does this suggest about the process of transmitting the Bible to other cultures? (Check your answer on p. 224.)

---

6. Latin Translations

Although Latin was the official language in the West, Greek retained its position as the literary language of the Roman world until the third century CE. By that time Old Latin translations of the Bible were already circulating widely in North Africa and in Europe. The **Old Latin Bible**, which was translated in North Africa from the Septuagint (LXX), was completed prior to 200 CE, for it appears to have been the Bible used by Tertullian and Cyprian during the second century. The unrevised Apocrypha of this translation was apparently added posthumously to Jerome's Vulgate Old Testament. Nothing else remains of the Old Latin text of the First Testament apart from fragments and citations in the early Church Fathers. The picture for the Old Latin text of the Second Testament, however, is quite different. Twenty-seven manuscripts of the Gospels have survived, along with seven from Acts, six from the Pauline epistles, and fragments of the general epistles and Revelation. These manuscripts date from the fourth through the

Old Latin translation of the Bible: Translation of the Bible from Greek into Latin in the first and second centuries CE, in various textual traditions, before the time of Jerome's Latin Vulgate.

Latin Vulgate: The translation of the Bible into Latin by Jerome, which became the authorized version in liturgical services of the Roman Catholic Church until modern times.

thirteenth centuries. In short, the Old Latin version continued to be copied long after it was displaced by the **Latin Vulgate** of Jerome.

The Old Latin New Testament is represented by two, and possibly three, different text types. The African text was used by Tertullian and Cyprian, a European text is preserved in the writings of Irenaeus and Novatian, and an Italian text is mentioned by Augustine—though some scholars regard this as simply a reference to the Vulgate itself (if so, there are only two different Old Latin texts of the New Testament). The African text, found in Codex Bobiensis, is a free and rough translation of the Greek text in the second century. The European text is represented by two codices: Codex Vercellensis, written by Eusebius of Vercelli (ca. 370-371); and Codex Veronensis, which is the basis of Jerome's translation of the Vulgate First Testament.

The numerous texts of the Old Latin Bible that had appeared by the last half of the fourth century led to the decision on the part of Damasus, bishop of Rome (366-384), to commission a revision of the Old Latin text that was to be a new and authoritative edition of the Bible for the Church in the West. Besides the confusion of Latin texts then in use, Damasus was concerned about the growing disputes between Christians and Jews and about the numerous disputations which followed the emergence of such heretical groups as the Marcionites, the Manichaeans, and the Montanists, who based their doctrine on their own canons and translations of the Bible. The Arian controversy led to the councils at Nicea (325), Constantinople I (381), and Ephesus (431). Moreover, the scholars of that era were calling for an authentic and standard text to carry out the teaching activities of the Church, its missionary programs, and its defense of the doctrines established at the great Church councils.

The controversy surrounding Jerome's translation of the First Testament from Hebrew reflects more than the conflicts between Christians and Jews. It was shaped by the popular notion held by many church leaders, including Augustine, that the LXX was actually the inspired and inerrant Word of God rather than a noninspired translation of the original Hebrew text.

St. Jerome: A Christian ascetic and biblical scholar (ca. 340-420 CE) who translated the Bible into Latin in Palestine under the auspices of Pope Damasus.

Sophronius Eusebius Hieronymus, better known as **St. Jerome** (ca. 340-420), was born in Stridon, Dalmatia, and went to Rome at age twelve to study Latin, Greek, and classical literary texts. He became a Christian at age nineteen and devoted himself to a life of monastic abstinence. He took up residence in the East near Antioch where, during the years from 374 to 379, he employed a Jewish rabbi to teach him Hebrew. After being ordained a presbyter at Antioch, he journeyed to Constantinople where he studied under Gregory Nazianzen. In 382, he was summoned to Rome to be the secretary of Damasus, bishop of Rome, who commissioned him to revise the Latin Bible. He was selected because of his training as a scholar and assumed the task because of his devotion to Damasus, in spite of the strong opposition he knew that task would precipitate.

A slightly revised Latin version of the Gospels was completed in 383, which was probably based on the European text of the Old Latin, which he corrected in accordance with an Alexandrian-type Greek text. Shortly after this, his patron died (384) and was succeeded by a new bishop of Rome. Jerome, who had aspired to that position, had already completed a hasty revision of Psalms when he returned to the East taking up residence in Bethlehem. Before his departure, he made a cursory revision of the rest of the Second Testament. Back in Jerusalem he turned his attention to a more careful revision of the Roman Psalter which he completed in 387. This revision, known as the **Gallican Psalter**, is currently included in the Vulgate Old Testament. It is actually a translation of the fifth column of Origen's *Hexapla.* As soon as he completed this task, Jerome began the revision of the Septuagint (LXX) while continuing to work on perfecting his knowledge of Hebrew so that he could make a fresh translation of the First Testament directly from the original language.

As he had anticipated years earlier, Jerome soon began to face suspicion and opposition to his work. When Jerome began to cast doubts on the "inspiration of the Septuagint," his opponents were outraged and accused him of judaizing. Among his many critics was **Augustine**, who was highly critical of Jerome's translation of the First Testament but wholeheartedly supportive of his Second Testament revisions after 398. Jerome's translation of the Hebrew Psalter never actually surpassed his earlier Gallican Psalter, or the Roman Psalter then in liturgical use, even though it was based on the original language instead of another translation. Jerome kept on translating the Hebrew Bible in spite of opposition and poor health, finally completing the Latin Vulgate in 405. Though it was not readily received, Jerome continued writing, translating, and revising the work. Since Jerome cared little for the Apocrypha,

Gallican Psalter: Jerome's translation of the Psalter into Latin, which is actually a translation of the fifth column of Origen's *Hexapla* rather than the Hebrew text.

Augustine: Bishop of Hippo, one of the Latin fathers in the early Christian Church (354-430 CE).

he reluctantly made a hasty translation of Judith, Tobit, the rest of Esther, and the additions to Daniel before his death. As a result, the Old Latin version of the Apocrypha was subsequently "brought into the Latin Vulgate Bible during the Middle Ages over Jerome's dead body." [9]

Shortly after Jerome's death in 420, his Old Testament translation gained a complete victory over its rivals and the Latin Vulgate subsequently became the unofficially recognized standard text of the Bible throughout the Middle Ages. It was not until the **Council of Trent** (1546-1563), however, that the Vulgate was officially elevated to that position within the Roman Catholic Church.

Council of Trent: An ecumenical council of the Roman Catholic Church which defined Church doctrine and condemned the Reformation (1546-1563 CE).

It was inevitable that the Vulgate text would suffer corruption in its transmission during the Middle Ages. Sometimes such corruption was simply the result of careless copying and the reintroduction of elements of the Old Latin text. Throughout the Middle Ages, several attempts were made in various monasteries at revision and recension of the Vulgate text, which led to the accumulation of more than eight thousand extant Vulgate manuscripts. Consequently, the Council of Trent ordered the preparation of an authentic edition of the Vulgate, but the papal commission which was committed to this task was unable to overcome the many difficulties it faced. Finally, in 1590, Pope Sixtus V published his own edition of the Vulgate. This **Sixtene edition** was rejected by the Jesuits, and Pope Gregory XIV (1590-1591) proceeded to revise the Sixtene text. His sudden death did not end the process of revision; for his successor Pope Clement VIII (1592-1605) took up the task and published a new "authentic" Vulgate edition of the Bible in 1604, which is known as the **Sixto-Clementine edition**. It differs from the Sixtene edition in some 4900 variants and was widely printed, surpassing even the Gutenberg edition of the printed Bible between 1450 and 1455. Since 1907, a critical revision of the Vulgate Old Testament has been undertaken by the Benedictines. The Vulgate New Testament was critically revised by a group of Anglican scholars at Oxford which was begun by Bishop John Wordsworth and Professor H. J. White between 1877 and 1926, and completed by H. F. D. Sparks in 1954.

Sixtene edition: An edition of the Latin Vulgate published by Pope Sixtus V in 1590 CE.

Sixto-Clementine edition: An edition of the Latin Vulgate published by Pope Clementine VIII in 1604 CE.

When Jerome's text of the Bible is recovered through textual criticism of the Vulgate, it reveals that Jerome's New Testament was a late fourth-century revision of the Old Latin; and his Old Testament was a late fourth- or early fifth-century version of the Hebrew text then in use in the East. Only a few of Jerome's many opponents acknowledged their error in accepting the LXX Old Testament as authoritative and inspired and openly gave their support to the accuracy of the Hebrew text underlying the Vulgate translation. Among Jerome's critics was Augustine, then bishop of Hippo, who subsequently became the dominant voice in the next several centuries of Christian history. During those centuries, the Vulgate became the authoritative edition of the Bible and served as the basis for most modern translations of the Bible prior to the nineteenth century.

Concept Check# 35

Do you see any irony in what was achieved by Jerome in his translation of the First Testament into Latin from the original Hebrew language in the Latin Vulgate? (Check your answer on p.224.)

---

7. Translations of Translations

From the beginning of Christianity on the day of Pentecost in Jerusalem, there were "Parthians, and Medes, and Elamites, and the dwellers in Mesopotamia, and in Judea, and Cappadocia, in Pontus and Asia, Phrygia, and Pamphilia, in Egypt, and in the parts of Libya about Cyrene, and strangers of Rome, Jews and proselytes, Cretans and Arabians" (Acts 2:9-11) among those who heard the preaching of the apostles. Such were in need of the Bible in their own languages. For all practical purposes, the Bible of primitive Christianity was the Septuagint (LXX) translation of the First Testament. That text was soon translated into a host of other target languages.

In Egypt, the Greek language, with seven demotic characters added to it, became the written form of Coptic before the emergence of Christianity. The Coptic dialect of southern Egypt (Upper Egypt) is known as Sahidic (Thebaic), with its center in the region of ancient Thebes (modern Luxor). The **Coptic versions** are translations of the Bible into the Coptic dialects, the most important of which are Sahidic and Bohairic. The Second Testament was translated into **Sahidic** by the beginning of the fourth century. Pachomius (d. 346), the great organizer of Egyptian monasticism, required the study of this text on the part of his followers. Meanwhile, in the Delta region of Lower Egypt near

Coptic versions: Translation of the Bible into Coptic, the language which developed from ancient Egyptian in several dialectal forms.

Sahidic: The Coptic dialect of southern Egypt (i.e., Thebes).

Bohairic: The Coptic dialect of Lower Egypt (i.e., Memphis and Alexandria).

Ethiopic: Stands for "Classical Ethiopic" or "Ge'ez," the language of ancient Ethiopia.

Ulfilas: "Apostle of the Goths" (311-381 CE), who translated the Bible into Gothic.

Memphis and Alexandria, **Bohairic** (Memphic) Coptic became the basic dialect of the Christian community in Egypt. The nearness to Alexandria, and continued use of the Greek language there, probably accounts for the fact that Bohairic versions of the Second Testament appeared somewhat later than their Sahidic counterparts. The only early Bohairic manuscript extant is Papyrus Bodmer III, the Gospel of John, which has a badly mutilated beginning. The third area of Coptic dialects, the Middle Egyptian Dialects, are classified as Fayumic and Achmimic. No entire Second Testament book survives in these dialects, though a copy of the Gospel of John is nearly complete. One fourth century papyrus codex in the Fayumic dialect, which contains John 6:11-15:11, is closer to Sahidic than to Bohairic. All of the First Testament manuscripts in Coptic dialects are translations from the Septuagint (LXX).

As Christianity spread through Egypt into Ethiopia, the Bible was translated into **Ethiopic**, beginning with the First Testament, which appears to have been revised in light of the Hebrew text in the fourth century, with the addition of the Second Testament in the seventh century. The work was done by Syrian monks who moved into Ethiopia during the so-called Monophysite Controversy (fifth and sixth centuries) and the rise of Islam (seventh and eighth centuries). The Ethiopic church continues to be Monophysite to the present time.

Recensions of the Ethiopic New Testament, which were made in the fifth and again in the twelfth centuries under the influence of Coptic and Arabic translations, may actually have been based on Syriac rather than Greek manuscripts. The Ethiopic Old Testament includes the noncanonical book of 1 Enoch (which is quoted in Jude 14-15) and the Book of Jubilees, which indicates that the Ethiopic Church accepted a broader canon than the Christian Church at large. More than one hundred manuscript copies of the Ethiopic Bible have survived, but none are earlier than the thirteenth century.

Though it is not clear exactly when Christianity spread into the region of the Germanic tribes between the Rhine and Danube rivers, it took place prior to the Council of Nicea (325), since Theophilus, bishop of the Goths, was a participant. The Goths played a significant role in European history during the fifth century. **Ulfilas** (311-381), the second bishop of the Ostrogoths, known as the "Apostle of the Goths," led his converts into what is now known as Bulgaria, where he translated the Greek Bible into Gothic. He is said to have created a Gothic alphabet and to have reduced the spoken language to writing in order to publish the Bible in a **Gothic version**. He made a remarkably faithful translation of the Lucianic recension of the First Testament into Gothic during the fourth century (ca. 350), of which very little remains. It is interesting to note that he felt the books of Samuel and Kings were too warlike to be transmitted to the Gothic tribes and intentionally omitted this material from his translation of the First Testament. The Gothic New Testament translated by Ulfilas, which is the earliest known literary monument in the Germanic dialect, survives only in fragmentary form. Its chief value lies in the simple fact that it is the earliest literary work in the Germanic language group to which English belongs. Six fragmentary manuscript copies survive, including Codex Argenteus ("the silver codex"), which is written on purple vellum in silver and some gold letters. All other Gothic manuscripts are palimpsests except for a single vellum leaf of a bilingual Gothic-Latin codex. Like Coptic, the Gothic language was reduced to written form expressly for the writing of the Bible into the vernacular of the people. All of the Gothic manuscripts date to the fifth and sixth centuries.

Gothic version: A translation of the Bible into the language of the Goths, who originated in Scandinavia migrating South and East in two branches during the early Christian centuries to settle in the Balkans and the Ukraine.

As the Syrian church spread, several secondary translations of the Bible were made, the most important of which is Armenian. Christianity was proclaimed the national religion of Armenia by Tiridates III in 304 CE; but the process in which the Bible was translated into the Armenian language is subject to debate. There are two traditions in regard to the origin of the **Armenian Bible**. One account credits St. Mesrob (d. 439) with the creation of a new alphabet to assist Sahak (Isaac the Great, 390-439) in translating the Bible from the Greek text. The other tradition claims that this translation was made from the Syriac text, which is more probable. The first Armenian translation of the First Testament, made in the fifth century, is a Hexaplaric recension revised in accordance with the Peshitta. The earliest Armenian translations were revised prior to the eighth century, to agree with certain "trustworthy Greek codices" obtained from Constantinople after the Council at Ephesus (431). This revision continues to be the most common Armenian text in use to the present time. The oldest extant manuscript of this revised text dates to the ninth century.

Armenian Bible: The translation of the Bible into the language of Armenia was done by the fifth century CE, though the details of this process are not clear.

By the middle of the fifth century CE, Georgia, the mountainous region between the Black and the Caspian seas to the north of Armenia, had its own version of the Bible which was translated from Armenian.

The Georgian alphabet, like the Armenian and Gothic, was developed expressly for the transmission of the Bible.

Christianity had spread to the Moravian empire in east-central Europe by the middle of the ninth century. When Rostislav, the founder of this kingdom, embraced the Christian religion, he requested that Slavonic priests be sent to conduct church services in the language of the people. In response, Emperor Michael III sent two monks from Constantinople. The monks were the brothers Methodius and Constantinus (who changed his name to **Cyril**), natives of Thessalonica, who devised a new alphabet for the task, known as the Cyrillic alphabet. It is composed of thirty-six letters and remains the basis of Russian, Ukrainian, Serbo-Croatian, and Bulgarian to the present time. The Cyrillic alphabet replaced the local Glagolitic alphabet in the tenth century. Commonly known as the "Apostles to the Slave," Cyril and Methodius first translated the Gospels into Old Slavonic and then set out to translate the First Testament. At one time, it was believed that their translation was made from the LXX; but it is now clear that it was made from the Latin Vulgate. Most of the extant Slavonic manuscripts are lectionaries.

Of the several other translations based on the Latin Vulgate, only the Anglo-Saxon and the Frankish translations require comment. The Frankish translation survives in a bilingual Latin-Frankish edition known from one fragmentary eighth-century manuscript which contains portions of Matthew. The Anglo-Saxon text is discussed below in the section on "Early English Translations."

Cyril: "Apostle of the Slavs" (827-869 CE), a Greek missionary to the Moravians and creator of the Cyrillic script.

Concept Check # 36

The spread of Christianity in early Church history is accompanied by the invention of new scripts explicitly for the translation of the Bible, namely: Gothic, Armenian, Georgian, and the Cyrillic alphabet among Slavic peoples in east-central Europe. What parallel do you see in modern times? (Check your answer on p. 224.)

---

8. Patristic Citations of the Biblical Text

The early **Church Fathers** saw the First Testament as a lasting record of God's revelation. For them, the very individuality of the separate

Church Fathers: Leaders of the early Christian Church fall into three groups: the Apostolic Fathers (70-150 CE); Ante-Nicene Fathers (150-300 CE); and Post-Nicene Fathers (300-430 CE).

human authors was of little consequence. For all practical purposes, they regarded the whole of the First Testament as simply one divine utterance, the "Word of God." Their use of the Second Testament, however, is somewhat different and more significant for our purposes here.

Though the extent of the Second Testament canon was not settled and acknowledged until the fourth century, that process was already underway as early as the last half of the first century, as witnessed in the biblical text itself: i.e., the process of selecting and sorting (Luke 1:1-4; 1 Thess 2:13), collecting (2 Pet 3:15-16), reading (1 Thess 5:27), circulating (Col 4:16), and quoting (1 Tim 5:18). In the first half of the second century, the apostolic writings were widely accepted as authoritative as well. The writings of the early Fathers were also widely read and circulated, and their quoting of the Second Testament in their struggles against heretical groups, their dialogues with unbelievers, and their exhortation against various vices tell us much about the history, beliefs, and practices of the early Church.

In the last half of the second century, the books of the Second Testament were explicitly cited as Scripture along with those of the First Testament. This was also a period of intense missionary activity in which the Scriptures were being translated into other languages. It was also during this period that commentaries began to appear, such as Heracleon's *Commentary on the Gospels*, and Melito's *Commentary on the Apocalypse*. The *Diatessaron of Tatian* also appeared on the scene. The writings of the Fathers are filled with citations from the Second Testament as authoritative Scripture.

During the third century, the Second Testament books were collected into a catalog of "recognized books" which were separated from other types of Christian literature. This century also saw a surge of intellectual activity within the Church, such as Origen's *Hexapla* (six-column Bible). Alongside the two classes of Christian literature (Scripture and writings of the Fathers), a body of apocryphal and pseudepigraphal literature emerged which made the official canonization of the Second Testament more and more necessary. By the time the fourth century began, the matter of the Second Testament canon was settled and widely acknowledged.

While the testimony of the early Church Fathers is older than the best codices, it is not always reliable. An individual writer may have quoted a variant reading from an existing manuscript, or the writing of that Father itself may have been subject to alteration or corruption during its own transmission, just as the Greek text of the Second Testament was. Moreover, the nature of individual citations ranged from verbatim accounts to paraphrase, or perhaps even a mere allusion. Even if the claim for the quotation was verbatim, it is not always clear whether it was cited from memory or read from a written text. All these difficulties notwithstanding, the evidence from the early Church Fathers is clearly of great importance in three ways: 1) they enable us to reconstruct the history of the text of the Second Testament in this period; 2) they provide the best evidence as to the canon of the Second Testament; and 3) they provide a means of dating the manuscripts of the Second Testament and assist us in determining the date and provenance of translations, versions, and revisions of the Second Testament text.

There are three broad classes of patristic writers: the Apostolic Fathers (70-150), the Ante-Nicene Fathers (150-300), and the Nicene and Post-Nicene Fathers (300-430). By the end of the first century, at least fourteen books of the Second Testament were cited as authoritative by the Fathers. By 110 CE, there were nineteen books recognized by citation; and within forty years (150), twenty-four books were so acknowledged. By the end of that century, twenty-six books had been so cited. Only 3 John, perhaps because of its small size and significance, was without such corroboration. But within a generation, Origen had confirmed the existence of 3 John, as did the Muratorian Canon and the Old Latin version.

Not only did the Church Fathers cite all twenty-seven books of the Second Testament, they quoted virtually every verse in all of these twenty-seven books. According to Geisler and Nix, five authors alone from Irenaeus to Eusebius made almost 36,000 quotations from the Second Testament.[10] Sir David Dalrymple claimed that he had found all but eleven verses of the entire Second Testament among the quotations of the second- and third-century Fathers. No other book from the ancient world exists in its entirety by way of thousands of quotations on the part of ancient authors. The amazing fact is that the entire Second Testament could be reconstructed simply from quotations made within two hundred years of its original composition.

In spite of its fanciful and sometimes heretical nature, the apocryphal literature from the second and third centuries also provides valuable attestation of the existence of the books in the Second Testament canon. In the first place, the very names of these books are often in clear imitation of the canonical Second Testament books. One can also demonstrate dependence on the canonical books in terms of both literary and doctrinal content. Their style and content are often clearly imitative of the first-century canonical books. Moreover, some of the third-century Gnostic books from Nag-Hammadi, Egypt (discovered 1946), actually cite various books of the Second Testament. The Epistle of Reginus, for example, cites 1 and 2 Corinthians, Romans, Ephesians, Philippians, Colossians, and the transfiguration narrative from the Gospels.

Concept Check # 37

How do you account for the fact that the Second Testament was quoted so often and so widely by the early Church Fathers? (Check your answer on p. 224.)

Thinking Exercise

On the Transmission of the Biblical Text

The critical thinking goal for this exercise is to clarify the process by which the biblical text emerged in antiquity.

How To Do This Exercise

Review the major divisions in sections A through C of this chapter, and the concepts and key words which appear there. Then answer the following:

1. Describe how the content of the Bible was known before the canonization process was completed.

_____

_____

_____

_____

2. The single most important translation of the First Testament in antiquity was the Greek Septuagint. What role did it play in the life of the early Christian and Jewish communities?

_____

_____

_____

_____

3. When Jerome decided to translate the First Testament from the original Hebrew text rather than the Septuagint, he encountered great resistance in the Church. What is the significance of his achievement, the Latin Vulgate?

_____

_____

_____

_____

D. The Development of Textual Criticism[11]

The history of the text of the Bible within the Christian Church may be divided into four periods, particularly in reference to the Second Testament: 1) the period of canonization of the Second Testament (to 325); 2) the period of standardization of the text (325-1500); 3) the period of publication (1500-1650); and 4) the period of criticism and revision (1650-present). Throughout the most recent period, an intense struggle has been waged between those who favor the "received text" (**textus receptus**) and those who seek to establish the "**critical text**." For the most part, the war, as such, is over. The battle for the Bible has been won by those who are intent on establishing the critical text as the authoritative basis of Christian faith. Although not many scholars today seriously defend the superiority of the received text, it should be noted that there is really no substantial difference between it and the critical text. What differences there are between these two traditions are essentially technical in nature, rather than doctrinal. Somewhat like a modern hologram, the integrity of the biblical text may be observed in spite of minor damage at specific points. One simply adjusts his or her view a bit to see past the specific problem to the underlying image contained in the Word of God, which is revealed on the pages of a human document with all its surface frailty. The great mystery of faith, like the mystery of the incarnation itself, is that a damaged "human" receptacle still remains "inerrant" so far as God's divine purposes are concerned.

1. The Period of Canonization of the Second Testament (to 325)

As early as the third century BCE, scholars in Alexandria set out to restore the texts of ancient Greek poets and other literary works of note. It was in this setting that the Septuagint (LXX) version of the Hebrew Bible was produced about 280-150 BCE. The city of Alexandria was subsequently a major center of Christianity until the rise of Islam in the seventh century. Thus, it is easy to understand why this city is also the home of early activities to restore the original text of the Bible. Nonetheless, there is no true textual criticism in the modern sense before the time of Origen (ca. 250 CE), particularly regarding the text of the Second Testament. Instead, the period from 100 to 325 CE is better described as one of reduplication of manuscripts within the canonical process that

Textus receptus: "Received text," a late and corrupt form of the Byzantine text type of the NT which dominated in the Western world for about three hundred years.

Critical text: The text of the Bible as restored to the presumed original Hebrew, Aramaic, and Greek by biblical scholars using the principles of textual criticism.

produced the Second Testament as the completion and culmination of the First Testament within Christian circles.

Meanwhile, Jewish scholars in Palestine were already at work in matters of textual criticism in the period between the Testaments (100 BCE to 100 CE). Study of evidence preserved in texts recovered from the Judean wilderness since 1947 reveals at least two recensions of the Hebrew Bible during this period. The proto-Lucianic recension, which predates the Christian era, is the first serious attempt to find an authoritative text of the Hebrew Bible amongst competing text types in the century before the Common Era (CE). And during the apostolic era in nascent Christianity, a second recension appeared known as the *Kaige* recension, which is essentially a proto-Masoretic Text of the Hebrew Bible.

The masoretic tradition which subsequently saw the fixing of the consonantal Hebrew text in Palestine, perhaps as late as the ninth century CE, also saw the fixing of a complex system of musical performance of that text through the accentual notation of the Masoretic Text which the masoretes had received through the ancestors of the ultra-conservative Karaite community known as the "**Elders of Bathyra**." For centuries this tradition of recitation of the Hebrew Bible was literally "in the hands" of highly trained tradants who had mastered the ancient practice of chironomy—to instruct those who were commissioned to sing the text in public worship—originally in the Second Temple in Jerusalem, but now in synagogues throughout the Jewish dispersion.

Elders of Bathyra: Predecessors of the Karaites from whom the masoretes received the accentual system of the Hebrew text of the First Testament.

During the second half of the first century CE, the various books of the Second Testament were first written on papyrus rolls. These so-called autograph copies have all subsequently been lost. But before they perished they were copied and circulated. These early copies, also written on papyrus rolls, were later recopied in papyrus codices, and still later on parchment and vellum. Very few, if any, of these early copies are extant today. While there were many copies made of the books which subsequently were included in the canon of the Second Testament, not all of them were of the same quality. As soon as copies began to appear, errors and misprints also were introduced into the developing textual tradition. By the time the apostolic period had come to a close, persecution was already widespread against the Christian community. Sporadic persecutions on the part of the Roman Empire culminated in two imperial pogroms under Decius (249-251) and Diocletian (284-305).

Christians suffered intense persecution, even death, and frequently saw their sacred writings confiscated and destroyed. Consequently, the Second Testament itself was in danger of being lost to the Church. Christians responded by making "unprofessional" copies, often in haste, with the subsequent result of still more errors being introduced.

Meanwhile in Alexandria, the Christian community undertook pioneering work at the local level, particularly in regard to textual criticism of the Greek translation of the First Testament, namely the Septuagint (LXX), in the period around 200-250 CE. Origen in Alexandria worked on his *Hexapla* and eventually wrote commentaries on books of the Second Testament as well. Other examples of early textual criticism which were done in places other than Alexandria include the Lucianic recension of the LXX, Julius Africanus' work on *Susanna*, and Theodore of Mopsuestia's *Song of Songs*. These early textual critics did important editorial revision of the biblical text, but their work did not stem the tide of casual, unsystematic, and largely unintentional creation of new variant readings in the transmission of the text of the Second Testament.

Concept Check # 38

Recensional activity to establish the official form of the Hebrew text of the First Testament within ancient Judaism took place centuries before similar activity among the Christians on the Greek text of the Second Testament. What prompted the standardization of the Greek text of the Second Testament? (Check your answer on p. 224.)

---

2. The Period of Standardization (325-1500)

Following the **Edict of Milan** (313), which removed the threat of persecution, the situation changed markedly so far as transmission of the biblical text is concerned. When the emperor Constantine wrote to Eusebius of Caesarea requesting fifty copies of the Christian Scriptures, a new direction emerged in the history of the Second Testament. The period of standardization of the text began, with careful copying of biblical manuscripts. At first, copies of manuscripts in a particular region were made by copyists of that region. But when Constantine moved the seat of government to the new capital, Constantinople, it was but a matter of time before that city would come to dominate the

Edict of Milan: The emperor Constantine granted equal rights for all religions and the property confiscated from the Christians was restored in 313 CE at Milan.

Greek-speaking world and its particular text type would become the standard text, particularly of the Second Testament. With the development of a standardized text, there was relatively little need for classification and critical evaluation of earlier manuscripts of the Second Testament. Consequently, the text remained relatively unchanged throughout this period. Moreover, at the end of this period, when Johann Gutenberg developed movable type for the printing press, the production of virtually identical copies of the Bible introduced a new era in the history of textual criticism.

As a result of the precedent set by Constantine, great numbers of manuscripts of the Bible were carefully produced throughout the Middle Ages; but official and carefully planned revision of the text was not common. Except for the efforts of scholars like Jerome (ca. 340-420) and Alcuin of York (735-804), efforts at critical revision of the biblical text in Christian circles were rare. The period between 500 and 1000, however, witnessed remarkable activity so far as the Hebrew Bible is concerned with the masoretic work in Tiberius which resulted in the received Masoretic Text in its fully vocalized form.

3. The Period of Publication (1500-1650)

Polyglot texts:
Multilingual printed editions of the Bible which contain the same text in several languages.

The concerns of the Protestant Reformation, together with the new situation introduced by the technology of the printing press, produced a new era in the history of textual criticism. Attempts were made to produce printed texts of the Bible as accurately as possible. One result was the series of **polyglot (multilingual) texts**, including such titles as the Complutensian Polyglot (1514-17), the Antwerp Polyglot (1569-72), the Paris Polyglot (1629-45), and the London Polyglot (1657-69). The standard edition of the Masoretic Text also appeared under the editorship of Jacob ben Chayyim (ca. 1525), a Hebrew Christian who based his text on fourteenth century manuscripts. This text is essentially a recension of the Masoretic Text as written by the Ben Asher family (ca. 920), which became the basis for all subsequent copies of the Hebrew Bible, whether in manuscript or printed form.

The first printed edition of the Greek New Testament was made in Spain in 1502 under the direction of Cardinal Francisco Ximenes de Cisneros (1437-1517). It was part of the Complutensian Polyglot, which contained Hebrew, Aramaic, Greek, and Latin texts. The work was published in the university town of Alcala (*Complutum* in Latin), from which it received its name. Even though this was the first printed edition of the Greek New Testament in 1514 and 1517, it was not the first to be placed on the market. Pope Leo X did not give his sanction for the release of the work until March 1520. Meanwhile Desiderius **Erasmus** (ca. 1466-1536) of Rotterdam received the honor of publishing the first printed edition of the Greek New Testament in March 1516. The first edition of Erasmus's Greek New Testament was done hastily and contained hundreds of typographical and mechanical mistakes. Moreover, the text itself was not based on early manuscripts, was not reliably edited, and therefore not trustworthy. The second edition, published in 1519, became the basis for Luther's German translation. Further editions of Erasmus's Greek New Testament, which became the so-called textus receptus ("received text"), appeared in 1522, 1527, and 1535.

Robert Estienne (Etienne; Latin **Stephanus**), the royal printer in Paris, published the Greek New Testament in 1546, 1549, 1550, and 1551. The third edition (1550) of this work, based on Erasmus's fourth edition, was the first to contain a critical apparatus, which was based on a mere fifteen manuscripts. After its publication, this third edition became the dominant text in England and the basis for the textus receptus. In his fourth edition, Estienne introduced the modern verse divisions. In this work, he also announced his conversion to Protestantism.

Theodore de Beze (Beza) (1519-1605), the successor to John Calvin in Geneva, published nine editions of the Greek New Testament after the death of Estienne in 1564, as well as a posthumous tenth edition in 1611. The most important of these editions appeared in 1582, which included a few readings from Codex Bezae and Codex Claromontanus. Beza's Greek New Testament was in general agreement with the 1550 edition of Estienne and served to popularize and stereotype the textus receptus. The King James translators used Beza's 1588-89 edition.

While the text of Stephanus (Estienne) held sway in England, the text of Bonaventure (1583-1652) and Abraham Elzevir (1592-1652) became the most popular on the Continent. Seven editions of their textus receptus were published in Leiden between 1624 and 1787. The 1624 edition was based on Beza's 1565 edition, and their second edition (1633) is the source of the title given to their text, namely that of textus receptus. The preface reads: *"Textum erao habes, nunc ab omnibus receptum: in quo nihil immutatum aut corruptum damus."* In short, a

Erasmus: A Dutch humanist, scholar, theologian, and writer (ca. 1466-1536), who published the first printed edition of the Greek New Testament (March 1516).

Robert Estienne (Stephanus): Published the first edition of the Greek New Testament with a critical apparatus (1550), which became the basis for the textus receptus. He introduced the modern verse divisions in the text of the Bible.

Theodore de Beze (Beza): John Calvin's successor in Geneva; popularized the textus receptus with some readings from newly discovered ancient manuscripts of the Greek New Testament.

publisher's blurb introduced the catchword (textus receptus = "received text") which designated the Greek text which had derived in turn from editions of Ximenes, Beza, and Stephanus. It should be noted that the textual basis for this work was very late, from but a handful of manuscripts, with several passages inserted with no textual support. Only the discovery of new manuscripts and consequent classification and comparison could remedy this situation.

> ### Concept Check # 39
>
> The invention of the printing press introduced a new era in the history of the transmission of the Bible. What was it about the first printed versions of the Bible that made the subsequent period of criticism and revision necessary? (Check you answer on p. 224.)

4. The Period of Criticism and Revision (1650-Present)

The gathering of new textual materials and their systematic collection and comparison characterizes the most recent era of textual criticism. The beginning of this process is illustrated in the publication of the London Polyglot, which was edited by Brian Walton (1600-1661) and included the Second Testament in Greek, Latin, Syrian, Ethiopic, Arabic, and Persian (the Gospels). It also contained annotations of variant readings in the recently discovered Codex Alexandrinus and a critical apparatus by Archbishop Ussher. In 1675 John Fell published an anonymous edition of the Greek New Testament in Oxford which contained evidence from the Gothic and Bohairic versions. In 1707, John Mill reprinted the 1550 Estienne text to which he added some thirty thousand variants from nearly one hundred manuscripts.

Richard Bentley (1662-1742), in a prospectus for a Greek New Testament which he never completed, challenged others to gather all available materials for intensive study. **Johann Albrecht Bengel** (1687-1752), who was among those scholars who responded, established one of the basic canons of modern textual criticism: the difficult reading is to be preferred to the easy. One of Bentley's colleagues, **Johann Jakob Wettstein** (1693-1754), published the first apparatus which identified the uncial manuscripts by capital Roman letters and the minuscules by Arabic numerals. He also is responsible for advocating the principle that

Johann Albrecht Bengel: Established the basic canon of modern textual criticism: The difficult reading is to be preferred to the easy.

Johann Jakob Wettstein: Published the first critical apparatus which identified the uncials by capital Roman letters and the miniscules by Arabic numerals.

manuscripts must be evaluated by their weight in significance rather than by their quantity in terms of numbers. The fruit of his forty years of careful study was published in Amsterdam in 1751-1752. A reprint of Wettstein's *Prolegomena* was issued in 1764 by **Johann Salomo Semler** (1725-1791), who is sometimes called the "father of German rationalism." Semler followed Bengel's example of classifying manuscripts by groups and introduced the term *recension* to groups of Second Testament witnesses. He identified three of these recensions: Alexandrian, Eastern, and Western. All later materials were regarded by Semler as mixtures of these three basic text types.

Johann Jakob Griesbach (1745-1812) brought Bengel's and Semler's principles to fruition by classifying the three groups of Second Testament manuscripts as Alexandrian, Western, and Byzantine. His work includes fifteen of the basic canons of modern textual criticism. Shortly after the publication of the first edition of his Greek New Testament (1775-1777), a number of other scholars published collations of textual evidence from the Church Fathers, various early versions, and the Greek text itself which set the stage for continued refinement in methodology.

Christian Friedrich Matthaei (1744-1811) published a critical apparatus in his Greek and Latin New Testament which included evidence from the Slavonic translations. Frary Karl Alter (1749-1804), a Jesuit in Vienna, added further evidence from Slavonic manuscripts and twenty additional Greek manuscripts. In 1788-1801 a group of Danish scholars, under the direction of Andrew Birch (1758-1829), published four volumes of textual work which included the readings of Codex Vaticanus for the first time. Meanwhile, Johann Leonhard Hug (1765-1846) and his student Johannes Martin Augustinus Scholz (1794-1852) advanced the theory that a "common edition" of the Greek New Testament emerged after the degeneration of the text in the third century. Scholz added 616 new manuscripts to the growing body of available materials and stressed, for the first time, the importance of assigning geographical provenance to certain groups of manuscripts, which was elaborated in 1924 by B. H. Streeter in his theory of "local texts."

The half century from 1831-1881 saw the first complete break with the tradition of the so-called textus receptus. **Karl Lachmann** (1793-1851) published the first Greek New Testament in the form of an eclectic critical text based on the evaluation of variant readings. In this period,

Johann Salomo Semler: Introduced the term "recension" to describe groups of New Testament textual traditions.

Johann Jakob Griesbach: Classified the three groups of New Testament manuscripts as Alexandrian, Western, and Byzantine.

Karl Lachmann: Published the first eclectic text of the Greek New Testament based on the evaluation of variant readings.

Tischendorf:
Discovered and
published important
manuscripts from St.
Catherine's
monastery in Sinai.

**Caspar Rene
Gregory**: His
publication of
Tischendorf's Greek
New Testament
(1894) provides the
main source of
textual materials on
which scholars still
depend.

Westcott and Hort:
Their "genealogical
theory" divided the
manuscript evidence
for the Greek New
Testament into four
types: Syrian,
Western, Neutral,
and Alexandrian.

Lobegott Friedrich Constantin von **Tischendorf** (1815-1874) discovered and published some of the most important biblical manuscripts from St. Catherine's monastery in Sinai. Henry Alford (1810-1871) convincingly discredited the unworthy and pedantic reverence for the received text in his numerous commentaries; and Samuel Prideaux Tregelles (1813-1875) was instrumental in persuading English scholars to reject the textus receptus.

Several other scholars deserve mention in regard to their role in the development of textual criticism. **Caspar Rene Gregory** completed the last edition of Tischendorf's Greek New Testament in 1894 with a prolegomenon which provides the main source of textual materials on which scholars still depend, as well as the basis for the universally accepted catalogue of manuscripts. Brook Foss Westcott (1825-1901) and Fenton John Anthony Hort (1828-1892) rank with Tischendorf in importance for the publication of their two volume work, *The New Testament in the Original Greek* (1881-1882). This work was used by the revision committee which produced the English Revised New Testament in 1881.

The so-called "genealogical theory" of **Westcott and Hort** divided the manuscript evidence into four types: Syrian, Western, Neutral, and Alexandrian. The Syrian text type included the Antiochian and Byzantine texts. Though the Western text type for Westcott and Hort derives from the Syrian church, it flourished in the western Mediterranean. The Neutral text type was considered Egyptian in origin and included Codex Vaticanus and Codex Sinaiticus. The fourth text type of Westcott and Hort was Alexandrian and included a small number of texts from Egypt which were not of the Neutral type. Westcott and Hort claimed that both the Neutral and Alexandrian text types come from a common ancestor.

The period since 1881 is characterized by reaction against the theory of Westcott and Hort. The chief opponents of the new critical text were John W. Burgon (1813-1888) and F. H. A. Scrivener (1813-1891), who argued as follows: 1) the traditional text used by the Church for fifteen hundred years must be correct because of its duration; 2) the traditional text had hundreds of manuscripts in its favor; and 3) the traditional text is better because it is older. Hermann Freiherr von Soden (1852-1914) rejected the notion about the Syrian recension as well as the Syrian text.

The results of such scholarly criticism is seen in the current status of the Westcott and Hort theory, which reflects a reinvestigation of the textual materials at their disposal. The text types have been reclassified by von Soden and other critics in that the Syrian family has been renamed as Byzantine or Antiochian so as not to be confused with the Old Syriac version. There is also general recognition of more intermixture between the Alexandrian and Neutral text types, and both of these are now considered to be variations of the same family. In short, the Alexandrian designation includes the Neutral text. In regard to the Western text type, scholars now find three subgroups: Codex Bezae (D), Old Latin, and Old Syriac. Moreover, a new text type has been discovered since the death of Westcott, Hort, and von Soden: namely, the Caesarean, which lies midway between the Alexandrian and Western texts, or possibly closer to the Western.

The most recent collations of these text materials are now available in Eberhard Nestle's *Novum Testamentum Graece* and *The Greek New Testament* of the United Bible Societies, edited by K. Aland and others. Scholars rank the manuscript evidence in the following descending order of importance: Alexandrian, Caesarean, Western, and Byzantine. Since the textus receptus essentially follows the Byzantine text type, it is obvious that its authority is not highly regarded in the mainstream of Second Testament scholarship.

A new attempt to provide more adequate tools for doing textual criticism of the Second Testament by **Reuben J. Swanson** is in process of publication. The first volume of his "Variant Readings Arranged in Horizontal Line Against Codex Vaticanus" under the title *New Testament Manuscripts, Part I: Matthew* (William Carey International University, 1994), includes a Foreword by Bruce Metzger, Chairman of the New Revised Standard Version Translation Project. The four-volume set on the Gospels was released in 1995, with the book of Acts to follow. The format is superior to that of the more traditional approach in that the reader has immediate access to the variant readings in more than fifty of the most significant manuscripts at a glance for each word in the Greek New Testament. Swanson has selected Codex Vaticanus as the base text (line 1) to which the other texts are compared, including previous critical texts (textus receptus, Wescott-Hort, **Nestle-Aland**, and the United Bible Societies text). Scholars who are interested may reconstruct any of the individual manuscripts collated, making this work a most valuable reference source for the study of the history of the text of the Greek New Testament.

Reuben J. Swanson: His "Variant Readings Arranged in Horizontal Line Against Codex Vaticanus" provides the student with access to the full textual evidence at a glance.

Nestle-Aland: A critical-eclectic Greek text of the First Testament originally published in 1898 by Eberhard Nestle, which has been continually revised with Kurt Aland as the current editor. In wording it is identical with the 3rd edition of the United Bible Societies text but differs in paragraphing, orthography, and punctuation.

The arduous task of reconstructing the presumed original text of the Bible from thousands of manuscripts which contain tens of thousands of variant readings is perhaps best appreciated by examining just how textual critics go about doing their job. The most practical way to do this is to observe the results by comparing the differences between the Authorized Version (KJV) of 1611, which is based on the textus receptus, with the American Standard Version (ASV) of 1901, the Revised Standard Version (RSV) of 1946 and 1952, the New International Version (NIV) of 1978, or the New Revised Standard Version (NRSV) of 1989.

The text of Deut 32:8 provides an instructive example. The Masoretic Text, followed by the KJV and the ASV reads, "The Most High gave to the nations their inheritance . . . He set the bounds of the peoples according to the number of the children of Israel." The RSV and NRSV follow the LXX rendition: "According to the number of the sons [or angels] of God." A fragment from Qumran supports the LXX reading. According to the principles of textual criticism, the RSV and NRSV are correct because: 1) this is the more difficult reading; 2) the reading is supported by the earliest known manuscript; 3) the reading is in harmony with the patriarchal description of angels as "sons of God" (cf. Job 1:6; 2:1; 38:7, and possibly Gen 6:4); and 4) this reading explains the origin of the other variant.

Zech 12:10 provides a similar situation. The KJV and ASV follow the Masoretic Text: "They shall look upon me [God is speaking] whom they have pierced." The RSV and the NIV follow the Theodotion version in rendering it, "When they look on him whom they have pierced." In this instance, the Masoretic Text preserves the preferred reading because it: 1) is based on the earlier and better manuscripts; 2) is the more difficult reading; and 3) can explain the other reading as theological prejudice against the deity of Christ or the influence of the Second Testament change from the first to the third person in its quotation of this passage (cf. John 19:37).

1 John 5:7 of KJV is omitted in the ASV, RSV, and NRSV. The NIV provides a note which indicates that the reference to the individual members of the Trinity here is not found in any Greek manuscript before the sixteenth century. There is virtually no textual support for the KJV reading among the Greek manuscripts, although there is ample support in the Vulgate. When Erasmus was challenged as to why he did not

include the verse in his Greek New Testament of 1516 and 1519, he hastily responded that he would insert it if anyone found even one manuscript to support it. When one sixteenth century Greek minuscule was produced to support it, the 1520 manuscript of the Franciscan friar Froy, Erasmus complied and included the verse in his 1522 edition. The KJV followed Erasmus's Greek text. In this case, the inclusion of the verse as genuine violates almost every major canon of textual criticism.

By way of summary, it should be clear that textual critics have at their disposal a series of rules, which for all practical purposes enable them to restore the exact text of the Hebrew and Greek in both testaments. The Bible is the best preserved book to survive from antiquity, with variant readings of any significance amounting to less than one half of one percent of the text, none of which affect any basic doctrine of faith.

Thinking Exercise

On the Development of Textual Criticism

The critical thinking goal for this exercise is to clarify the concept and development of textual criticism.

How To Do This Exercise

Textual criticism is essentially the gathering of textual materials and their systematic collection and comparison in an attempt to reconstruct the original text of the Bible. Review the concepts and key words as they appear above in Section D, "The Development of Textual Criticism." Then answer the following questions:

1. What happened between the time of Jesus and the invention of the printing press that made the establishment of a critical text of the Bible necessary?

_____

_____

_____

2. What makes textual criticism in the modern era different from what Origen attempted for the Septuagint in the 3rd century CE)?

_____

_____

_____

3. Textual criticism of the Hebrew Bible today is based on a critical edition of one of the most trustworthy manuscripts from antiquity, namely that of the Leningrad Codex (1008 CE); whereas the standard critical edition of the Greek New Testament is eclectic in nature. Is either of these two models of greater intrinsic worth for doing textual criticism?

_____

_____

_____

E. A Brief History of the English Bible[12]

1. Partial Translations of the Bible into English (450-1350)

In some respects the early history of the transmission of the Bible in English translation resembles that of the canonical process itself in ancient Israel; for, at first, the Bible was known only in aural and visual form—as experienced within the context of public worship. The story begins with **Caedmon** (d. ca. 680), as recorded in Bede's *Ecclesiastical History*. This relatively simple laborer in the monastery at Whitby in Yorkshire, Northumbria, is said to have left a party one night for fear that he might be called upon to sing. Later that night he dreamed that an angel commanded him to sing songs about God's creation, which he then produced. Other songs followed as Caedmon began to paraphrase in song the full story of Genesis, Israel's Exodus from slavery in Egypt, and on to the Second Testament account of the incarnation, passion, resurrection, and ascension of Jesus, the coming of the Holy Spirit, the teachings of the apostles, and the growth of the early Christian Church. His works became the popularized people's Bible of that day and were memorized and disseminated widely throughout the land.

Shortly after 700, **Aldhelm** (640-709), the first bishop of Sherborne in Dorset, translated the Psalms into Old English. This was technically the first true formal translation of any actual portion of the Bible into Old English. **Egbert** of Northumbria, the archbishop of York and teacher of Alcuin, translated the Gospels into Old English about 705. He was subsequently summoned by Charlemagne to establish a school at the royal court of Aix-la-Chapelle (Aachen).

The Venerable Bede (674-735), the most eminent scholar in England and one of the greatest in all Europe at that time, wrote his *Ecclesiastical History* at Jarrow-on-the-Tyne in Northumbria. His other works include a translation of the Gospel of John, perhaps to supplement the earlier work of Egbert. According to tradition, Bede completed this translation at the very hour of his death in 735.

Besides being king of England (870-735), Alfred the Great was a scholar of the first rank. It was during his reign that the so-called Danelaw was established under the Treaty of Wedmore (878), in which the entire populace was ordered to submit to Christian baptism and

Caedmon: Popularized the Bible in musical form in 7th century England (Northumbria).

Aldhelm: His translation of the Psalms was the first true formal translation of any portion of the Bible into Old English (ca. 700 CE).

Egbert: Translated the Gospels into Old English (705 CE).

loyalty to the king. Alfred translated Bede's *Ecclesiastical History* from Latin into Anglo-Saxon. He also translated the Ten Commandments, portions of Exodus 21-23, Acts 15:23-29, and a negative form of the Golden Rule.

Aldred: Translated the Gospels into Northumbrian (ca. 950).

Sometime around 950, a scholar by the name of **Aldred** wrote a Northumbrian translation of the Gospels between the lines of a late seventh-century Latin manuscript. It was from this Latin copy of Eadfrid, bishop of Lindisfarne (698-721), that Aldred's work received its name, the *Lindisfarne Gospels*. A generation or so later, the Irish scholar MacRegol produced a similar text known as the *Rushworth Gospels*.

Aelfric: Translated portions of both testaments from Latin into the dialect of Wessex (ca. 1000).

Aelfric, bishop of Eynsham in Oxfordshire, translated portions of the first seven books of the First Testament from Latin into the dialect of Wessex around the year 1000. These texts, along with other portions of the Bible which he translated and cited in his homilies, were intended to supplement the so-called *Wessex Gospels*, which had been translated before Aelfric's time.

The period of Saxon domination in England came to an end with the Norman Conquest of 1066, which introduced a period of Norman-French influence on the language of the people. This political and social reality is reflected in the attempts made to translate the Bible. Around the year 1200, an Augustinian monk by the name of **Orm** wrote a poetic paraphrase of the Gospels and Acts, accompanied by a commentary. This work, known as the *Ormulum*, is preserved in a single manuscript in which the language is Teutonic, but the cadence and syntax reflects Norman influence.

Orm: An Augustinian monk (ca. 1200), who wrote a poetic paraphrase of the Gospels and Acts in Teutonic.

William of Shoreham is credited by some with writing the first prose translation of a portion of the Bible into a southern dialect of English in the year 1320. Richard Rolle (ca. 1320-1340), the "Hermit of Hampole," translated the Psalms from the Latin Vulgate into the North English dialect. This work was widely known in its time.

Concept Check # 40

How do you account for the fact that the earliest "translations" of the Bible into English were in poetic form and sometimes set to music? (Check your answer on p. 224.)

2. Complete Translations and Revisions in English (1350-1611)

John Wycliffe (ca. 1320-1384), "the Morning Star of the Reformation," represents the dawn of a new era in Bible translation. A contemporary of Geoffrey Chaucer and John of Gaunt, Wycliffe lived during the so-called Babylonian Captivity in the Roman Catholic Church and found himself in the limelight as an opponent of the papacy. Casting aside scholastic Latin as a vehicle for communicating the Scriptures to the English people, Wycliffe organized an order of itinerant preachers called the Lollards (the "poor priests") who traveled about preaching, reading, and teaching the English Bible. To aid them in this task, a new translation was needed. Wycliffe completed the New Testament in 1380 and the Old Testament in 1388. Although the complete translation is generally credited to Wycliffe, it was actually finished after his death by Nicholas of Hereford.

The Wycliffe translation was made from contemporary manuscripts of the Latin Vulgate. Though the textual base on which the translation was based was generally of poor quality, the work itself introduced a new epoch in the history of Bible translation. This is due to the simple fact that the translators determined to use the simplest and most common language, which, at the same time, would also be as much like the Latin as possible, so that those who knew no Latin might by the English come to learn many Latin words.

John Purvey (ca. 1354-1428), Wycliffe's secretary, is credited with making a revision of the earlier Wycliffe Bible in 1395. Though this revision is commonly known as the Later Wycliffe Version, the term *version* does not strictly apply. Purvey's revision replaced many latinized constructions with native English idiom. It also replaced Jerome's preface with one written by Purvey, which contributed to the weakening influence of the papacy in England. It should be noted that the Wycliffe Bible was produced, revised, and circulated prior to the work of John Hus (ca. 1369-1415) on the Continent in Bohemia. It was also done before the invention of the printing press by Johann Gutenberg (ca. 1454). The technology of modern printing was introduced in England by William Claxton in 1476, which set the stage for a new era in the transmission of the English Bible; for by the year 1500, there were already more than eighty editions of the Latin Bible published in Europe.

John Wycliffe: Translated the entire Bible into English for his itinerant preachers ("Lollards") from the Latin Vulgate (1380-1388).

John Purvey: Revised Wycliffe's Bible by replacing many latinized constructions with native English idiom and removing the preface by Jerome.

William Tyndale:
Translated the Bible into English against severe opposition which cost him his life; he was executed for heresy on October 6, 1536.

Miles Coverdale:
Tyndale's assistant, produced the first complete English Bible in 1535.

Thomas Matthew (Matthew's Bible):
Pen name of John Rogers, who published the second licensed English Bible in circulation within a year of Tyndale's execution.

William Tyndale (ca. 1492-1536) took up the task of translating the Bible in England. Following unsuccessful attempts in his home country, Tyndale set sail for the Continent in 1524 where he finally printed his English translation of the Second Testament in Cologne in late February 1526. This was followed by the printing of Tyndale's translation of the Pentateuch at Marburg (1530) and of Jonah at Antwerp (1531). Because of his use of the works of Wycliffe and Luther, Tyndale was under constant threat for his very life such that his translations of the Bible had to be smuggled into England. Copies of these texts were purchased by Cuthbert Tunstall, bishop of London, who had them burned publicly. Even Sir Thomas More (1478-1535), the Lord Chancellor of England under Henry VIII and author of the *Utopia*, openly attacked Tyndale's translation as the product of some "pestilent sect," like that of Luther's German translation. In 1534, Tyndale began his work on a revision of the Second Testament. Shortly after completing this revision, he was forcibly removed from Antwerp and taken to a fortress at Vilvorde in Flanders, where he continued his work on translating the First Testament. In August, 1536, he was tried and found guilty of heresy, defrocked from his priestly office, and turned over to the secular authorities for execution. At the moment of his execution on October 6, Tyndale cried out, "Lord, open the King of England's eyes." That prayer was answered within a year.

Miles Coverdale (1488-1569), Tyndale's assistant and proofreader at Antwerp, was instrumental in producing the first complete English Bible in 1535. Coverdale introduced chapter summaries and set the precedent for separating the First Testament from the Apocrypha. Coverdale's translation was reprinted twice in 1537, again in 1550, and once more in 1553. Nonetheless, the true successor to the 1535 edition was the so-called *Great Bible* of 1539.

John Rogers (ca. 1500-1555), another assistant of Tyndale and the first martyr of the persecutions of Mary Tudor, took up the pen name of **Thomas Matthew** and published another English Bible in 1537 which combined the First Testament texts of Tyndale and Coverdale with the 1535 revision of Tyndale's New Testament. In 1549, a slightly revised edition appeared; and in 1551, a Bible was published under the designation "Matthew's" on the title page, which contained Taverner's Old Testament and the 1548 edition of Tyndale's New Testament. John Rogers added copious notes and references to the work of Tyndale and

Coverdale, and borrowed heavily from the French editions of Lefevre (1534) and Olivetan (1535). His 1537 edition was published with the approval of Henry VIII and took its place as the second licensed English Bible in circulation within a year of Tyndale's execution.

Richard Taverner (1505-1575) published a revision of Matthew's Bible in 1539 which made better use of the Greek article. His work, however, was soon surpassed by still another revision of Matthew's Bible, the so-called *Great Bible* of 1539. Thomas Cromwell (ca. 1485-1540), Protestant Lord Chancellor under Henry VIII, was authorized to produce a translation of the Bible without the prologues and notes of Coverdale and Matthew which had offended many. With further approval by Thomas Cranmer (1489-1556), the first Protestant archbishop of Canterbury, Miles Coverdale prepared a new text which used the work of others in preference to his own recently published work. The result was the *Great Bible* of 1539, which received its name because of its great size and format—it was larger than any previous edition and richly adorned. Its title page was a fine woodcut attributed to Hans Holbein, which shows Henry VIII, Cranmer, and Cromwell distributing Bibles to the people who in response cry out, "Vivat rex" and "God save the King." The Apocrypha was removed from the text of the First Testament and placed in an appendix titled "hagiographa" (holy writings). It should be remembered that most of the bishops of the church in England at this time were still Roman Catholic. Consequently, although the *Great Bible* was authorized to be read in the churches in 1538, it remained controversial and was challenged as being neither a version nor a revision of a version, but rather a revision of a revision.

Great Bible: A revision of Matthew's Bible in 1539 published with the approval of Cromwell and Cranmer, which received its name from its great size and format.

A second edition of the *Great Bible* was published in April 1540, which was called Cranmer's because it contained a preface by Thomas Cranmer, then archbishop of Canterbury. This was followed by five other editions before the end of 1541. The preface of Cranmer's Bible includes this statement: "This is the Byble apoynted to the use of the churches." In the third and fifth of the six editions of Cranmer's Bible, a note was included on the title page that Bishops Tunstall and Heath had "overseen and perused" the work. The irony is that Tunstall, as bishop of London, had condemned Tyndale and his work five years earlier.

During the persecutions of Mary Tudor (1553-1558), many reformers in England fled to the Continent for safety. Among these were Miles

Coverdale and John Knox (ca. 1513-1572) who joined a group of scholars in Geneva. In 1557, **William Whittingham**, a member of that group and a brother-in-law of John Calvin, published a revision of the Second Testament which marked the first time the English text was divided into modern verses, following the example of the 1551 Greek New Testament of Stephanus and earlier Latin and Hebrew editions of the Bible. Italics were also introduced to indicate where English idiom required a departure from a literal translation of the original text. Shortly after this New Testament was published, work began on a careful revision of the entire English Bible. In 1560, the long and eventful history of the *Geneva Bible* began; and by 1644, this work had gone through 140 editions. Its popularity withstood the challenge of both the *Bishops' Bible* (1568) and the first generation of the authorized King James Version (1611). Its text is repeatedly quoted in Shakespeare's plays, it was used extensively by the Puritans, and was even used in the address from "The Translators to the Readers" in the 1611 translation authorized by King James.

Though the *Geneva Bible* was not sponsored by the established church in England, it quickly became the household Bible of the realm. Its success prompted officials in the church to produce an authorized version. This work was taken up by a group of scholars which included eight bishops, hence the name the *Bishops' Bible* which was published in 1568 in London, "cum privilegio regiae majestatis." The pages of the New Testament were on thicker paper than the Old Testament in order to survive greater wear. It contained the preface by Cranmer and another by Matthew Parker, then archbishop of Canterbury. From 1568 to 1611, this compromise translation was used widely in the churches throughout England. Nonetheless, the *Geneva Bible* retained its prominence in the homes of the English people. The *Bishops' Bible* was the basis for the famous Authorized King James revision of 1611.

Concept Check # 41

What single characteristic distinguishes the process of Bible translation in England from the work of John Wycliffe (14th century) to the *Bishops' Bible* of 1568? (Check your answer on p. 224.)

3. The Rheims-Douay Bible (1582-1635)

After the death of the Roman Catholic queen Mary Tudor in 1558, Elizabeth I ascended the throne as a Protestant and the picture was quickly reversed. Now Roman Catholic exiles on the Continent took up the task of vernacular translation of the Bible for use in England to compete with the Protestant Bibles. In 1568, a group of these scholars founded the English College at Douay in Flanders where they sought to train leaders of the church who would preserve their Catholic faith in England under the leadership of William Allen (1532-1594). The college was moved to Rheims in 1578, where it came under the direction of Richard Bristow (1538-1581), who had gone to Douay in 1569. Meanwhile, Allen was called to Rome, where he founded another English College and became cardinal before returning to Douay in 1593.

The task of translating the Latin Vulgate into English at the college in Douay was taken up by Gregory Martin (d. 1582), Richard Bristow, and William Allen. Martin worked on the translation of the Old Testament until his death in 1582. Shortly before Martin's death, the New Testament was published with notations by Bristow and Allen. This so-called **Rheims New Testament** translation (1582) was intended for use in England in place of the existing Protestant translations. It was a relatively poor rendition of the text, however, and was based on the Latin Vulgate rather than the original Greek New Testament. In the copious notes they included, the translators made no secret of the fact that theirs was a polemical work. The Rheims New Testament was republished in 1600, 1621, and 1633. Meanwhile, the publication of the Douay Old Testament was delayed until 1609, in spite of the fact that it was actually translated earlier than the Rheims New Testament of 1582. A second edition of this translation of the First Testament appeared in the **Rheims-Douay Bible** of 1635. The Rheims New Testament was in circulation long enough to have its influence on the English Bible translators of 1611. The Douay Old Testament, however, was not published in time to influence the work of those scholars. With a Protestant queen on the throne in England who was succeeded by a Protestant king, the Rheims-Douay Bible had little possibility of success in competition with the Protestant translations already available. The second revised edition of the Rheims-Douay Bible did not appear until 1749-1750, under Richard Challoner, bishop of London.

Rheims New Testament: A Roman Catholic translation of the Second Testament into English from the Latin Vulgate (1582).

Rheims-Douay Bible: A Roman Catholic English Bible translated from the Latin Vulgate (1635).

Concept Check # 42

How did the Protestant Reformation complicate the process of Bible translation in England? (Check your answer on p. 224.)

4. The Authorized King James Bible (1611)

In January, 1604, James I was summoned to the Hampton Court Conference in response to the so-called Millenary Petition in which nearly one thousand Puritan leaders had signed a long list of grievances against the Church of England. James I treated the Puritans with rudeness at first, until John Reynolds, Puritan President of Corpus Christi College in Oxford, proposed an authorized version of the English Bible for all parties concerned. The king favored the proposal because it provided the opportunity for him to win personal support among the English people by replacing both the *Geneva Bible* and the *Bishops' Bible*. Six groups of scholars were chosen for the task: two at Cambridge to work on 1 Chronicles through Ecclesiastes and the Apocrypha; two at Oxford to work on Isaiah through Malachi, the Gospels, Acts, and the Apocalypse; and two at Westminster to work on Genesis through 2 Kings and Romans through Jude. The fifty-four men chosen for this task were instructed to follow the text of the *Bishops' Bible* unless they found that the translations of Tyndale, Matthew, Coverdale, Whitchurche, and Geneva agreed more with the original. Since the 1516 and 1522 editions of Erasmus's Greek New Testament provided their base text, the interpolation of 1 John 5:7 was included. Moreover, the translators made no use of a number of superior texts which had come to light since Erasmus completed his work; and, of course, they did not have access to some of the most important of the great uncial manuscripts such as Codex Alexandrinus, which reached England in 1621, and Codex Sinaiticus, which did not come to light until 1844. The decision to use the *Bishops' Bible* as their base text also meant that many of the old ecclesiastical words were retained.

No marginal notes were added to the revision of 1611 which came to be known as the **King James Version**. Nonetheless, it should be noted that this work was never actually authorized so far as the Puritans and others in the Church of England were concerned, nor was it a version. It simply replaced the Bishops' Bible in the churches of England because no editions of that older work were published after 1606. The decision

King James Version: The revision of the English Bible done under the auspices of King James I (1611) which replaced the *Bishops' Bible* in official circles and eventually displaced the *Geneva Bible* in popular usage.

to use the format of the *Geneva Bible* gave the 1611 publication further impetus for general acceptance and eventual replacement of its chief rival. Three editions of the Authorized (King James) Version appeared in 1611 and its growing popularity continued to call for new printings. During the reign of Charles I (1625-1649), the so-called Long Parliament called for further revision of the Authorized Version or a new translation altogether. Nonetheless, only minor revisions were introduced in 1629, 1653, 1701, 1762, 1769, and two later editions. The revisions introduced by Dr. Blayney of Oxford in the eighteenth century included some 75,000 minor departures from the 1611 edition. Slight changes continued to appear as recently as 1967, in the text which accompanied the New Scofield Reference Edition.

In 1975, an international group of 130 scholars, editors, and religious leaders launched a project which culminated in the publication of a more thorough revision, the *New King James Bible* in 1982 in the United States. The project was initiated and sponsored by Thomas Nelson, Inc., under the leadership of its president, Sam Moore.

The continuing vitality of the King James Version of the Bible is evident from still other efforts. In 1990, Jay P. Green published what is called the *Modern King James Version*; and in 1991, a translation of the New Testament appeared, along with Psalms, Proverbs, and Ecclesiastes, which was labeled as volume one of the *21st Century King James Bible*.

> ### Concept Check # 43
> How do you account for the lasting popularity of the Authorized King James Version of the English Bible? (Check your answer on p. 224.)

5. Roman Catholic Translations and Versions (1635-1970)

The Rheims-Douay Bible began slowly but gradually made its way to dominance by 1635. Richard Challoner published a second revised edition of this work in 1749-1750, which came to be known as the **Rheims-Douay-Challoner Bible**. This work made use of the 1718 translation of the Vulgate New Testament by Cornelius Nary and the revised edition of the Rheims New Testament by Robert Witham in 1730.

Rheims-Douay-Challaner Bible: The second revised edition of the Roman Catholic Rheims-Douay Bible (1749-50) published by Richard Challoner.

Challoner's Bible, which went through further revisions and editions, dominated the field for two hundred years. The first Roman Catholic Bible published in the United States (1790) was an edition of the Douay Old Testament and the Rheims-Challoner New Testament, which also was the first quarto Bible of any kind published in North America. Francis Patrick Kenrick produced a revision of the Challoner Bible in six volumes (1849-1860).

In 1936, a revision of the Rheims-Challoner New Testament was sponsored by the Episcopal Committee of the Confraternity of Christian Doctrine. The *Confraternity Bible* was the work of a committee of twenty-eight scholars under the direction of Edward P. Arbez using the Latin Vulgate text as its basis, but with use of recent developments in biblical scholarship. The Confraternity New Testament appeared in 1941. The Old Testament eventually followed in 1967, but with a most important change in procedure. The encyclical of Pope Pius XII known as *Divino Afflante Spiritu* appeared in 1943, which stated that translations of the Bible could be based on the original Hebrew and Greek texts rather than merely on the Latin Vulgate. This was a historic departure from earlier tradition; for Pope Pius IX had condemned Bible societies as pestilent sects in his famous *Syllabus of Errors* (1864). Before 1943, all official Roman Catholic translations of the Bible were based on the Latin Vulgate. In 1955, the Roman hierarchy gave its official sanction to the translation of Monsignor John Knox, who based his work on the Sixto-Clementine Vulgate text of 1592. This translation, the *Confraternity Bible*, became the official Roman Catholic Bible in Great Britain.

When the restrictions of World War II were lifted, the Confraternity did what had not been done for more than 1500 years. They published a translation of the First Testament from the original Hebrew; and work was begun under the direction of Louis F. Hartman on a similar version of the Second Testament. In 1970, **the New American Bible** was published, which was based on the most recent developments of textual criticism and was translated directly from the Hebrew and Greek texts. The translation committee was made up of fifty-nine Catholic and five Protestant scholars who were members of the Catholic Biblical Association of America. The translation of the books of Samuel in this edition was done by Professor Frank Cross, a Protestant scholar at Harvard University, and was first published in 1969 in *The Holy Bible: Translated from the Original Languages with Critical Use of All the Ancient*

Confraternity Bible: A Roman Catholic revision of the the Rheims-Douay-Challoner Bible (1967) sponsored by the Episcopal Committee of the Confraternity of Christian Doctrine.

New American Bible (NAB): A Roman Catholic translation of the Bible directly from the Hebrew and Greek texts (1970) done by members of the Catholic Biblical Association of America.

Sources by Members of the Catholic Biblical Association in America. The "Textual Notes" in this volume remain the handiest access to a critical English translation of the books of Samuel, which in many respects is closer to the Old Palestinian textual tradition as preserved in the manuscript from the Dead Sea Scrolls known as 4QSam^a and the early Lucianic recension of the Septuagint (LXX) than it is to the received masoretic tradition.

Concept Check # 44

What is the single most important development within Roman Catholic tradition in the twentieth century so far as the translation of the Bible is concerned? (Check your answer on p. 225.)

---

6. Official Protestant Revisions from 1611 to 1970

When the *Authorized King James Bible* appeared in 1611, none of the great manuscripts had been discovered other than Codex Bezae (D), which was used very little by those scholars. With these new discoveries, came attempts to revise the work accordingly. All of the revisions of the King James Bible for more than two hundred years were made without official ecclesiastical or royal authorization. In fact, no official revision took place for over a century after the work of Dr. Blayney (1769). Some of the revisions that were published were ill-advised, like the additions of Ussher's chronology. Nonetheless, there were exemplary attempts at unofficial revision, like the anonymous edition of *The Holy Bible Containing the Authorized Version of the Old and New Testaments with Many Emendations* (1841). In the preface to this work, the author states explicitly that he made use of manuscripts not available in 1611.

The first official revision was that of R. L. Clark, Alfred Goodwin, and W. Sanday who published *The Variorum Edition of the New Testament of Our Lord and Saviour Jesus Christ* (1880), which was done at "his majesty's special command." The **Variorum Bible** followed the tradition of Tyndale, Coverdale, Great, Geneva, Bishops', and the editions of the King James Bible and prepared the way for the English Revised Bible.

Variorum Bible: The first official revision of the New Testament of the Authorized King James Bible (1880), which prepared the way for the English Revised Bible.

The growing desire for an official revision of the Authorized Bible led to the convocation of the Province of Canterbury in 1870, in which Samuel Wilberforce, bishop of Winchester, proposed a revision of the Second Testament where Greek texts revealed inaccurate or incorrect translations in the King James text. Bishop Ollivant followed with a motion to include the First Testament and Hebrew texts in the project. Two groups of scholars were appointed, which was subsequently enlarged to include some sixty-five revisers from various denominations. They began their work in 1871 and were joined in 1872 by a group of American scholars. The Old Testament was released in 1885, the Apocrypha in 1896 (1898 in the United States), and the entire Bible was published in 1898. More than three million copies were sold in less than a year. Some of the renderings of this **English Revised Bible** were not accepted by the American revision committee. In 1901, *The American Standard Edition of the Revised Version* was published. Further revisions were made, such as the change from *Lord* to *Jehovah* and *Holy Ghost* to *Holy Spirit.* Paragraph structures were revised and shortened, and page headings were added. Slowly this **American Standard Version** (ASV) won acceptance in the United States and remains the preferred translation in some circles. Though the ASV lacks much of the beauty of the King James Bible, its more accurate readings have made it popular among teachers and students of the Bible.

Like the earlier translations which were built on the foundation of William Tyndale, the ASV was the work of many hands over generations of time. In 1928, the copyright passed from Thomas Nelson and Sons to the International Council of Religious Education (an association of the educational boards of forty major Protestant denominations), which took up the task of a new revision in 1937, designed to utilize the great advances in continued biblical scholarship. The revision committee was made up of thirty-two outstanding scholars who were to follow the ASV unless two-thirds of the committee agreed to change the reading. They decided to make use of simpler and more current forms of pronouns except in reference to God, and to utilize more direct word order. Delayed by World War II (1939-1945), the New Testament did not appear until 1946, with the Old Testament following in 1952 and the Apocrypha in 1957. The completed work, known as the **Revised Standard Version** (RSV), was launched with a tremendous publicity campaign which unfortunately resulted in a backlash of critical opposition in some circles. The RSV was accused of blurring traditional messianic passages in the First Testament, such as the substitution of "young woman" for "virgin" in Isa 7:14. All of the criticism notwithstanding, the RSV provided the English-speaking Church with an up-to-date revision of the Bible based on the "critical text."

English Revised Bible (ERB): An authorized revision of the English Bible (1885) to which the Apocrypha was added in 1898.

American Standard Version (ASV): The American version of the English Revised Bible (1901).

Revised Standard Version (RSV): A revision of the American Standard Version (1957), which subsequently became the first truly Common Bible when it was officially sanctioned by the Roman Catholic Church (1973) and the Orthodox Churches (1977).

A revision of the American Standard Version was attempted in the 1960s under the auspices of the Lockman Foundation (founded in 1942). The New Testament appeared in 1963 followed by the Old Testament in 1970. **The New American Standard Bible** (NASB) attempted to renew the American Standard Version, the "rock of biblical honesty." Recognizing that the ASV was clearly a monument of the best scholarship in the English-speaking world of the latter half of the nineteenth century, the Lockman Foundation sought "to rescue this noble achievement from what appeared to be an inevitable demise, to preserve it, as a heritage for coming generations, and to do so in such a form as the demands of passing time dictate." The product of their efforts, the NASB, represents a conservative and literal approach to the translation of the Bible which failed to reach its stated goal of putting the Scriptures in "a fluent and readable style according to current English usage." It retains the value of the original ASV as a useful study Bible.

New American Standard Bible (NASB): A revision of the American Standard Version (1970), under the auspices of the Lockman Foundation.

Concept Check # 45

What is the lasting value of the American Standard Version (ASV)? (Check your answer on p. 225.)

7. Jewish Translations and Versions (1789-1990)

As early as the third century BCE, Jews found it necessary to translate the Hebrew Bible into vernacular Greek in Alexandria. Their translation of most of the First Testament into Aramaic also testifies to the fact that the Jewish people were not always able to study the Scriptures in the Hebrew language. Throughout the Middle Ages, the conditions under which Jews lived were not conducive to scholarship in general. Nonetheless, by about 1400, they had begun to make new translations of the Hebrew Bible into various languages. It was not for another four hundred years, however, before Jews began to translate the Hebrew Bible into English.

In 1789, a Jewish version of the Pentateuch appeared in English that claimed to be an "emendation" of the King James Bible. In 1839, a somewhat similar work was published by Salid Neuman. Between 1851 and 1856, Rabbi Abraham Benisch produced the first complete Bible (the First Testament) for English-speaking Jewry. And finally, in 1884,

The Hebrew Bible (Leeser): The first Jewish translation of the Hebrew Bible for American Jewry, by Isaac Leeser (1853).

The Holy Scriptures (1917): An English translation of the Hebrew Bible published by the Jewish Publication Society, which parallels the American Standard Version.

Tanakh: The Holy Scriptures (1985): An English translation of the Hebrew Bible by the Jewish Publication Society, sparked by the Revised Standard Version and the New English Bible.

Michael Friedländer made a further attempt to "emend" the King James Bible for use by Jews in what was called "A Jewish Family Bible."

In 1853, Isaac Leeser of Philadelphia produced the first Jewish translation for American Jewry in his version of *The Hebrew Bible*, which enjoyed popularity in British and American synagogues for more than a generation as the standard Bible for English-speaking Jews in America. The Jewish Bible Society (founded in 1888) decided to revise Leeser's translation at their second biennial convention in 1892. As work proceeded, it soon became evident that an entirely new translation was needed. The Jewish Publication Society subsequently published its version of the Hebrew Bible in 1917, *The Holy Scriptures According to the Masoretic Text, A New Translation*, a work modeled after the classic style of the King James Version which closely paralleled the American Standard Version (1901).

Following the release of the Revised Standard Version and activity in England toward the publication of the New English Bible, the Jewish Publication Society began to publish a new translation of the Hebrew Bible at their annual meeting in 1953. Harry M. Orlinsky served as editor-in-chief of the project, along with H. L. Ginsberg and Ephraim A. Speiser as fellow editors. *The Torah: A New Translation of the Holy Scripture According to the Masoretic Text* appeared in 1962, followed by *The Five Megilloth and Jonah* (1969), *The Prophets* (1978), and *The Writings* (1982). These volumes, with revisions, were combined in a single volume under the title *Tanakh: The Holy Scriptures. The New JPS Trans- lation of the Traditional Hebrew Text* (1985), a work which popularly acclaimed to be "The Standard Jewish Bible for the English-speaking world." This work is not a revision of any other version, Jewish or Christian. It is a completely fresh translation of the traditional Hebrew text in living, up-to-date, and highly readable English. The goal of the translators was to provide a translation which carried the same message in the modern setting to that of the original in the world of ancient times. It is not a mechanical, word-by-word translation like that of the 1917 version, but rather a conscious attempt to break away from the traditional English translations with a version in contemporary idiomatic English. It is winning a hearing among Christians as well as Jews.

Aryeh Kaplan translated the Torah and Haftaroth readings for synagogue use in an English and Hebrew edition, which appeared as *The Living Torah* in 1981. His translation was designed to bring the Torah to life in simple, clear, and modern language. It includes extensive notes and a comprehensive index.

Hugh J. Schonfield, a distinguished Jewish scholar, attempted to reconstruct what he called the "authentic" New Testament Jewish atmosphere for Gentile readers in *The Authentic New Testament* (1955). *The Jewish New Testament* (1989) was written by David Stern, a Messianic Jew who lives in Jerusalem, to express the "original and essential Jewishness" of the New Testament. The translation was based on the United Bible Societies' 3rd edition of the Greek text, and tends toward the "dynamic equivalence" method of translating. The translation of the Second Testament by Heinz Cassirer, *God's New Covenant*, also appeared in 1989. This work by a Jewish Christian was based on the Greek editions of Nestle and the United Bible Societies with the goal of displaying "attentiveness to Jewish sensibilities."

Concept Check # 46

How do you explain the fact that English-speaking Jews did not produce an independent translation of the Hebrew Bible until well into the 20th century? (Check your answer on p. 225.)

---

8. The Revised Standard Version Becomes a Common Bible (1973)

In 1965, *The New Testament: Revised Standard Version Catholic Edition* marked a milestone in the English translation of the Bible. With about twenty-four basic changes (listed in an appendix) and the addition of notes, the RSV was officially approved for use by Roman Catholics. The age of ecumenical translations and versions of the Bible had begun.

In 1969, the RSV Committee was extended to include six Roman Catholic scholars, two of which were to represent Great Britain and one from Canada. In 1972 a representative from the Greek Orthodox Church was added to the committee which led to the publication of the *RSV Common Bible with the Aprocrypha* in 1973, which appeared during the "Week of Prayer for Christian Unity" in England (in February) and during Lent in the United States.

To include other Eastern Orthodox churches (Russian, Ukrainian, Bulgarian, and Armenian) three other additions were made to the

Apocrypha and Deuterocanonical works, namely 3 and 4 Maccabees and Psalm 151. In 1977, an expanded edition appeared which contained these three additional texts which are accepted by Eastern Orthodox communions. The RSV thus gained the distinction of being officially authorized for use by all major Christian churches: Protestant, Anglican, Roman Catholic, and Eastern Orthodox.

New Revised Standard Version (NRSV): A revision of the Revised Standard Version (1989).

The Revised Standard Version Bible Committee is a continuing body, made up of about thirty members. The committee includes several Roman Catholics, an Eastern Orthodox member, and a Jewish member—along with others from various Protestant denominations. This committee issued a second edition of the RSV New Testament in 1971, and in 1974 authorized the preparation of a revision of the entire RSV Bible which was published in 1989 as the **New Revised Standard Version** (NRSV) under the leadership of Bruce M. Metzger. The NRSV attempts to correct linguistic sexism arising from the inherent bias of the English language towards the masculine gender, a bias that in the case of the Bible has often restricted or obscured the meaning of the original text. At the same time, this new version seeks to preserve all that is best in the English Bible as it has been known and used through the years.

A condensation of the RSV was published in 1982 as *The Reader's Digest Bible.* Bruce Metzger served as General Editor of the project which resulted in a reduction of the biblical text by forty percent. A somewhat similar work was done earlier by Charles Kent, with the help of four other editors, who produced *The Shorter Bible* (1921)—an abridgement of the ASV which omitted two-thirds of the Old Testament and one-third of the New Testament. *The Dartmouth Bible* (1950) is an abridgement of the King James Version which omitted about one-half of the total text. That work was done under the auspices of Dartmouth College for student needs.

> ## Concept Check # 47
> What distinguishes the Revised Standard Version (RSV) from all other English translations of the Bible in modern times? (Check your answer on p. 225.)

9. Official English Versions from 1970 to 1990

Not convinced that the Revised Standard Version was in fact a continuation of the long-established tradition of earlier English Bible translations, the General Assembly of the Church of Scotland met in 1946 to consider a new official translation. A joint committee was appointed in 1947 with three groups of scholars chosen for the task: one for the Old Testament, one for the New Testament, and one for the Apocrypha. The project was under the direction of C. H. Dodd. The New Testament of **The New English Bible** (NEB) appeared in 1961, followed by the Old Testament and Apocrypha in 1970. The aim here was to present a genuinely English idiom which would be "timeless," one in which the language was plain enough to convey its meaning without being bald or pedestrian. The hope was to produce a translation which would become a second authoritative version alongside the King James Bible. More than four million copies of the NEB were sold during its first year of publication. The NEB has been criticized for its anglicisms and its concentration on intelligibility over literalness of meaning, as well as its critical rearrangement of some sections of the First Testament. In 1974, the Joint Committee of the Churches of England set in motion what was to be become a major revision of the NEB, which appeared in 1989 as the **Revised English Bible** (REB).

The American Bible Society published its *Good News for Modern Man* (1966), which is also known as **Today's English Version** (TEV). Within two years, over ten million copies were sold, and some thirty-five million copies within the first six years of its existence. Its popularity continues in editions under several different titles. The translation was prepared by Robert Bratcher, who submitted his work for suggestions and approval to translation consultants of the American Bible Society, and to the Translation Department of the British and Foreign Bible Society. The popularity of this readable work was enhanced by the addition of a series of more than six hundred artistic line drawings by the French artist Annie Vallotton.

Another translation project was taken up by the New York Bible Society which was published under the title, *The Holy Bible: New International Version* (NIV), which was published in 1978. The project included more than a hundred scholars who worked directly from the best available Hebrew, Aramaic, and Greek texts. The project began in 1965, after several years of deliberation on the part of committees from the

New English Bible (NEB): A translation of the Bible from the original languages (1970), by the Church of Scotland, which was intended to replace the King James Bible in official usage.

Revised English Bible (REB): A revision of the New English Bible (1989) by the Churches of England.

Today's English Version (TEV): A translation by the American Bible Society (1966), which attempts to render the Bible in vernacular English.

New International Version (NIV): A translation of the Bible by the New York Bible Society (1978), which was done by a group of evangelical scholars and endorsed by many Protestant denominations in 1966.

Christian Reformed Church and the National Association of Evangelicals. The project was endorsed by a large number of leaders from many denominations who met in Chicago in 1966. The translation of each book of the Bible was assigned to a team of scholars. Their work was revised by one of the Intermediate Editorial Committees whose work went on to one of the General Editorial Committees. The work was then reviewed by the Committee on Bible Translation, which made further changes and released the completed work, which is championed as the more-or-less official version of the Evangelical Theological Society.

> ### Concept Check # 48
>
> How would you explain the fact that, in terms of general sales, the NIV is outselling the RSV? (Check your answer on p. 225.)

10. Other English Translations for Roman Catholics

A host of translations of the Bible for Roman Catholics in modern speech appeared in the last two centuries, the earliest of which include: *Coyne's Bible* (1811), *Haydock's Bible* (1811-1814), the *Newcastle New Testament* (1812), *Syer's Bible* (1813-1814), *MacNamara's Bible* (1813-1814), *Bregan's New Testament* (1814), and *Gibson's Bible* (1816-1817). *The Layman's New Testament* was published in 1928, which contained Challoner's text of the Old Testament on the left page with polemical notes on the right. Cuthbert Lattey, S.J., edited the *Westminster Version of the Sacred Scriptures*, which appeared in 1935. The Second Testament in this edition was based on the Greek New Testament rather than the Latin Vulgate. The translation of the First Testament from Hebrew was not yet completed at the time of Lattey's death in 1954.

The revised form of the Rheims-Douay version was the only Catholic Bible to have official approval until the translation of the New Testament by Monsignor Ronald Knox in 1945, which was made from the Latin Vulgate. Knox's translation of the Old Testament was published in 1948 but, unlike the New Testament, was not approved as an official version. The significance of this translation is the simple fact that it broke once and for all the shackles of the tradition of the Rheims-Douay version in Roman Catholic tradition. Since the work of Knox, we now have Catholic Bibles consistently based on the original languages and using contemporary speech.

In 1956, James A. Kliest and Joseph L. Lilly published *The New Testament Rendered from the Original Greek with Explanatory Notes*. The French translation of the Bible by Dominican priests, *La Bible de Jerusalem* (1961), led to one of the most widely received Roman Catholic Bibles in America, **The Jerusalem Bible** (JB), which was published in 1966 and has the distinction of being the first complete Catholic Bible to be translated into English from the original languages. The introduction and notes in this volume, which were translated directly from French into English, represent the work of the so-called "liberal" wing of Catholic biblical scholarship. In 1973, a new edition of *Bible de Jerusalem* appeared, which warranted a new edition of JB, the **New Jerusalem Bible** (NJB), which appeared in 1985.

> ## Concept Check # 49
>
> What was the significance of the translation of the Bible by Monsignor Ronald Knox for the Roman Catholic Church? (Check your answer on p. 225.)

11. Other Translations and Editions of the English Bible

Alongside the official translations of the Bible in the eighteenth and nineteenth centuries, a host of unofficial translations and versions were published. For example, Daniel Whitby produced a *Paraphrase and Commentary on the New Testament* in 1703. Edward Wells followed with what he called *The Common Translations Corrected* (1718-1724); William Whiston published his *Primitive New Testament* in 1745, John Wesley introduced some 12,000 changes in the text of the Authorized Bible, and Edward Horwood made a *Liberal Translation of the New Testament* in 1768.

Efforts to translate the First Testament began to appear in the nineteenth century, beginning with Charles Thompson's publication of *The Septuagint Bible* in 1808. Lancelot Brenton followed with his edition of the *Septuagint Version of the Old Testament* (1844). Samuel Sharpe published his *New Testament* in 1840 followed by the *Old Testament* in 1865. Meanwhile, Robert Young published his *Literal Translation of the*

Jerusalem Bible (JB): An English translation (1966) adapted from the French translation (1961) by Dominican priests in Jerusalem working from the original Greek and Hebrew texts.

New Jerusalem Bible (NJB): A revision of the Jerusalem Bible (1985).

Bible in 1862, and Dean Alford published his *Greek New Testament* and a revision of the Authorized Bible in 1869. Somewhat later, John Nelson Darby, leader of the Plymouth Brethren and the one who shaped the system of theological thought called Dispensationalism, published a *New Translation of the Bible* (1871, 1890), while Joseph Bryant Rotherham was publishing *The Emphasized Bible* (1872, 1902). Thomas Newberry's *The Englishman's Bible* also appeared in the 1890s.

The twentieth century saw such a proliferation of English Bible translations that it is no longer feasible to mention them all. All the great manuscripts from antiquity were now known and the public sentiment for colloquial translations was such that the time was ripe for the happy confusion of translations and commentaries which continues to flood the market. There are now more translations of the Bible in English than all other modern languages combined.

One of the more significant developments in English Bible translation within the twentieth century emerged with the publication of multivolume commentary series in which individual scholars present their own translation of the original biblical text along with detailed scholarly discussion. The International Critical Commentary, which began to appear at the turn of the twentieth century and has been resumed in recent years, was a significant step in this direction. The Anchor Bible Commentary series (1964 – present) is perhaps the most outstanding current example of the trend. Some commentaries in this series, such as the three volumes on Psalms by Mitchell Dahood, are little more than annotated translations of the biblical text based on comparative philology. Other such commentary series of note, containing new translations of individual books of the Bible, include: The Old Testament Library (1962 – present; though some of the volumes translated from German have the RSV), the New International Commentary on the Old Testament (1976 – present) and the New Testament (1950s – present), the Hermeneia series (1972 – present), the Word Biblical Commentary (1982 – present), and Continental Commentaries (1984 – present).

The parade of scholars with their translations appears to be gaining in momentum as the century draws to a close. Arthur S. Way led the parade with his translation in 1901. The next year saw the publication of *The Twentieth Century New Testament*, which was based on the text of Westcott and Hort. Richard Francis Weymouth, who was a consultant in this project, published his own work, *The Resultant Greek Testament,* in 1903 (which appeared posthumously). James A. Robertson published a thoroughly revised edition in 1924.

When Weymouth retired from his work as headmaster of Mill High School in London, he produced a modern speech version of the New Testament which was published after his death in 1902 by his friend, Ernest Hampden-Cook. The first of five editions of Weymouth's work, *The New Testament in Modern Speech*, appeared in 1903. The most thorough-going revision of this work was the fourth edition (1924), the work of "several well-known New Testament Scholars."

Ferrar Fenton published *The Holy Bible in Modern English* (1895, 1903), which may well be the most pretentious of all the works by a single scholar. Fenton claims to have based his work on Hebrew, Chaldee, and Greek manuscripts.

James Moffat, an Oxford scholar, followed with *The New Testament* (1913), *The Old Testament* (1924), and *A New Translation of the Bible* (1924). Moffat's work is characterized by his own Scottish style with its modernistic theological bias. The American counterpart to Moffat's work is that of Edgar J. Goodspeed (New Testament) and J. M. Powis Smith (Old Testament), *The Complete Bible: An American Translation* (1931). The intent of this translation was to produce a work "based upon the assured results of modern study, and put into the familiar language of today."

The *Concordant Version of the Sacred Scriptures* (New Testament completed in 1926; translation of the First Testament still in progress) sought to provide an English equivalent for every word in the original languages. G. W. Wade attempted to present a fresh translation of the Second Testament in what he believed to be the chronological order of the books in *The Documents of the New Testament* (1934). In 1937, Charles B. Williams published *The New Testament in the Language of the People*, in which he attempted to convey the exact meaning of the Greek verb tenses. Gerald Warre Cornish's *St. Paul from the Trenches* (1937) appeared that same year, published posthumously. W. C. Wand published *The New Testament Letters* (1943) in the format of a bishop writing a monthly letter to his diocese. J. H. Hooks chaired a committee which published *The Basic English Bible* (1940-1949), in which the translation is limited to one thousand "basic" English words. Charles Kingsley Williams attempted a similar work in *The New Testament: A Translation in Plain English* (1952).

Modern Language Bible (MLB): A translation under the direction of Garrit Verkuyl (1971), which was commonly known as the Berkeley Version (1945, 1959).

An attempt to provide a conservative counterpart to the Revised Standard Version (RSV) was published under the direction of Garrit Verkuyl of Berkeley, California, entitled *The Berkeley Version in Modern English* (1945, 1959), which was revised and published in 1969 as *The Holy Bible: The New Berkeley Version in Modern English;* and more recently as the **Modern Language Bible** (1971).

The Jehovah's Witness publications, under the name of the Watchtower Bible and Tract Society, published *The New World Translation of the Christian Greek Scriptures* (1950) and *The New World Translation of the Hebrew Scriptures* (1953). When the Watchtower Bible and Tract Society published *The Bible in Living English* in 1972, it was thought at first that it was a revised edition of its earlier New World Translation. This is not the case, however. The work is an entirely new translation by Steven Byington (1868-1957), who was not a Jehovah's Witness. According to Byington's own comments, the work "is a commentary rather than a translation"—one which the publishers found useful because it renders the name of God as "Jehovah."

The Amplified New Testament (1958), produced by the Lockman Foundation, was followed by *The Amplified Bible* in 1964, which was published by Zondervan Publishing House. Its purpose is "to reveal, together with the single-word English equivalent to each key Hebrew and Greek word, any other clarifying shades of meaning that may be concealed by the traditional word-for-word method of translation." It seeks to make the Bible understandable through amplification.

Following the release of several popular translations in his attempt to make the New Testament understandable to a London youth group, J. B. Phillips published *The New Testament in Modern English* in 1958. The great popularity of this work lies in its freshness of style and readability. A revised edition appeared in 1972. In the meantime, Phillips also published a translation of Amos, Hosea, Isaiah 1-35, and Micah under the title, *Four Prophets* (1963).

Kenneth S. Wuest followed the example of J. B. Phillips in publishing his *Expanded Translation of the New Testament* (1959), which combined the several installments he released in prior publications. His work, along with the Lockman Foundation publication of *The Amplified Bible* (1958, 1964) follows the tradition of Charles B. Williams. In 1961, Olaf M. Norlis published *The Simplified New Testament in Plain English* and R. K. Harrison translated *The Psalms for Today* to accompany it.

William Barclay, long-known for his popularization of scholarly work in *The Daily Study Bible* (17 vols.), published a two-volume translation of the New Testament (1968-69), which appeared in a one-volume paperback edition in 1980. Though Barclay's express purpose was "to make a translation which did not need a commentary to explain it," he also admits that translation "will necessarily involve what is known as paraphrase."

Eugene Peterson published *The Message: New Testament in Contemporary English* (1993), followed by *The Message: The Psalms* (1994). The immediate popularity of his works has led some to call him "America's J. B. Phillips."

Concept Check # 50

What is the primary objective in Bible translation from the New Testament of Weymouth (1903) to that of Eugene Peterson (1993)? (Check your answer on p. 225.)

12. Translations Done Expressly for Children

Beginning in 1956 on the book of Romans, Kenneth Taylor set out to produce a modern speech rendering of the Scriptures which grew out of his frustration with his reading of the classic KJV to his own children. His attempts to explain the passages of the Bible in simple, everyday English they could understand culminated in *The Living Bible* (1971), which has sold millions of copies.

Living Bible (LB): Kenneth Taylor's translation of the Bible (1971) in simple, everyday English.

The need to put the biblical text into simple language that even a child could understand has long been a concern in the translation of the Bible. In recent years, this goal has produced a growing number of translations which are expressly designated as Bibles for children.

In 1960, Jay Green published *The Children's "King James" Bible: New Testament*, followed by what he called a Teen-age Version (1962) and *The Children's Version of the Holy Bible* (1962).

First published as *The Children's New Testament* in 1969, Gleason Ledyard completed his *New Life Version* of the Bible in 1986. This translation uses a vocabulary of about 850 words. It is claimed that "even educated adults who are familiar with the Scriptures find themselves startled into new insights by its blunt simplicity."

International Children's Bible (ICB): A translation by the World Bible Translation Center (1986), which claims to be "the first translation of the Holy Scriptures prepared specifically for children."

In 1984, the *New Century Version* of the New Testament was published under the auspices of the World Bible Translation Center in Fort Worth, Texas. The complete Bible appeared in 1986 as the ***International Children's Bible,*** which claims to be "the first translation of the Holy Scriptures prepared specifically for children." Published by Word Publishing Company with a paperback edition entitled *The Answer to Happiness, Health, and Fulfillment in Life: The Holy Bible: A Translation of Our Time*, it includes selected writings from a wide range of well-known persons, including Billy Graham, Robert Schuller, Catherine Marshall, Mother Teresa, etc.

The New Evangelical Translation, produced by God's Word To The Nations Bible Society, claims to be done at a reading level "accessible to children without being condescending to adults." The New Testament appeared in 1988 and went to a second edition in 1992. The translation of William Beck, *An American Translation* (1976), was used as a base for this version involving twenty-five scholars who claim to be working "directly from Greek texts." The complete Bible, published in 1995 as *God's Word: Today's Bible Translation That Says What It Means,* claims to be written at a fourth or fifth grade reading level.

Contemporary English Version (**CEV**): A translation by the American Bible Society (1995), which attempts to put the Bible in language a child can readily understand.

The ***Contemporary English Version*** (CEV) was published by the American Bible Society in 1995 (the New Testament in this version appeared in 1991). This translation attempts to take into consideration the needs of the *hearer*, as well as those of the reader, who may not be familiar with traditional biblical language. Written as a Bible for children by Dr. Barclay Newman, who led a team of three translators and one editorial associate in the basic translation work, it was tested in the First Baptist Church of Springfield, Missouri, with the second and third grade departments. The goal of this project was to produce a text a child eight or nine years of age could read aloud, without stumbling, and communicate to another child of five or six with understanding. At the same time, the translators sought to make the translation of such a nature that parents would listen with appreciation and enjoyment because of a lucid and lyrical style.

> ### Concept Check # 51
> How do you explain the phenomenon of the growing number of "children's Bibles" since 1960? (Check your answer on p. 225.)

13. Study Bibles

In the Middle Ages, illuminated Bibles provided helps for the reader in terms of marginal commentaries on the sacred text, illustrations, and ornamentation. Parallel passages, especially in the four Gospels of the New Testament, were noted. Red ink marked the words of Jesus, and elaborate covers and pigments derived from precious metals and other materials made these handwritten manuscripts works of art.

Study Bibles today are less ornate than their medieval counterparts; but they offer an abundance of information that embellishes and explicates the biblical text with indexes, maps, cross references, and glossaries. With more than six hundred such Study Bibles currently available it is not feasible here to survey them all. The "1995 Review of Study Bibles," published in *Biblical Archaeology Review* (September/October 1995, pp. 72-76) covers fifty-one examples which include all of the major English versions and several individual translations of the Bible.

Thinking Exercise

On the History of the English Bible

The critical thinking goal for this exercise is to clarify the major phases in the history of the English Bible.

How To Do This Exercise

Review the major divisions in section E of this chapter, "A Brief History of the English Bible," and the concepts and key words which appear there. Then answer the following:

1. Describe briefly how the Bible was known in ancient England from ca. 600 to 1300 CE.

_____

_____

_____

_____

_____

2. The second phase in the history of the English Bible was initiated by John Wycliffe (1380) and completed by the publication of the Bishops' Bible (1568). Describe what happened and explain why.

_____

_____

_____

_____

_____

3. The third phase in the history of the English Bible began in 1611 with the publication of the Authorized King James Version (KJV) within the context of the English Reformation. Trace the history of the KJV from 1611 to the present.

_____

_____

_____

_____

4. The fourth phase in the history of the English Bible (the twentieth century) begins with the English Revised Biblc (ERB) of 1898 and the American Standard Version (ASV) of 1901. It culminates in the RSV Common Bible of 1973. Explain the significance of the ASV and trace its history from 1901 to the present.

_____

_____

_____

_____

5. The fifth phase in the history of the English Bible is marked by fresh translations of the Bible from the best known Hebrew and Greek manuscripts within Protestant, Roman Catholic, and Jewish circles. Discuss this process in terms of the NIV (Protestant), the *New American Bible* (Roman Catholic), and the *Tanakh* (Jewish).

_____

_____

_____

_____

6. Explain how the New International Version (NIV) differs from the New Revised Standard Version (NRSV) and discuss the relative importance of these two translations.

_____

_____

_____

_____

Discussion Questions

1. Since the Greek translation of the Hebrew Bible (the Septuagint) was used widely by the Jews in antiquity and became established as the Bible of the early Christian Church, why is it important that modern translations of the Old Testament be based on the Hebrew text?

2. If the Bible is the best preserved of all texts from antiquity, why is it important to establish a "critical text" of the Old and New Testaments?

3. Evaluate the validity of the claim that Reuben Swanson's *New Testament Greek Manuscripts* is "the greatest breakthrough in New Testament study tools in 500 years."

4. Discuss the role of the Authorized King James Bible (1611) in the history of the English Bible. How do you account for the dominant role it has played?

5. Discuss the significance of Kenneth Taylor's translation, *The Living Bible*.

Concept Map: The Bible in Antiquity

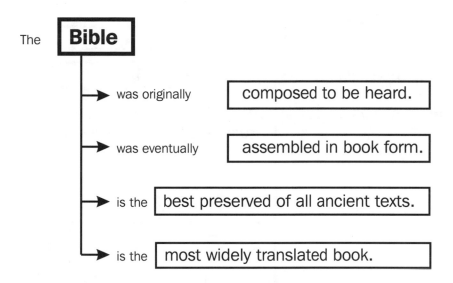

The **Bible**

→ was originally   composed to be heard.

→ was eventually   assembled in book form.

→ is the   best preserved of all ancient texts.

→ is the   most widely translated book.

Bible translation began in antiquity.

Concept Map: Transmission of the Text of the Bible

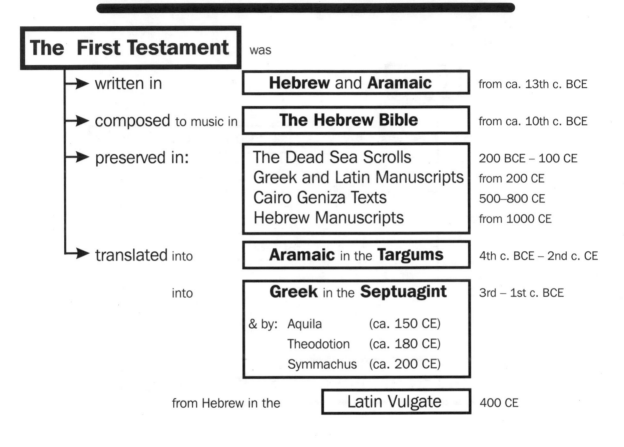

The First Testament was

→ written in   **Hebrew** and **Aramaic**   from ca. 13th c. BCE

→ composed to music in   **The Hebrew Bible**   from ca. 10th c. BCE

→ preserved in:

The Dead Sea Scrolls	200 BCE – 100 CE
Greek and Latin Manuscripts	from 200 CE
Cairo Geniza Texts	500–800 CE
Hebrew Manuscripts	from 1000 CE

→ translated into   **Aramaic** in the **Targums**   4th c. BCE – 2nd c. CE

into   **Greek** in the **Septuagint**   3rd – 1st c. BCE

& by: Aquila   (ca. 150 CE)
          Theodotion   (ca. 180 CE)
          Symmachus   (ca. 200 CE)

from Hebrew in the   Latin Vulgate   400 CE

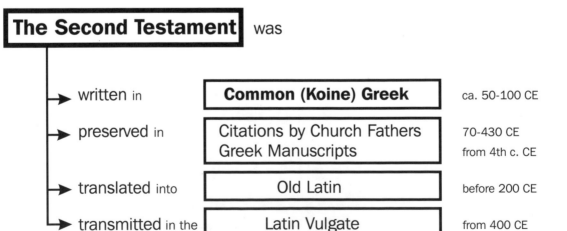

The Second Testament was

→ written in   **Common (Koine) Greek**   ca. 50-100 CE

→ preserved in

Citations by Church Fathers	70-430 CE
Greek Manuscripts	from 4th c. CE

→ translated into   Old Latin   before 200 CE

→ transmitted in the   Latin Vulgate   from 400 CE

Concept Map: Textual Criticism of the Bible

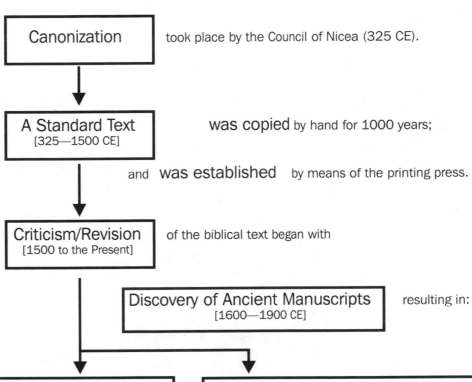

Canonization took place by the Council of Nicea (325 CE).

A Standard Text [325—1500 CE] was copied by hand for 1000 years; and was established by means of the printing press.

Criticism/Revision [1500 to the Present] of the biblical text began with

Discovery of Ancient Manuscripts [1600—1900 CE] resulting in:

The Critical Text of the First Testament

Jacob ben Chayyim text (1525)

Biblia Hebraica, ed. R. Kittel
(3 editions, 1906-1937)

Biblia Hebraica Stuttgartensia (1976)

BHS revision [Leningrad Codex]
(in progress)

Hebrew Univ. Bible [Allepo Codex]
(in progress)

The Critical Text of the Second Testament

Textus Receptus [1633] (Oxford, 1873)

Westcott-Hort, NT in Original Greek (1935)

Nestle-Aland, Novum Testamentum Graece
(1898-1979)

United Bible Society, The Greek NT
(4th ed., 1993)

Swanson, NT Greek Manuscripts
(1994 - in progress)

Concept Map: History of the English Bible

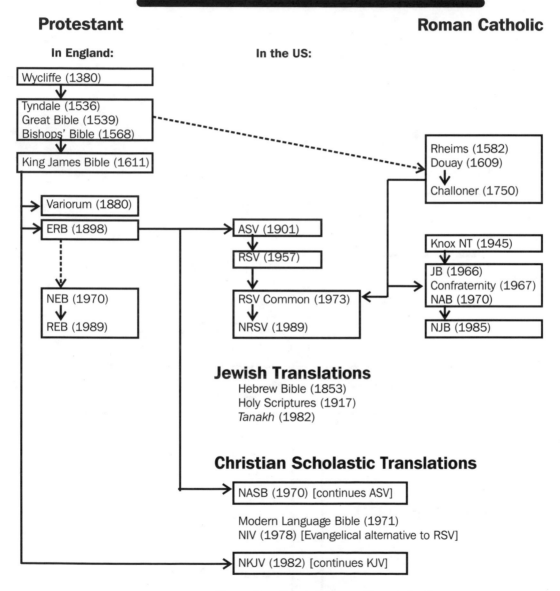

Protestant   **Roman Catholic**

In England: In the US:

Wycliffe (1380)

Tyndale (1536)
Great Bible (1539)
Bishops' Bible (1568)

King James Bible (1611)

Variorum (1880)

ERB (1898)

NEB (1970)
REB (1989)

ASV (1901)

RSV (1957)

RSV Common (1973)

NRSV (1989)

Rheims (1582)
Douay (1609)
Challoner (1750)

Knox NT (1945)

JB (1966)
Confraternity (1967)
NAB (1970)

NJB (1985)

Jewish Translations
Hebrew Bible (1853)
Holy Scriptures (1917)
Tanakh (1982)

Christian Scholastic Translations
NASB (1970) [continues ASV]

Modern Language Bible (1971)
NIV (1978) [Evangelical alternative to RSV]

NKJV (1982) [continues KJV]

Popular Language Translations
Today's English Version (1966)
Living Bible (1971)
International Children's Bible (1986)
Contemporary English Version (1995)
God's Word (1995)

5 The Authority of the Bible

Learning Objectives

After studying this chapter, you should be able to:

1. Explain why the Bible is **normative**.
2. Take a position on the question of the **inerrancy** of Scripture and argue your case.

We sometimes hear it said that we should read the Bible as if it were a letter from a loved one. There is much to be said for this, but it does not go far enough; for the One who speaks to us is not far away in some distant place. He is more present to us than we are to ourselves, as Saint Augustine once put it. We ought not to merely *read* the Bible, but *listen* to it; for God is present and speaks to us through the words of this ancient book. God speaks to us now, to where we are. Old familiar passages often carry old familiar messages, for that is what we need to hear now; but sometimes that same familiar text carries a new and fresh word of life. This too is part of the process we call revelation.

A. Who Wrote the Bible?

Before we take up the difficult and controversial topic of biblical inerrancy, I would like to share a personal experience that took place in a church in Boston some years ago. The whole thing was set up in order to make a point. In preparation for a talk with a group of senior high-school students, a copy of Webster's *Intercollegiate Dictionary* was

Normative: Of or pertaining to a standard; the authoritative basis for behavior and beliefs.

Inerrancy: The teaching within Jewish, Christian (and Muslim) tradition that the Bible (and the Koran) is free from error, which is a logical consequence of the belief that the Bible (and the Koran) is the "word of God."

placed on top of a piano. That evening, during the course of my address, I made the following statement: "Now, according to Webster (and I pointed to the dictionary), nuclear fission is 'the splitting apart of the nucleus of an atom into fragments, usually two fragments of comparable mass, with the evolution of approximately 100 million to several hundred million electron volts of energy.'"[1] What was I saying? I knew full well that when Noah Webster first compiled his dictionary of the English language neither he nor anyone else knew anything about subatomic physics. Was I lying when I said "Webster says"? No, all I was saying is: "It stands written in the book that you and I know as Webster's Dictionary."

It is a bit like the phrase "Hoyle says" among card players. There is no game in the current issue of *Hoyle's Card Games* that is still in the actual form of the first edition of this particular reference work.[2] More-over, some of the games discussed in the latest edition emerged long after the death of Sir Edmund Hoyle in 1769. When we say "Hoyle says," to settle an argument in a game, we are not making a statement on matters of **higher criticism**. We are only saying, "It is written in the bible of the card player that such and such is the case." Similarly when the New Testament states that "Moses says" or "Moses wrote," Jesus and the apostles are saying nothing more than "It stands written in the books that you and I recognize as the Torah of Moses, the Pentateuch." Nothing is said here on matters of so-called higher criticism.

Higher criticism: The study of the Bible, having as its object the establishment of such facts as authorship and date of composition.

When it comes to ascribing authorship of sacred tradition within a community of faith, we should be careful that we do not say more than we mean. When Robert Robinson wrote the words of the hymn "Come, Thou Fount of Every Blessing" almost two hundred years ago, the second stanza began with the words "Here I raise mine Ebenezer." In a widely used modern hymnal, the words are "Here I raise to Thee an altar."[3] We can readily understand why the editors of this hymnal made the change. The reference to the story of Ebenezer in 1 Samuel 7 is not as familiar to the average worshiper today as it was two hundred years ago. But at the top of the page, the author of the hymn is still Robert Robinson. Did he write the hymn as it stands in this popular hymnal? Well, yes and no. He is the author of the hymn, though all of the individual words we sing are not his—at least not in the manner in which he originally composed them.

My own research in the book of Deuteronomy over the course of the past several years suggests that the Hebrew text in its present form, as preserved by the masoretes, is a musical composition.[4] The canting tradition of the synagogues preserves memory of the original perform-ance of the text during the period of the Second Temple in Jerusalem and perhaps even earlier, if Suzanne Haïk-Vantoura is correct.[5] In short, though details in her decipherment of the musical information pre-served in the accentual system of the Hebrew Bible may change with further research, much of Haïk-Vantoura's work is likely to withstand the test of time. The Bible as we have it is not a collection of independent books, which certain scribes in antiquity gathered together into a library. It is a single book, by a single author—if we are to give credence to the common affirmation in public worship that it is the "Word of God." That being the case, we can now say much more about the actual canonical process that brought the book to us than could our predecessors. We have attempted to do that, at least in broad outline, in chapter 2 of this book.

The doctrinal basis of the Evangelical Theological Society speaks of the Bible as "inerrant in the **autographs**." What, however, is an auto-graph within the canonical process, at least in its earlier stages in ancient Israel? The book of Deuteronomy was the center of a complex process of canonical activity, from at least the time of Josiah to the dedication of the Second Temple in Jerusalem at the end of the sixth century BCE. So far as Deuteronomy is concerned, that process included much more than the mere compilation of the Pentateuch. It also included the Former Prophets, or what some would call the Deuteronomic History, within a still larger canonical entity that David Noel Freedman has called the "Primary History."[6] It may have included both the Latter Prophets and the Writings as canonical categories as well, though perhaps not in the form we now know, as we have argued in chapters 2 and 3 of this book.

The sharp distinction which is generally made between prose and poetry in the Bible has prevented scholars from seeing clearly the actual genre of much of the Bible, and the book of Deuteronomy in particular. This book enjoyed generations of use within public worship in ancient Israel before its use at the center of canonical activity in the time of Josiah. Like other law codes throughout the Mediterranean, the book of Deuteronomy was sung at the festivals of antiquity. This fact was

Autographs: Manuscripts in the handwriting of their author; the original text of the manuscripts of the books of the Bible as composed by the individual authors or their amanuenses (persons employed to write what another dictates).

noted in passing more than two hundred years ago by Bishop Robert Lowth, in his famous *Lectures on the Sacred Poetry of the Hebrews*.

As was the case with the laws of ancient Greece, the laws of ancient Israel were chanted to music by the Levites—the same persons who also were entrusted with the transmission of the whole of the sacred canonical tradition which ultimately became the Hebrew Bible.

T. Georgiades has shown convincingly, at least for ancient Greek literature, that the distinct concepts of music and poetry as we understand them today were not known in antiquity:[7]

> The ancient Greek verse line was a singular formation for which there is no analogy in Western Christian civilization. It was, if you will, music and poetry in one, and precisely because of this it could not be separated into music and poetry as two tangibly distinct components. For this particular vehicle of meaning the Greeks, however, had a special term: *mousiké.*

The work of Haïk-Vantoura is built on the same observation. Like ancient Greek literature, the Hebrew Bible emerged in the form of *mousiké*—a combination of music and language. Haïk-Vantoura has used the Greek term *melos* ("melody-text") to describe what she observed. It should be noted that the same term is used in the Greek translation of Jesus, son of Eleazar, son of Sirach, in what is sometimes called the "Song of the Levites," to describe how the singers led the people of Israel in worship in the time of Simeon II, son of Jochanan (i.e., 219-196 BCE, see Sir 50:18).[8]

The book of Deuteronomy is poetry in its entirety, at least in the very broadest sense of that word, as I have argued elsewhere.[9] Though it contains a lyric poem in the "Song of Moses" (chap. 32), the entire book is in the form of didactic poetry of a lesser nature, so far as heightened speech goes. The composer of the original was Moses, but the text as we have it enjoyed a life of its own for generations in the public worship of ancient Israel. Like Robert Robinson's hymn, individual words no doubt changed in usage through time. Indeed the very structure of the greater "Song of Moses," which we now call Deuteronomy, may have changed as it developed in public performance by a long line of singers in the festivals and in Levitical circles of ancient Israel through hundreds of years.[10] The concentric structural patterns, found at virtually all levels of analysis, bear witness to its tightly woven composition. That structure points to an author. On one level of observation that author is Moses, who composed the original Torah in musical form. But on another level, the author is God himself, at work through a long chain of poet-prophets (like Moses) in ancient Israel who recited this text in public worship and who made it the center of an elaborate canonical process that gave us the Bible itself as the Word of God.

The symmetries in structure and in total length of corresponding sections of the canon of sacred Scripture, which are discussed in chapters two and three above, bear witness to the fact that God was involved in the process of canonization, promulgation, and preservation of the biblical text. The Bible is no ordinary book. It is the vehicle through which God has communicated his purposes to his people in times past and through which he continues to communicate in the present. In short, the Bible is the Word of God.

Though the canon of sacred Scripture is normative, before that canon received its final form there were already norming principles operating within the experience of ancient Israel. Ultimately, God himself is the norming norm; but the God of Israel is a God who reveals himself concretely in history, as the late G. Ernest Wright was wont to say.[11] Such a view of history is theological and requires a different **hermeneutic** than that of a view of history that empirically focuses on cause and effect only. The theological hermeneutic sees the horizontal procession of history from a vertical relation. If God is ultimately the norming norm who reveals himself within the history of Israel, and if history is shaped by real persons, then we are in a position to affirm the person of Moses as a normative influence within the history of the people of ancient Israel. So in this sense (of a creative norming event happening through a particular person for a particular people) we can claim Moses' authorship of the Pentateuch.[12]

When a significant event occurs in a person's life, its full meaning is not often made clear until some time has passed and until a remembrance, a making present of that event through time, has been allowed to leaven that personal history. This is all the more true when God comes into a person's life. The meaning of an event where God touches a human life is unraveled in time. It is the event itself that holds the significance and truth, but the full meaning of it is made manifest when the initial event has time to touch, arouse, and suppress all the various energies that constitute a human life and history. This is also—and

Hermeneutics: The theory of interpretation of texts, which begins with determination of the original meaning of a text (exegesis) and leads to elucidation of its sense for modern readers (exposition, paraphrase, or sermon).

especially—true with Moses and the people of Israel. The event of the life of Moses, especially the Moses of Sinai, is the moment in time when God revealed himself and called a people to himself. The full revelation is made manifest when the people of God continue to remember and respond to the event. Out of this remembering and response comes a Scripture that continually looks back to the event for its authority and power. So it is that Moses is the authority within the Pentateuch. Future generations would remember the authority, the authorship, of their covenant with God and the law by which they are called to obey him by recognizing and claiming the man Moses in their midst.

In our time, the historical-critical method, as practiced within the professional guild of scholars, may mark a period of individuation that makes it possible to reengage with the biblical text in greater integrity and freedom. The individuation process achieves its purpose only to the extent that the new individual reengages with the community and tradition creating that community. The new engagement is characterized by a greater integrity to the whole person and a more profound freedom that must be exercised. The historical-critical method creates a new context from which a theological hermeneutic may proceed with greater integrity and greater freedom, and therefore with greater participation in the life of Scripture.

In Scripture, the apparent contradictions and ambiguities constitute part of the revelation. The Word of revelation comes into history, not to obliterate it or to make it nonhistorical but to enter into it as a recreating force. As Robert Alter once put it: "The biblical outlook is informed, I think, by a sense of stubborn contradiction."[13] The apparent contradictions and ambiguities in Scripture reveal not an abstract God but a God who actually enters into the human process.

Normative hermeneutic: The principle of interpretation of sacred texts within a given community which is authoritative, or binding, on members of that community.

The underlying view of reality and history in the pure historical-critical mind makes the concept of Mosaic authorship of the Pentateuch inconceivable to many. The absence of a **normative hermeneutic,** or the belief that there cannot be one, cuts them off from the hermeneutic world of Scripture, which has as its foundation a hermeneutic of participation in the life of God's Word as living, judging, and transforming. The historical-critical mind reads a text; it does not hear Scripture. The theological testimony of the whole Scripture, which evolved out of the normative influence of Moses on generations who looked back to him to make present his authority, is validated in the experience of the hearing community. What is called for, so it seems, is a calculated naiveté which submits not only to the integrity of the whole text but also to the hearing of Scripture within the community that remembers and therefore interprets its own historical situation under God and his prophet Moses.

Remembering means making the past present. Remembering is presence. It suggests more than a mere recall of data. It is a making present of the past that recreates the present through presence. Remembering signals the transmission of the norming presence from generation to generation.

Much of Scripture as we know it, particularly the First Testament, was probably performed and sung in liturgical settings in ancient Israel, and thus the form of Scripture is essentially poetic. Poetry is the ideal tool for theology. It is a way of seeing that is not just a system for interpretation, but a way of life—a way of making present that which lies beyond the bounds of human experience and understanding. Scripture is a symbolic theology in which symbols actually communicate the presence of that which they symbolize. The power is in the event itself, which becomes a transforming symbol actually making present the event through time. The nature of the symbol is intimately related to the nature of sacred time. Even the material on which the law was written was treated as having presence and power. Only a symbolic consciousness can know presence. The fact that the poem of Scripture was probably sung at a special set-apart time suggests a quality of *ekstasis* in worship, in which remembering is acted out by the whole person and by the whole community. It is a remembering that is larger than the individual or even the community. It is a remembering of the prophet Moses, who was chosen by God to reveal his presence—and of the prophet greater than Moses, who invited his people to actually participate in his death, burial, and resurrection through symbolic remembrance in what we call the Eucharist or the Lord's Supper.

Concept Check # 52

What is meant when we say the Bible is the authority for our faith? Why is poetry an appropriate vehicle for the expression of normative principles of faith? (Check your answer on p. 225.)

B. Is the Bible Inerrant?

Tension between the claims of modern science and time-honored beliefs about the Bible have been the focus of conflict for centuries. The most famous example of this controversy, the familiar story of Galileo in the seventeenth century, illustrates the problem.[14] When Galileo looked out at the heavens through the telescope which he had invented, he observed phenomena which could not easily be reconciled with common beliefs about the world and the cosmos. According to the popular version of this story, the leaders of the Roman Catholic Church at that time refused to look through his telescope; for, if they had, they would have seen for themselves the movement of the planets and moons, which confirmed the views of Copernicus that the earth was not the center of the universe. Galileo was forced, by threat of death, to recant and acknowledge the folly of science as he knew it in the face of the revealed truth which religious leaders believed was grounded in their particular reading of the Bible.

Though there is some truth in this popular account, it does not do justice to the actual events of that time. As Nancy Pearcey has shown,[15] the pope who condemned Galileo was not opposed to his scientific ideas as such. In fact, he once belonged to a group of Galileo's supporters. What concerned the pope was the way Galileo had chosen to use science to assail Aristotelian philosophy. In the Middle Ages, Thomas Aquinas adapted Aristotle's philosophy to Christian teaching. But many of Aristotle's scientific ideas were mistaken. Galileo not only championed the view of Copernicus over that of Aristotle regarding the earth as the center of the planetary system, he launched scathing attacks on Aristotle's entire philosophy. In so doing, he brought down the wrath of the religious establishment on both himself and the science he embodied.

The tension between science and Christianity today is different in its focus, because of the theory of evolution, as championed by Charles Darwin, and the field of geology, as developed by Charles Lyell, in the nineteenth century. This "new science" appeared to be in flat contradiction to the teaching of the book of Genesis as popularly understood. Fundamentalist attacks on Darwinism and counterattacks by scientists and pseudo-scientists escalated in the United States after the 1925 Scopes trial in which William Jennings Bryan, three-time presidential candidate and noted fundamentalist, handled the prosecution of a biology teacher who intentionally defied Tennessee's law against teaching evolution in the public schools. Though Scopes was found guilty, as expected, the more important aspect of this trial for our purposes is what happened in the witness chair when the defense attorney Clarence Darrow forced Bryan to admit that the six, consecutive, twenty-four-hour periods he affirmed as *the* biblical truth of creation must be incorrect.

In 1961, Henry Morris, a civil engineering professor, and John Whitcomb, a theology professor, published a book entitled *The Genesis Flood*.[16] This lengthy volume dealt with much more than the Flood. It was a treatise on creation according to what is sometimes called the young universe time scale of thousands of years as opposed to the billions of years, which evidence from the fields of geology and astronomy suggest. To fundamentalists, *The Genesis Flood* provided the scientific respectability they had been seeking to combat science with science, or so it seemed. Actually, what has taken shape is a new assault on modern science by one part of the religious establishment, which has led some scientists to denounce religion itself as "anti-science," as witnessed by a recent article in *Nature,* a prestigious science journal. Such a conclusion would certainly come as a big surprise to the people who *founded* modern science, as Charles Colson has noted. As he put it, "Most of the early scientists were devout Christians: Copernicus, Boyle, Newton, Pasteur. In fact, historians tell us Christianity helped inspire the scientific revolution."[17]

By the early 1970s, as Hugh Ross has observed, "the supposed irreconcilability of Genesis 1 (and other portions of Scripture) with the scientific record was giving impetus to revision of the long-held views of biblical authority and inerrancy."[18] A number of evangelical seminaries replaced the word *inerrant* with the word *infallible* as the appropriate adjective to describe the Bible. *Infallible* would mean that the Bible is wholly trustworthy on matters of Christian faith and practice, but not necessarily so on matters of science, history, and geography.

In an attempt to counter this revisionist movement, a group of Christian scholars founded the International Council on Biblical Inerrancy (ICBI) in 1977. The concern of this body was to defend and apply the doctrine of biblical inerrancy as "an essential element for the authority of Scripture and a necessity for the health of the church."[19] The 1982 ICBI Summit focused attention on the matter of the ages of the universe and the earth, with three full-length papers: 1) Walter Bradley, professor of mechanical engineering, presented the case for interpreting the Genesis creation days as long epochs; 2) Henry Morris, founder and president of the Institute for Creation Research, presented the case for six consecutive twenty-four-hour creation days; and 3) Gleason Archer, professor of Old Testament and Semitics, presented his analysis of the original language of the Genesis text. The conclusion of this body, after lengthy discussion, was that adherence to six consecutive twenty-four-hour creation days is not essential to belief in biblical inerrancy. The Summit participants then framed the following list of affirmations and denials with respect to natural science. All but Morris signed the document.

ICBI Affirmations and Denials on Scripture and Natural Science[20]

We *affirm* that any preunderstanding which the interpreter brings to Scripture should be in harmony with scriptural teaching and subject to correction by it.

We *deny* that Scripture should be required to fit alien preunderstandings, inconsistent with itself, such as naturalism, evolutionism, scientism, secular humanism, and relativism.

We *affirm* that since God is the author of all truth, all truths, biblical and extrabiblical, are consistent and cohere, and that the Bible speaks truth when it touches on matters pertaining to nature, history, or anything else. We further affirm that in some cases extrabiblical data have value for clarifying what Scripture teaches, and for prompting correction of faulty interpretations.

We *deny* that extrabiblical views ever disprove the teaching of Scripture or hold priority over it.

We *affirm* the harmony of special with general revelation and therefore of biblical teaching with the facts of nature.

We *deny* that any genuine scientific facts are inconsistent with the true meaning of any passage of Scripture.

We *affirm* that Genesis 1-11 is factual, as is the rest of the book.

We *deny* that the teachings of Genesis 1-11 are mythical and that scientific hypotheses about earth history or the origin of humanity may be invoked to overthrow what Scripture teaches about creation.

As Hugh Ross has noted, "In the council's opinion, belief in biblical inerrancy required no immutable assertion of the cosmic or geologic ages. Belief in a finite date for creation was viewed as sufficient."[21] Unfortunately, the hopes of the council as regards reconciling opposing points of view and lessening the growing schism between modern science and the popular teaching of such Christian leaders as Henry Morris did not materialize.

The question of inerrancy of the Bible in Roman Catholic circles has taken a different direction than that of Protestant Christianity, largely because of a remarkable article written by Norbert Lohfink, S.J., "The Inerrancy of Scripture," which first appeared in English translation in 1968. The article was written as a position paper in preparation for Vatican Council II (1962-65) and does not address the issue of science and religion. For Lohfink the matter of inerrancy of Scripture is a given, as stated in the opening sentence of his article: "If it is necessary today to discuss the inerrancy of the Bible, it is not the idea itself which is under dispute, for this is an ancient and unequivocal tradition of faith."[22] Lohfink goes on to discuss in detail the three ways in which this doctrine has been discussed in times past: 1) of the Bible as a whole; 2) the individual books of the Bible; and 3) the biblical writers. The ensuing discussion is fully cognizant of the accomplishments in modern biblical scholarship. Lohfink argues convincingly that the arguments which focus on inerrant writers or inerrant books are no longer useful. It is the Bible as a whole which must be the focus of our inquiry when it comes to the question of inerrancy. Lohfink concludes that, "In practice, one will reach the inerrant sense of Scripture only in biblical theology."[23] In short, "in the light of the theses we have propounded, biblical inerrancy is seen to be simply a special aspect of the truth of divine revelation." Lohfink's final sentence is a quotation of the ancient words of Hugo St. Victor, "The whole divine Scripture is one book, and this one book is Christ."

What Lohfink has done here is to foreshadow current discussion of the canonical process, as discussed in chapters 1 and 2 of this book. The time has come to search for new analogies to explain how the Bible, like the incarnation of Jesus Christ as the "Word of God," is at the same time a human book, with all its consequent limitations, and the revelation of God. The term "inerrancy" remains useful in that it points to the mystery of this book as being revelation. As the revealed "Word of God," the Bible is inerrant.

> ## Concept Check # 53
>
> In what ways is the concept of inerrancy still a useful one in discussing the normative function of the Bible in Christianity and Judaism, in spite of past and current controversy? (Check your answer on p. 226.)

C. New Ways of Thinking About the Bible

The most useful analogies I have found for thinking about the mystery of the Bible as the revealed "Word of God" are the modern hologram and the 3-D stereogram, the new computer art form.[24] The hologram remains a mystery to me, even when the physical principles which make it possible are explained. The fact that I can look on a two-dimensional surface and observe a three-dimensional object is mysterious enough. What is more astounding is the simple fact that superficial irregularities, or "errors" on the surface of the hologram do not effect the underlying image as such. When one observes such an irregularity, all one needs to do is to move a bit so that the eye looks around the irregularity to see the image beneath the surface. The Bible is a bit like that. On the one hand, there are surface irregularities, or what often look like errors or even flat, outright contradictions. But such "surface irregularities" do not effect the image "within." Moreover, one quickly learns the danger in focusing one's attention too closely on a single text in isolation from the whole of the Bible; for if we focus our attention on the surface, we cannot see the image within the hologram.

A simple example may be useful at this point.[25] About forty years ago, a coal miner in West Virginia "took hold of the message" of Mark 16:17-18, which includes the statement that followers of Jesus Christ "shall take up serpents; and if they drink any deadly thing, it shall not hurt them." He founded a church. As he put it, "You have got to do what the Word says, not talk about it, but put it in action. And there ain't too many people that want to put their life on the line for the Word." His church teaches that handling a deadly snake is God's will; it is God's test for a true believer. But is it? Only if you focus your full attention on this single "surface irregularity" and lose sight of the detailed image beneath the surface.

There have been seventy confirmed deaths in the history of Appalachian serpent handling—about the same number as died in the Waco inferno under David Koresh. Two occurred in this one West Virginia church. The first was a twenty-two-year-old who died of a snake bite in 1961. Her mother was standing next to her when the rattler struck. The mother said: "I've often looked back to what happened and I've never seen the real power of God on anybody like it was on her. She had a glorified look."

That mother is now seventy-two years of age and has survived seventeen snake bites herself. When asked why she does this, her reply was: "A carnal mind can't understand snake handling. It takes a spiritual mind." Her son has been bitten 106 times and has the scars on his hands, arms, and face to prove it. He says: "See, I handle serpents because it's in the Bible, like a commandment. And I drink poison, like strychnine, because the Bible says it won't hurt me. Now, either every word in the Bible is right or it's wrong."

The second death in that West Virginia church occurred in 1992, when another member was struck by a rattlesnake on the left wrist and died thirteen hours later. His widow said, "He believed it, he lived it, and he died for the Word. He never once asked why; he never complained about the pain; and I know he's in a better place right now than I am." She continues to attend the services. Her son-in-law, a twenty-five-year-old with a picture of Jesus on his belt buckle, sums it up this way: "The Bible says every man has got an appointed time to die. If it's driving the car, or handling serpents, or sitting here talking to you." His brothers and sisters have been trying to get him to leave the church. His response: "I ain't going to hell for nobody!"

When another woman in that church was asked why she allowed her children to participate in the service, she replied: "My children take up serpents and I worry because I am a mother. I can't tell them not to do that because I would be telling them not to obey the Lord. See, you can't hide anything from the Lord. If I sit here and told you it didn't scare me, that would be a lie because God knows it does."

All these people risk their lives and the lives of their children "because it is God's will." How do they know it is God's will? They know that it is God's will because they read the words in their Bible and they believe that every single word in that book is the inerrant "Word of God."

The mysterious truth is that the Bible is the inerrant "Word of God" in ways these poor people do not understand. They have exercised the so-called left brain of logical analysis and have focused their attention on the detail of one single "surface irregularity." And in so doing, they have lost sight of the marvelous image there beneath the surface which invites them to explore its mystery in new ways of thinking and of personal experience.

This brings us to the second analogy, that of the 3-D stereogram. I remember my first experience with this new art form in the Lawrence Hall of Science in Berkeley. My daughter told me to stare at a huge picture on the wall. I still am not able to explain what became visible. It's a mystery. Somehow the whole picture suddenly changed as my focus shifted to a point beyond, or inside, the picture. At that point a new picture emerged which was three-dimensional in nature. And no matter how much I try to explain it to others, they cannot understand what I saw until they share that same experience of discovery. Moreover, having that experience tends to be addictive. One wants to experience it again and again, and to share it with others.

The experience of seeing a stereogram utilizes another part of the brain, the so-called right brain. This experience of seeing is not achieved through logical analysis. To me, this way of seeing is a bit like the role of icons in Eastern Church traditions. In my Baptist tradition, icons do not play a significant role, unless of course, as some more liberally oriented critics would have it, the Bible itself becomes an icon.

My introduction to the field of iconography was a meditation by Henry Nouwen on "Rublev's Icon of the Trinity" in the *Harvard Divinity Bulletin* (June-August 1984). I was struck with how deeply Rublev's icon spoke to Nouwen, and to others as well, who have taken the time to enter deeply into its structure and symbolism.

Let's take a brief look at this remarkable work, considered by some "to be one of the most perfect achievements in the history of art."[26] Nouwen was experiencing what he called "a hard period of (his) life, in which verbal prayer had become nearly impossible." It was "a long and quiet presence to this Icon (which) became the beginning of (his) healing."

Rublev painted his icon in memory of St. Sergius, in a desire to bring fifteenth-century Russia together around the name of God so that its people would conquer "the devouring hatred of the world by the contemplation of the Holy Trinity." He chose a moment in the Old Testament narrative of Abraham's three heavenly visitors in Genesis 18 to portray the Trinity. In the icon, the table which Abraham set for his three guests beneath the oak of Mamre becomes an altar on which the flesh of the freshly slaughtered calf is placed in a chalice. The picture is shaped by two geometric forms. On the one hand, the figures compose a circle with the chalice at the center and each of the three figures speaks by means of their right hands. For Nouwen, the central figure is God the Father and his two fingers point to the chalice and to God the Son.

The message is clear. It is a message of the incarnation itself; and the Son, understanding its full significance, accepts that painful task in the gesture of the hand. The Holy Spirit opposite extends a hand of blessing on the action thus signified and at the same time directs the viewer's attention to the peculiar opening beneath the chalice. It is here, according to Nouwen, that the viewer is drawn literally inside the icon itself in an upward direction—through the chalice, to God the Father, and then to a tree.

At that point the second structural pattern in Rublev's icon becomes clear. For together with the alignment of the three faces, we now have a cross which speaks of the profound mystery of God's self-revelation. As Nouwen put it, "It is a mystery beyond history, yet made visible through it. It is a divine mystery, yet human too. It is a joyful, sorrowful, and glorious mystery transcending all human emotions, yet not leaving any human emotion untouched."

Is this a proper way in which to read the Bible? Are we permitted to use a single episode in a narrative complex in the book of Genesis as a window through which to view the whole of the Scriptures, as Rublev has done? In light of what we have presented above regarding the canonical process, the answer to these questions must be a resounding yes, in spite of the obvious tension such a reading creates with the historical-critical method itself.

Rublev's Icon of the Trinity

What we are suggesting here is that we should press the analogy a bit further; in that the Bible itself, as a whole, is to be read in a manner somewhat like Nouwen has read Rublev's icon. If we take the long hours necessary to contemplate the structural detail of the Bible taken as a whole, it is possible to see the hand of an artist at work in the formation and structure of the canon of sacred Scripture. Moreover, it is clear that such contemplative insight may touch our emotions and ultimately transform us.

In short, it is possible to see two structural configurations in the canon of the First Testament that seem to intersect and point beyond themselves to the same redemptive, revelatory act of God which Nouwen has seen in Rublev's icon. The first of these structures is concentric in nature and embraces what we commonly call the Law and the Prophets. At the center we have two groups of four books in the Hebrew canon: Exodus, Leviticus, Numbers, Deuteronomy // Joshua, Judges, Samuel, Kings.

The first group appears at first glance to be the story of Moses, beginning with his birth (Exodus 1-2) and ending with his death (Deuteronomy 34). A closer look at the detail within Exodus and Deuteronomy reveals further aspects of a concentric arrangement. There are two "Songs of Moses" (Exodus 15 and Deuteronomy 32), which frame two great covenant ceremonies under Moses' leadership—one at Mount Sinai (Exodus 19) and the other on the Plains of Moab (Deuteronomy 29-31). The first of these is concluded by the giving of the "ten commandments" (Exodus 20) followed by the "Covenant Code" (Exodus 21-23); whereas the second is preceded by a second giving of the "ten commandments" (Deuteronomy 5) followed by the "Deuteronomic Code" (Deuteronomy 12-26). And the books of Exodus and Deuteronomy frame the two parallel wilderness books of Leviticus and Numbers. As Edward Newing has shown, this concentric structure has a center in Exodus 33, which he calls the "Promised Presence," where Moses gets a glimpse of the glory of Yahweh.

According to A. H. van Zyl, the so-called Deuteronomic History in the parallel group of four books also has a concentric structural design. We move from the conquest of the land under charismatic leadership (Joshua) to the loss of the land under monarchic government (2 Kings). In between, we have the possession of the land under charismatic leadership (Judges and 1 Samuel) set against the possession of the land under monarchic government (2 Samuel and 1 Kings). This section, too, has a center which consists of two parallel mountaintop experiences on the part of Elijah. In 1 Kings 18, Elijah calls down fire from heaven in the great contest with the prophets of Baal on Mount Carmel. In the next chapter, Elijah makes his way to Mount Horeb, the mountain of God's revelation to Moses, where he too gains a glimpse of the glory of Yahweh. But after each theophanic visitation, the narrator is careful to comment that God was not present in the wind, nor the earthquake, nor the fire. This time God communicates his glory through the awesome silence of his absence. Needless to say, the confluence of these two encounters with God on that same sacred mountain point beyond themselves to another mountaintop experience where Moses and Elijah are joined by a prophet greater than either of them, through whom the glory of God is revealed in what the Gospel writers call the transfiguration of Jesus.

The two groups of four books in the Law and the Former Prophets focus on Moses, set against the subsequent succession of leaders in ancient Israel which extends from Joshua to Jehoiachin, the last king of Judah, who was released from prison in Babylon. These eight books are framed by the stories of the "Ancestors" (Abraham, Isaac, Jacob, and Jacob's twelve sons—Genesis 12-50) and the "Prophets" (Isaiah, Jeremiah, Ezekiel, and the twelve minor prophets). The designation of Abraham in the book of Genesis as a prophet (Gen 20:7) who is the recipient of God's covenant promise thus takes on a deeper dimension. In the words of the great classical prophets of ancient Israel, the old epic story received a powerful new meaning. Here we meet another structure which points beyond itself as well.

The primary epic story of the Old Testament may be outlined in linear form (as we argued in chapters 2 and 3) in terms of a journey out of bondage in Egypt, through the waters into the wilderness, en route to the Promised Land. And though these terms are rooted in past events, however elusive they prove to be to the historian, in the hands of the great prophets of Israel each of these symbols is transformed and projected beyond history into an eschatological dimension. The creation stories of Genesis 1-11 anticipate a new *Opus Dei* ("work of God") in the city of God which is described as a "New Jerusalem." The people of God see themselves as once more in exile and bondage, awaiting a new deliverance which will carry them through the waters and the wilderness of a New Exodus to a New Conquest which will become the Kingdom of God.

Is it any wonder that Luke, in his description of the transfiguration of Jesus, describes the conversation between Moses, Elijah, and Jesus as focusing on "his Exodus" which was to be accomplished at Jerusalem (Luke 9:28-31)? As Rublev saw, in his own way, it is an empty tomb that draws each one of us inside the icon of sacred Scripture to discover the meaning of its intriguing structures. Those structures converge in a cross and a great circle, where the end is also the beginning.

In spite of the controversy of recent years on the question of the inerrancy of Scripture, the term remains useful. To claim that the Bible is trustworthy is simply not sufficient. The road maps produced by the American Automobile Association are trustworthy; but they are not Scripture. To claim the inerrancy of Scripture is to claim God as author. The Bible is "God's Story" revealed in human history. As such, the Bible shares in the mystery of the incarnation of Jesus Christ as the creative "Word of God" (John 1:1). On the one hand, the Bible is a human book produced by fallible men and women in times past. At the same time, the Bible is also the product of a divine author. And no matter how much we progress in our understanding of the historical process God used to give us this book, it will forever remain a mystery beyond rational analysis, at least in its essence. That's what we mean when we insist that the Bible is the inerrant Word of God; and, as such, that it preserves for us the normative written record of "God's Story in Human History."

Thinking Exercise

On the Authority of the Bible

The critical thinking goal for this exercise is to clarify the concept of the Bible as the revealed inerrant word of God.

How To Do This Exercise

Norbert Lohfink has argued that the concept of inerrancy of the Scriptures has been used in three different ways in church history: 1) inerrant authors; 2) inerrant books of the Bible; and 3) inerrancy of the Bible as a whole. With these three distinctions in mind, answer the following:

1. What problems do we face when we think of authorship of individual books of the Bible, like the book of Isaiah, when we have in mind a single author writing a book on paper at a particular point in time?

_____

_____

_____

_____

_____

2. What problems do we face when we think of particular books in the Bible, such as the book of Nahum, without taking into account its context within the Book of the Twelve in relation to the book of Habakkuk?

_____

_____

_____

_____

_____

3. What evidence can you cite to argue for a coherency of the Bible taken as a whole which points toward the existence of an author as such?

_____

_____

_____

_____

_____

4. If you decide to designate this "author" of the Bible as a whole to be God, what concepts can you think of which may prove useful in terms of logical, objective description of this phenomenon?

_____

_____

_____

_____

_____

5. What terms, metaphors, and analogies can you think of which may be useful to communicate the concept of the Bible as the revealed inerrant word of God?

_____

_____

_____

_____

_____

Discussion Questions

1. Is Moses the author of the Pentateuch?

2. Is the Bible "inerrant in the autographs," as claimed by members of the Evangelical Theological Society?

Concept Map: Summary of Chapter 5

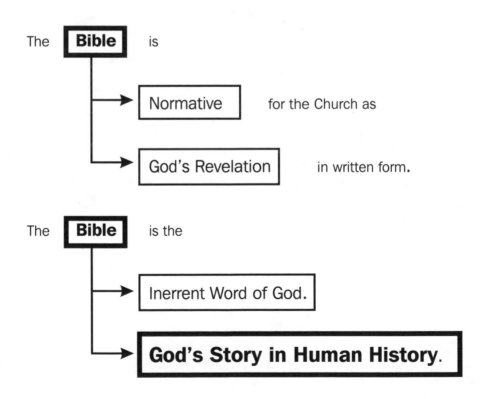

Notes

Notes to preface

1. See Jo Milgrom, *Handmade Midrash: Workshops in Visual Theology* (Philadelphia, New York, Jerusalem: Jewish Publication Society, 1992). A briefer presentation of this method may be found in "Encountering the Exodus Story Through Handmade Midrash," by D. L. Christensen and Jo Milgrom, in my book, *Experiencing the Exodus from Egypt* (Berkeley: BIBAL Press, 1988), pp. 3-36.

2. W. Gordon, *Synectics: The Development of Creative Capacity* (New York: Harper and Row, 1961), pp. 117-19.

3. See my article, "The Akedah in Genesis 22:1-19: An Invitation to Jewish-Christian Dialogue," *American Baptist Quarterly* 4 (1985), pp. 340-46; which is reprinted as Appendix B in *Experiencing the Exodus from Egypt* (Berkeley: BIBAL Press, 1988), pp. 89-95.

4. J. Sanford, *The Man Who Wrestled With God* (Paulist Press, 1981), p. 5.

5. C. L'Heureux, *Life Journey and the Old Testament: An Experiential Approach to the Bible and Personal Transformation* (Paulist Press, 1986), p. vii.

Notes to chapter 1

1. K. E. Christopherson, "Fundamentalism: What Led up to It, How it Got among Us, and What We in Academe Do about It," an unpublished paper used in a course on "Judaeo-Christian Life and Thought," at Pacific Lutheran University, dated August 29, 1979.

2. R. Polzin, *Moses and the Deuteronomist: A Literary Study of the Deuteronomic History* (New York: Seabury Press, 1980).

3. N. Lohfink, *The Inerrancy of Scripture and Other Essays* (Berkeley: BIBAL Press, 1992), pp. 24-51 (especially p. 39).

4. For a similar bipolar concept of authority, i.e., "Authority of the Word" vs. "Authority of the Spirit," see D. M. Lloyd-Jones, *Authority* (Chicago: Inter-Varsity Press, 1958). I am grateful to John Olley of the Baptist Theological College of Western Australia for this reference.

5. R. B. Laurin, ed., *Contemporary Old Testament Theologians* (Philadelphia: Judson Press, 1970), p. 18.

6. M. W. Wallbank, et al, *Civilization Past and Present*, vol. 1, 6th ed. (Glenview, IL: Scott, Foresman and Co., 1969), p. 398.

7. M. Brauch, "Theological Education: The Glory and the Agony," *TSF Bulletin* 9/2 (Nov.-Dec. 1985), p. 4.

Notes to chapter 2

1. Though the number of books in earliest Jewish tradition was increased from twenty-two to twenty-six in some circles, and ultimately to twenty-four in the Talmud, the actual order of the books remains the same. To get twenty-four, Ezra-Nehemiah and 1 and 2 Chronicles are considered to be single books.

2. See the recent publication of the Hebrew Bible, *Tanakh: The Holy Scriptures* (The Jewish Publication Society, 1988).

3. D. L. Christensen, "Josephus and the Twenty-Two-Book Canon of Sacred Scripture," *Journal of the Evangelical Theological Society* 29/1 (1986), 37-46.

4. N. Sarna, *Understanding Genesis* (New York: McGraw-Hill, 1966), p. 84; and C. Labuschagne, "The Literary and Theological Function of Divine Speech in the Pentateuch," in *Vetus Testamentum* Supplement 36 (1985), p. 171. Labuschagne's arguments are spelled out in detail in his book, *Vertellen met getallen* (Zoetermeer, 1992); which, hopefully, will be available in English translation shortly.

5. See D. N. Freedman's article, "Canon of the OT," in *The Interpreter's Dictionary of the Bible,* Supplementary Volume (Nashville: Abingdon, 1976), pp. 131-32.

6. F. M. Cross, Jr., *Canaanite Myth and Hebrew Epic: Essays in the History of the Religion of Israel* (Cambridge: Harvard University, 1973), pp. 99-111.

7. D. L. Christensen, "Num 21:14-15 and the Book of the Wars of Yahweh," *Catholic Biblical Quarterly* 36 (1974), pp. 359-60; "Book of the Wars of the Lord," *Anchor Bible Dictionary*, vol. 6 (Garden City, NY: Doubleday, 1992), p. 880.

8. E. G. Newing, "A Rhetorical & Theological Analysis of the Hexateuch," *South East Asia Journal of Theology* 22 (1981), pp. 1-15.

9. The diagram here is taken from Jacob Milgrom's commentary, *The JPS Torah Commentary: Numbers* (Philadelphia/New York: The Jewish Publication Society, 1990), p. xviii.

10. See my article, "Jonah and the Sabbath Rest in the Pentateuch," in *Biblische Theologie und gesellschaftlicher Wandel*, Festschrift für Norbert Lohfink, S.J., eds. G. Braulik, W. Groß, S. McEvenue (Freiburg, Basel, Wien: Herder, 1993), pp. 57-58.

11. Robert R. Wilson, *Prophecy and Society in Ancient Israel* (Philadelphia: Fortress Press, 1980), pp. 223 and 234.

12. R. Wilson, *Prophecy and Society*, p. 245, where Wilson is citing S. Dean McBride.

13. On the connection between the Decalogue in Deut 5 and Deut 12-26, see S. Kaufman, "The Structure of the Deuteronomic Law," *MAARAV* 1 (1979), pp. 105-58, who argues that Deut 12:1-25:16 is in fact a literary expansion on the part of a single author. See also G. Braulik, "The Sequence of the Laws in Deuteronomy 12-26 and the Decalogue," in *A Song of Power and the Power of Song: Essays on the Book of Deuteronomy*, ed. D. L. Christensen (Winona Lake, IN: Eisenbrauns, 1993), pp. 313-335.

14. See note 7 above.

15. A. H. van Zyl, "Chronological Deuteronomic History," *5th World Congress of Jewish Studies*, vol. 1 (1969), pp. 12ff.

16. The situation is similar in the Latter Prophets, particularly in Isaiah 40-55. See my article, "A New Israel: The Righteous from among All Nations, " in *Israel's Apostasy and Restoration: Essays in Honor of Roland K. Harrison*, ed. A. Gileadi (Grand Rapids, MI: Baker Book House, 1988), pp. 251-259.

17. Cf. Samuel Terrien, *The Elusive Presence: Toward a New Biblical Theology* (Harper & Row, 1978), pp. 227-36 and 422-28.

18. J. Watts, *Isaiah 1-33*. Word Biblical Commentary, vol. 24 (Waco, TX: Word Books, 1985), p. li.

19. J. Watts, *Isaiah 1-33*, p. li.

20. D. L. Christensen, "Jonah and the Sabbath Rest in the Pentateuch," in *Biblische Theologie und gesellschaftlicher Wandel: Für Norbert Lohfink, S.J.*, eds. G. Braulik, W. Groß, S. McEvenue (Freiburg, Basel, Wien: Herder, 1993), pp. 48-60.

21. See J. Magonet, *Form and Meaning: Studies in Literary Techniques in the Book of Jonah* (BEvT 2; Bern and Frankfurt/M.: Lang, 1976), pp. 44-50.

22. D. L. Christensen, "The Book of Nahum: The Question of Authorship within the Canonical Process," *Journal of the Evangelical Theological Society* 31/1 (March 1988), pp. 51-58.

23. J. Blenkinsopp, *Prophecy and Canon: A Contribution to the Study of Jewish Origins* (Notre Dame: University of Notre Dame Press, 1977), pp. 120-21 and G. Ostborn, *Cult and Canon* (Uppsala, 1950), p. 44, which is cited by Blenkinsopp.

24. The term is borrowed from Samuel Terrien, *The Elusive Presence*, p. 380.

25. The pioneering work on the reconstruction of the readings for the triennial cycle is Adolf Büchler, "The Reading of the Law and Prophets in a Triennial Cycle," *Jewish Quarterly Review* 5 (1893), pp. 420-468 and 6 (1894), pp. 1-73. See also Nahum Sarna, *Journal of Biblical Literature* 87 (1968), p. 102.

26. N. Snaith, "The Triennial Cycle and the Psalter," *Zeitschrift für die alttestamentlicher Wissenschaft* 51 (1933), p. 304. Psalm 119 with its interest in the law would have formed an excellent companion to the commencement of the book of Deuteronomy. In the midrash on Psalm 119 (*Midrash Tehillim*) there are twenty-one quotations from Deuteronomy.

27. The diagrams are taken from an article by I. Abrahams, "E. G. King on 'The Influence of the Triennial Cycle upon the Psalter,'" *Jewish Quarterly Review* 16 (1904), pp. 580-581.

28. M. D. Goulder, *The Psalms of the Sons of Korah*. (JSOT Press, 1982), argues that the Korah Psalms originated in Dan.

29. See my articles, "Job and the Age of the Patriarchs in Old Testament Narrative," *Perspectives in Religious Studies* 13/3 (1986), pp. 225-28; and "A New Israel: The Righteous from among All Nations," in *Israel's Apostasy and Restoration: Essays in Honor of Roland K. Harrison* (Grand Rapids, MI: Baker, 1988), pp. 256-258.

30. See *Interpreter's Dictionary of the Bible* (1962), vol. 2, p. 911.

31. This particular point was stressed in his presidential address, "The Old Testament in Twenty Minutes," which was presented to the Society of Biblical Literature during its Pacific Coast Region annual meeting on March 29, 1985.

32. The number 110 for the age of Joseph is sometimes related to a presumed ideal age in Egyptian literary tradition. See N. Sarna, *Understanding Genesis* (New York: McGraw-Hill, 1966), pp. 226, 231, who mentions twenty-seven such references in Egyptian literature. Even so, it seems preferable to explain the number on the basis of a mathematical schema within the biblical material itself.

33. F. L. Meshberger, "An Interpretation of Michelangelo's *Creation of Adam* based on Neuroanatomy," *Journal of the American Medical Association* 264 (1990), 1837-1841.

34. D. L. Christensen, "Josephus and the Twenty-two-book Canon of Sacred Scripture," *Journal of the Evangelical Theological Society* 29/1 (1986), pp. 37-46.

35. See Moses Stuart, *Critical History and Defense of the Old Testament Canon* (Andover: Warren F. Draper, 1872), p. 404.

36. M. Stuart, *Old Testament Canon*, p. 258.

37. M. Stuart, *Old Testament Canon*, p. 415.

38. See Menahem Haran, "Book-Scrolls in Israel in Pre-Exilic Times," *Journal of Jewish Studies* 33 (1982), pp. 161-173.

39. See David Noel Freedman, "The Undiscovered Symmetry of the Bible," *Bible Review* 10/1 (February 1994), pp. 34-41; "The Symmetry of the Hebrew Bible," *Studia Theologica* 46 (1992), pp. 83-108; and *The Unity of the Hebrew Bible* (Ann Arbor: University of Michigan, 1991). On the data for the New Testament, see Robert Morganthaler, *Statistik des Neutestamentlichen Wortschatzes* (1958).

40. Dan Olson, "The Biblical Center and the Canonical Process: Reflections on the 'Pentateuchal' Model and the Book of Enoch," unpublished paper submitted in a course on the Pentateuch at Fuller Theological Seminary, Menlo Park (May 21, 1993).

41. Eliezer Shulman, *The Sequence of Events in the Old Testament*, trans. Sarah Lederhendler (Israel: Investment Co. of Bank Hapoalim and Ministry of Defense, 1987), p. 22.

42. D. L. Christensen, "Janus Parallelism in Genesis 6:3," *Hebrew Studies* 27 (1986), pp. 20-24.

43. Isaac M. Kikawada and Arthur Quinn, *Before Abraham Was* (Abingdon, 1985), pp. 119-126.

44. The only explicit citation is in Heb 11:17 (cf. Rom 8:32).

45. D. Garrett, *Rethinking Genesis* (Baker, 1991), pp. 121-125; G. Rendsburg, *The Redaction of Genesis* (Eisenbrauns, 1986), pp. 53-69.

46. See J. Z. Smith, "The Prayer of Joseph," in J. Neusner (ed.), *Religions in Antiquity: Essays in Memory of Erwin Ramsdell Goodenough* (Leiden: Brill, 1968), pp. 253-294.

47. I owe this observation to my student, Dan Olson.

Notes to chapter 3

1. N. Lohfink, "The Inerrancy of Scripture," in *The Inerrancy of Scripture and Other Essays* (Berkeley: BIBAL Press, 1992), p. 39.

2. See, in particular, the work of Aaron Wildavsky, *The Nursing Father: Moses as a Political Leader* (University of Alabama Press, 1984); and *Assimilation versus Separation: Joseph the Administrator* (New Brunswick, NJ: Transaction Publications, 1993).

3. M. Weinfeld, "Deuteronomic Literature and Wisdom Literature," in *Deuteronomy and the Deuteronomic School* (Oxford University Press, 1972), pp. 244-281.

4. See my article, "Num 21:14-15 and the Book of the Wars of Yahweh," *Catholic Biblical Quarterly* 36 (1974), pp. 359-360.

Notes to chapter 4

1. See my article, "Josephus and the Twenty-Two-Book Canon of Sacred Scripture," *Journal of the Evangelical Theological Society* 29/1 (March 1986), pp. 37-46.

2. Robert Lowth, *Lectures on the Sacred Poetry of the Hebrews*, trans. G. Gregory (London, 1815), pp. 54-55.

3. Suzanne Haïk-Vantoura, *The Music of the Bible Revealed: The Deciphering of a Millenary Notation*, translated by Dennis Weber and edited by John Wheeler (Berkeley: BIBAL Press, 1991).

4. See John Wheeler, "Afterword by the Editor," in *The Music of the Bible Revealed*, p. 494; and Paul Kahle, *The Cairo Geniza*, 2nd ed. (New York: Frederick Praeger, 1960), pp. 82-85, 103.

5. On the Kodaly method, see Lois Choksy, *The Kodaly Method: Comprehensive Music Education from Infant to Adult*, 2nd ed. (Englewood Cliff, NJ: Prentice Hall, 1987).

6. In addition to the work of Suzanne Haïk-Vantoura, one should also see Anne Kilmer, Robert Brown, and Richard Crocker, "Sounds from Silence: Recent Discoveries in Ancient Near Eastern Music," Stereo LP, with 24 page booklet. Bit Enki Records 101 (1976)—the publication of a Hurrian cult hymn and tuning text from Babylonia.

7. The balance of this chapter is dependent on the work of Norman L. Geisler and William E. Nix, *From God to Us: How We Got Our Bible* (Chicago: Moody Press, 1974), chs. 12-20, pp. 139-255. The material in this section is an abridged adaptation of pp. 139-154 with some additions from other sources.

8. See note 7. The material in this section is based on Geisler & Nix, pp. 154-157; 191-196; 200-212; and 217-226.

9. Quoted from Geisler & Nix, p. 222.

10. See Norman L. Geisler and William E. Nix, *A General Introduction to the Bible* (Chicago: Moody Press, 1968), p. 357.

11. See note 7. The material in this section is based on Geisler & Nix, pp. 162-173 and 183-184.

12. See note 7. The material in this section is based on Geisler & Nix, pp. 227-253.

Notes to chapter 5

1. This particular quotation is taken from *The American Heritage Dictionary of the English Language* (Houghton Mifflin, 1969), p. 496.

2. E. Hoyle, *The Accurate Gamester's Companion* (9th ed.; London: Osborne and Reeve, 1748), evolved into the standard bible of the card player, *Hoyle's Card Games* (New York: Methuen, 1979).

3. *Praise: Our Songs and Hymns* (Grand Rapids: Zondervan, 1983 [1979]), p. 35.

4. See D. L. Christensen, "Form and Structure in Deuteronomy 1-11," in *Das Deuteronomium* (Bibliotheca ephemeridum theologicarum lovaniensium, 68; 1985), pp. 135-144; and *Deuteronomy 1-11*, Word Biblical Commentary, vol. 6A (Dallas, TX: Word Books, 1991).

5. S. Haïk-Vantoura, *La Musique de la Bible Révélée* (Paris: Dessain et Tolra, 1976), now available in English translation, *The Music of the Bible Revealed*, trans. by D. Weber (Berkeley: BIBAL Press, 1991).

6. D. N. Freedman, "Canon of the Old Testament," in *Supplement Volume to Interpreter's Dictionary of the Bible* (Abingdon, 1976), pp. 131-132.

7. T. Georgiades, *Music and Language: The Rise of Western Music as Exemplified in Settings of the Mass* (Cambridge: Cambridge University, 1982), pp. 1-6.

8. I am indebted to John Wheeler for this observation.

9. See D. L. Christensen, "Prose and Poetry in the Bible: The Narrative Poetics of Deuteronomy 1,9-18," *Zeitschrift für die alttestamentliche Wissenschaft* 97 (1985), pp. 179-189.

10. One of my students, Michael Lannon, argued this point with unusual force in an unpublished paper (1985), "Deuteronomy: A Song of Power and the Power of Song." I borrowed this concept from him in the title of a recent book, *A Song of Power and the Power of Song: Essays on the Book of Deuteronomy* (Eisenbrauns, 1993).

11. See G. Ernest Wright, *God Who Acts: Biblical Theology as Recital* (Studies in Biblical Theology, 8; London: SCM, 1952).

12. The thoughts expressed in the following paragraphs are largely those of Marcel Naruki. See our joint article, "The Mosaic Authorship of the Pentateuch," *Journal of the Evangelical Theological Society* 32/4 (December 1989), pp. 465-471.

13. R. Alter, *The Art of Biblical Narrative* (New York: Basic Books, 1981), p. 154.

14. See Charles E. Hummel, *The Galileo Connection: Resolving Conflicts between Science & the Bible* (Downers Grove, IL: Inter-Varsity Press, 1986).

15. Nancy Pearcey and Charles Thaxton, *The Soul of Science: Christian Faith and Natural Philosophy*. Turning Point Christian Series (Crossway Books, 1994).

16. J. C. Whitcomb, Jr., and Henry Morris, *The Genesis Flood* (Philadelphia: Presbyterian and Reformed, 1961).

17. Charles Colson, "Are Christians 'Anti-Science'?", *Jubilee: The Monthly Newsletter of Prison Fellowship* (November 1994), p. 7.

18. Hugh Ross, *Creation and Time: A Biblical and Scientific Perspective on the Creation-Date Controversy* (Colorado Springs: NavPress, 1994), p. 155.

19. James Montgomery Boice, *Does Inerrancy Matter?* (Oakland, CA: International Council on Biblical Inerrancy, 1979), p. 2.

20. E. Radmacher and R. Preus, eds., *Hermeneutics, Inerrancy, and the Bible: Proceedings from the ICBI Summit 11, 1982, in Chicago, IL* (Grand Rapids, MI: Academie Books, 1984), pp. 901-903.

21. Hugh Ross, *Creation and Time,* p. 157.

22. Norbert Lohfink, "Inerrancy of Scripture," *The Inerrancy of Scripture and Other Essays* (Berkeley: BIBAL Press, 1991), p. 24.

23. Lohfink, *Inerrancy*, p. 51.

24. See T. Nemoto, M. Tokuyama, and N. Tsukahara, eds., *Super-Stereogram* (San Francisco: Cadence Books, 1994).

25. This illustration is taken from an article by Jim Myers, "Either every word in the Bible is right or its wrong!," in his newsletter *Discovering the Bible*, vol. 6, No. 10 (1994), pp. 1, 6.

26. Sr. M. Helen Weier, O.S.C., *Festal Icons of the Lord* (Collegeville, MN: The Liturgical Press, 1977), p. 45.

Answers to Concept Checks

1. The word "old" is often pejorative in English usage suggesting to many Christians that the Old Testament is of little importance, having been superseded by the New Testament. Since the entire Bible is canonical Scripture, it is wise to use neutral language in referring to the two major sections of the canon.

2. Yes, at least from a practical point of view. The professional journals and academic societies, which are structured around these disciplines, are traditional in nature.

3. No, the omission of the word "holy" in the title in such editions as the Harper Collins Study Bible (NRSV) is not a statement against the belief in revelation as such. It is true, however, that few Christians and Jews revere the sacred text today in the manner described in the Talmud and practiced widely in the Muslim world so far as the Koran is concerned.

4. Yes it would. In addition to the obvious value in terms of deepening the dialogue between Jews and Christians, there are heuristic values as well, which will become increasingly evident in further study of this textbook. The structure of the Hebrew Bible, as preserved in the Masoretic Text, reflects in broad measure the canonical process itself, which produced the Bible as we know it. It is easier to *think biblically* with this structure.

5. Yes it is. We will explore this possibility in depth in Chapter 3.

6. It is important to note the fact that numbers were used theologically in the scribal circles of ancient Israel. Not only does this fact help us to avoid the difficulties with respect to numbers that appear to be excessive, it also directs our attention toward more important issues in matters of theology.

7. The central theological consequence in the story of the Exodus from Egypt is the experience of the presence of God on the part of the people of Israel.

8. A good king in the Former Prophets is one who listens to the prophet and shares his rule over the people of Israel with the prophet. His "goodness" has nothing to do with morality as such.

9. Concern for women in the Former Prophets is part of a larger concern for the powerless, which focused specifically on the widow, the orphan, and the resident alien.

10. The book of Deuteronomy functions as a literary bridge connecting the Pentateuch and the Former Prophets.

11. Yes, the book of Isaiah is a collection of material which is to be read over against the Book of the Twelve (minor prophets). It is not to be read as an isolated book by a single individual written at a point in time in the eighth century BCE.

12. Yes, the destruction of the Temple in Jerusalem was central so far as the canonical process is concerned. Jeremiah ministered primarily in Jerusalem before the destruction of the Temple and subsequently died in exile in Egypt. Ezekiel was exiled to Babylon ten years before the destruction of the Temple. Both prophets are transitional—bridging the era of ancient Israel and that of early Judaism.

13. More than half of the 150 psalms in the Hebrew Bible are ascribed to authors other than David, including one to Moses (Psalm 90). The correspondence between individual psalms and the corresponding readings from the Torah suggest that the psalms were adapted to prescribed readings in the Pentateuch such that

individual psalms were altered, or perhaps even written, for specific occasions in the worship cycle of the Second Temple in Jerusalem.

14. If the literary scheme is to place Job among the Ancestors in the book of Genesis, then the writers are also suggesting that God's purposes extend beyond the people of ancient Israel as such. The thrust of the Writings as a whole seems to imply a universalism in God's purposes among the nations.

15. The fundamental teaching in the religion of ancient Israel is that God is one. At the same time, there is a profound mystery here; for God is beyond gender. The figure of Lady Wisdom addresses this mystery. According to the book of Proverbs, she was there before the creation of the universe. In a sense then, she is part of the godhead.

16. Though people knew how to read, the culture was not literate in the modern sense. Literature was written by hand on scrolls or on individual leaves made of papyrus or parchment. Consequently written documents were expensive. The parchment scrolls were made for public reading aloud, generally within the context of worship in the synagogues and early church meeting places. The idea of reading silently from a manuscript was virtually unknown in antiquity. The "reading" of the Scriptures on the part of the disciples was in the form of public recitation, primarily within the context of a community assembled for worship and study.

17. The book of Daniel is difficult to classify from a literary point of view. Though it is commonly listed among the prophets in Christian tradition, in terms of canonical structure it belongs to the Writings as the only example of full-blown apocalyptic literature, which includes a collection of wisdom tales (chs. 1-6). As such it functions as a bridge connecting the Former Prophets, the Latter Prophets, older "Wisdom," and the historical tradition of the so-called Chronicler. Its theme is that of the four great kingdoms which sets the stage for the "Kingdom of God."

18. It is easy to remember. The structure consists of a simple chiasm, with a center. That center tends to constitute the central point, which is often reinforced in the first and last elements of the five-part structure. Moreover, the pattern produces an aesthetic feeling of balance and beauty for both the performer and the audience, as musicians have known through the centuries. The principle of "nesting" in certain computer programming witnesses to the fact that concentric design is a basic part of the structuring process of the human psyche—a way the mind organizes material and retains it through extensive periods of time. It is akin to what some have called the "right-brain" logic of the human brain.

19. Jesus, like Isaac, is presented as the only "beloved son" of his father who decided to offer him up as a sacrifice as God had decreed. Isaac carried the wood for the burnt offering on his back, as Jesus carried his own cross to Golgotha. The unique ram, who is substituted at the last minute for Isaac and offered as a burnt offering in his place, is paralleled in the Christian understanding of Jesus as the "Passover lamb" who died in our place.

20. The Day of Atonement is the most solemn moment in the religious calendar of the Jews, ancient and modern. Christians saw the symbolism of the account in Leviticus 16 as fulfilled in the atoning work of Jesus. He is the scapegoat as well as the ultimate sacrificial offering itself, which achieves atonement for sin—but, in this instance, not merely "once a year for all the sins of the Israelites" (Lev 16:34). For the Christians, "we have been made holy through the sacrifice of the body of Jesus Christ once for all" (Heb 10:10).

21. The "Kingdom of God" in the teaching of Jesus, becomes the fifth and final monarchy in Christian tradition—the culmination of human history.

22. Yes, it does. It is difficult to conceive of a design as intricate as what is observed here without a designer. Traditional explanations within the faith communities of both Judaism and Christianity, which claim that the Bible is the "Word of God," see God as the "author." It is also possible to explain the phenomena, at least in part, in terms of what depth psychology calls the "collective unconscious" within the historical process of a given community.

23. The implications are profound. Jesus patterned a servant model of leadership which is sadly lacking in many Christian institutions, where leaders act in terms of political "Machiavellian" models instead.

24. Yes, it does. The culmination of the canonical process in ancient Israel is found in the person and work of Jesus Christ as interpreted by the early Christian Church, which emerged within the context of the so-called Pax Romana ("Roman peace") that Paul had in mind.

25. The Gospel accounts of the transfiguration do not appear to be commentary on any specific Old Testament texts so much as they are an explosive series of associations which link Moses and Elijah with Jesus. The point is what is communicated by God himself at this decisive moment in the narrative, when Jesus consciously commences a journey of suffering: "This is my Son, hear him as you would Moses and Elijah!"

26. The significance lies in the fact that it directs our attention to liturgical performance of the biblical text in antiquity, and to the music of the Bible in particular. The ancient scribes have left us a wealth of information to reconstruct how the Hebrew Bible was written to be heard as "music" within the context of worship in the Second Temple in Jerusalem.

27. The Bible is cross-cultural in its appeal such that manuscripts survive in virtually every cultural context in which literature was known in antiquity.

28. In terms of hard evidence, it extends our knowledge of the Hebrew text of the First Testament back a thousand years earlier in time.

29. The uncials appear to be the first official copies of the Greek text made on vellum so as to preserve the text for future generations. The fact that proper word division, punctuation, and organization of the text into chapters and verses took place later, over centuries of time, illustrates the dynamic nature of the biblical text, which was composed primarily to be heard in public recitation rather than to be read in private.

30. The most important consequence of this evidence is the fact that the Greek language of the Second Testament is the common language of the first century, and not some "perfect language" from God as some of the early Church Fathers assumed. The meaning of the vocabulary of the Bible has been illuminated enormously by study of this evidence.

31. From earliest times, the biblical text has been interpreted, and even altered, to suit the needs of specific groups of people. The official text represents the fixing of a developing tradition within the mainstream of the community of faith.

32. Official Targums appeared only for those texts which were read on a regular basis in public worship within ancient Judaism. As the Hebrew language became less and less familiar to the worshipers, they became more

and more dependent on the Aramaic paraphrases.

33. Translation is by its essential nature always interpretation as well; and interpretation is shaped by the world view and the specific life situation of the translator. This is why the process of translating the biblical text is never complete.

34. The biblical tradition is dynamic in nature and the "Word of God" is not limited to any single written text or translation of that text. Churches in the West, both Roman Catholic and Protestant, have much to learn from the orthodox churches of the East.

35. Jerome opposed the belief of Augustine and other early Church Fathers who thought that the Greek Septuagint was the authoritative "Word of God," rather than the original Hebrew text of the First Testament. His own Latin translation subsequently took the place of the Septuagint as the inspired "Word of God" within the Roman Catholic Church until the twentieth century.

36. The largest missionary agency in the twentieth century is that of the Wycliffe Bible Translators and the Summer Institute of Linguistics. Their express purpose is to devise the means of putting the biblical text in previously unwritten languages among all the various people groups in the world today.

37. These early writers considered these texts to be authoritative and not always readily available and known to their opponents, whether heretical groups or unbelievers.

38. As was the case with the First Testament in ancient Judaism, the establishment of the canon of the Second Testament had to take place before there was a felt need to establish a standardized text as such. During the period in which the canon of the Second Testament was taking shape,

widespread copying of manuscripts introduced errors and misprints. Roman persecution and the confiscation and destruction of manuscripts led to the production of "unprofessional" copies of the Second Testament, often done in great haste, which added to the problem.

39. The first edition of Erasmus's Greek New Testament was done hastily and contained hundreds of typographical errors. Of even greater importance, however, is the simple fact that the translation itself was based on contemporary handwritten copies of the Bible, which in turn were the products of copying such texts over the course of hundreds of years. The rediscovery of ancient copies of the biblical text was to take place in the subsequent era.

40. The content of the Bible story is more easily communicated and retained when it engages the so-called "right brain" of the recipient. People have known this fact intuitively through the centuries. The primary concern of these early Christians was to communicate the content of the biblical story, not any specific textual form of it.

41. The process is one of validation—from the work of individual scholars to official authorized version under the auspices of the king of England.

42. The political division into two separate camps (Protestant and Roman Catholic) necessitated two different "authorized" versions of the English Bible.

43. The reason for its popularity is in part political. King James I used the occasion to win personal support from the English people and the hierarchy in the established Church of England. The new version replaced both the *Geneva Bible* (among the populace) and the *Bishops' Bible* (within the established Church of England). It's lasting popularity was enhanced by the fact that the task was taken up by a most

competent team of scholars, under the auspices of the royal court which involved both of the major universities in England (at Oxford and Cambridge).

44. The most important single development in Roman Catholic tradition in the twentieth century so far as Bible translation is concerned is the turning away from the Latin Vulgate as the official text of the Bible. The papal encyclical of 1943 opened the door. The publication of *The New American Bible* (1970) and the RSV Common Bible (1973) completed the process.

45. The ASV retains, and perhaps exaggerates, the literalness of its predecessor by following the Hebrew and Greek word order closely. It is easy for the student to get back to the original languages.

46. It was the great influx of Jews from western Europe to the American continent in the late 19th century that produced the need for an improved version of the Hebrew Bible in English for use in synagogue, school, and home.

47. The RSV is the only truly ecumenical Bible, in the sense that it is officially accepted in all major church traditions: Orthodox, Protestant, and Roman Catholic.

48. Since the organizational meeting in Chicago in 1966, the NIV has had the backing of a large number of evangelical organizations in the United States. The evangelical community outnumbers the liberal establishment of the older denominations by a wide margin and the Bible is central in the expression of their faith. Moreover, many ordinary Christian believers simply find the NIV to be more readable. It is a fresh translation from the original Hebrew and Greek texts and not a revision of older works within the old King James tradition.

49. The approval of Knox's translation of the New Testament from the Latin Vulgate within the Roman Catholic Church broke the long established tradition of the Rheims-Douay-Challoner Bible. Rejection of his translation of the Old Testament opened the door to an official translation based on the original Hebrew and Greek texts in *The Jerusalem Bible* (1966) and *The New American Bible* (1970).

50. The primary objective for Weymouth, Peterson, and a number of others has been that of putting the text into contemporary English usage so that the message can be easily understood. Other objectives include that of clarifying the meaning of the text in terms of increases in our knowledge of the best manuscript tradition and the fruits of critical scholarship in terms of recovering the meaning of the language of the Bible itself in its original setting.

51. The ultimate test of intelligibility among professionals in the field of communication is that of putting the message in language a child can understand. Kenneth Taylor's remarkable success with *The Living Bible* (1956-71) encouraged others in this direction.

52. The place of reason in matters of faith is a central issue in religious history and philosophy. As the revealed "word of God," the Bible is the standard to which we must turn to settle matters of dispute. The Scriptures are essentially poetic in form. Poetry is a way of seeing that makes present what lies beyond the bound of human experience and understanding. Theology deals with what is beyond the powers of analytical left-brain reasoning alone. The language of poetry enables us to make use of the full range of human reasoning, including the affective intuitive powers of the so-called right brain.

53. The concept of the inerrancy of Scripture has a long history in Christian and Jewish tradition. Suggested terms to replace the controversial word itself, such as infallible or wholly trustworthy, tend to cut us off from this heritage. It is preferable to focus our attention on the different ways of defining the term "inerrancy," as Norbert Lohfink has done, and to update past discussion in ways that take into account the current state of affairs in theological reflection.

Glossary

Abiathar—one of the two high priests in the time of David, whom King Solomon exiled to Anathoth.

Abimelech—the son of Gideon who actually ruled as king in Israel for three years until his assassination, which occurred a century before the official inauguration of kingship under Saul.

Abraham—a Hebrew patriarch in the book of Genesis and an important figure in three major religions: Judaism, Christianity and Islam. Known earlier as Abram, he is called "the father of many nations" (Gen 17:5) and the friend of God (2 Chr 20:7).

Accentual system—a complex system of marks added above and below the consonantal text of the Hebrew Bible to indicate how the text was canted in public recitation. The system is essentially a form of musical notation.

Aelfric—translated portions of both testaments from Latin into the dialect of Wessex (ca. 1000).

Akedah—the "binding" of Isaac (Gen 22:1-19); the mysterious story of the testing of Abraham who was commanded by God to offer his son Isaac as a burnt offering on Mount Moriah (later identified as the Temple Mount in Jerusalem).

Aldhelm—his translation of the Psalms was the first true formal translation of any portion of the Bible into Old English (ca. 700 CE).

Aldred—translated the Gospels into Northumbrian (ca. 950).

Aleppo Codex—the oldest copy of the Hebrew Bible (930 CE) in the tradition of the Ben Asher family of the masoretes at Tiberias.

Alexandrian text type—a type of text of the Greek NT current in Egypt as early as the second century CE.

American Standard Version (ASV)—the American version of the English Revised Bible (1901).

Amos—a Hebrew prophet of the 8th century BCE from Judah who ministered in the northern kingdom of Israel as well as in Judah before the fall of Samaria in 722/21 BCE. The book of Amos is the third book in the Book of the Twelve (minor prophets).

Anathoth—a town associated with the Levitical priests in ancient Israel, located about two miles NE of Jerusalem, and the birthplace of the prophet Jeremiah.

Apocalyptic—literature taking its name from the book of Revelation (Greek *apokalypsis*) that reports mysterious revelations mediated by angels.

Apocryphon—a religious writing of uncertain origin regarded by some as inspired, but rejected by most authorities.

Aquila's version—a slavishly literal translation of the Hebrew Bible into Greek which enjoyed popularity in Jewish circles (ca. 130-150 CE).

Armenian Bible—the translation of the Bible into the language of Armenia was done by the fifth century CE, though the details of this process are not clear.

Astarte—a Canaanite goddess who was the consort of Baal and a popular deity among the common people in ancient Israel.

Augustine—bishop of Hippo, one of the Latin fathers in the early Christian Church (354-430 CE).

Autographs—manuscripts in the handwriting of their author; the original text of the manuscripts of the books of the Bible as composed by the individual authors or their amanuenses (persons employed to write what another dictates).

Azazel—a demonic figure to whom the sin-laden scapegoat was sent on the Day of Atonement (see Lev 16:8-26).

Baal—the great storm and fertility god of the Canaanites who was a rival to the Israelite god Yahweh in the time of the prophet Elijah.

Barak—the military leader in the book of Judges who, together with the prophetess Deborah, fought against the Canaanite general Sisera (ca. 12th century BCE).

Bengel, Johann Albrecht—established the basic canon of modern textual criticism: the difficult reading is to be preferred to the easy.

Bethel—the religious center of the northern kingdom of Israel, and one of the two places in which King Jeroboam erected golden calves to replace the ark of the covenant as a primary religious symbol.

Beze, Theodore de (Beza)—John Calvin's successor in Geneva; popularized the textus receptus with some readings from newly discovered ancient manuscripts of the Greek New Testament.

Bishop's Bible—the authorized version of the English Bible (1568), which became the basis for the King James Version (1611).

Bohairic—the Coptic dialect of Lower Egypt (i.e., Memphis and Alexandria).

Caedmon—popularized the Bible in musical form in 7th century England (Northumbria).

Caesarean text type—a text type of Greek MSS of the NT which lies between the Alexandrian and Western with affinities to both. It was used by Origen in Caesarea.

Cairo Geniza—the storage place for sacred manuscripts and books which were worn out or otherwise no longer useable, found in a synagogue in Cairo in the latter part of the 19th century CE.

Canon—the official authoritative collection of sacred documents for a given religious body.

Canonical process—the historical process in which the individual books of the Bible took their present shape as an authoritative (i.e., canonical) text of sacred Scripture within the context of ancient Israel, early Judaism, and the early Christian Church.

Chiasm—the principle of arranging items in a four-part structure, with two pairs arranged so that one pair frames the other: i.e., in an a-b-b'-a' pattern.

Chironomy—the "sheet music" of antiquity; music was transmitted to individual performers by means of an elaborate system of hand signs—somewhat like "signing for the deaf" today.

Church Fathers—leaders of the early Christian Church fall into three groups: the Apostolic Fathers (70-150 CE); the Ante-Nicene Fathers (150-300 CE); and the Post-Nicene Fathers (300-430 CE).

Cipher—a coded message, writing done in a secret manner which conveys a message hidden from those who do not have the key to decode the mystery.

Codex (pl. codices)—a manuscript in the form of a leaf book rather than a scroll, with separate leaves sewn together. The idea apparently developed from parchment notebooks (*membranae*; cf. 2 Tim 4:13), an adaptation of the multileaved Greek and Roman tablets made of thin boards fastened together by a thong hinge. All extant MSS of the NT appear to be in this form.

Codex Alexandrinus—a well-preserved uncial text of the Septuagint and the Greek New Testament (mid-5th century CE) from Alexandria in Egypt.

Codex Sinaiticus—an important uncial text of parts of the Septuagint and the Greek New Testament (4th century CE), found by Tischendorf at the Monastery of St. Catherine in Sinai.

Codex Vaticanus—the oldest and one of the most important uncial texts of the Septuagint and the Greek New Testament (mid-4th century CE).

Confraternity Bible—a Roman Catholic revision of the Rheims-Douay-Challoner Bible (1967) sponsored by the Episcopal Committee of the Confraternity of Christian Doctrine.

Contemporary English Version (CEV)—a translation by the American Bible Society (1995), which attempts to put the Bible in language a child can readily understand.

Coptic versions—translation of the Bible into Coptic, the language which developed from ancient Egyptian in several dialectal forms.

Council of Nicea—the first major ecumenical council in the early Church which was convened in 325 CE to deal with the Arian heresy.

Council of Trent—an ecumenical council of the Roman Catholic Church which defined church doctrine and condemned the Reformation (1546-1563 CE).

Coverdale, Miles—Tyndale's assistant, produced the first complete English Bible in 1535.

Critical text—the text of the Bible as restored to the presumed original Hebrew, Aramaic, and Greek by biblical scholars using the principles of textual criticism.

Cyril—"Apostle of the Slavs" (827-869 CE), a Greek missionary to the Moravians and creator of the Cyrillic script.

Daniel—a prophet in ancient Israel who was exiled to Babylon, in the time of Jeremiah and Ezekiel, where he subsequently assumed a high position in the government of the Persian Empire (much like Joseph in Egypt). The book of Daniel, which belongs among the Writings, is the only example of fully developed apocalyptic writing in the First Testament.

David—the most powerful king of biblical Israel (ca. 1000 to 970 BCE) who established Jerusalem as the capital and is reputed to have written many of the psalms in the Psalter. He was the successor of King Saul and built an empire in which the people of Israel occupied the whole of the Promised Land for the first time.

Day of Yahweh—a central feature in the message of the Hebrew prophets, which originally referred to the time when Yahweh would vindicate his people Israel by defeating their enemies. It came to mean an eschatological day of judgment for Israel and foreign nations.

Dead Sea Scrolls—leather, papyrus, and copper scrolls dating from ca. 100 BCE to 135 CE containing complete and partial texts of most of the books of the Hebrew Bible, which were discovered at or near Qumran on the west side of the Dead Sea in 1947 and the years following.

Deborah—a woman prophet and a judge in ancient Israel who, together with Barak as military commander, defeated the Canaanite forces of Sisera in the 12th century BCE.

Diatessaron of Tatian—a harmony of the Gospels which was regarded as an authoritative gospel text by the early Syriac-speaking Church.

Edict of Milan—the emperor Constantine granted equal rights for all religions and the property confiscated from the Christians was restored in 313 CE at Milan.

Egbert—translated the Gospels into Old English (705 CE).

Eisodus—the epic journey of the people of Israel into the Promised Land under the leadership of Joshua.

Elders of Bathyra—predecessors of the Karaites from whom the masoretes received the accentual system of the Hebrew text of the First Testament.

Elijah—the historical Hebrew prophet of the 9th century BCE who plays a pivotal transitional role in the development of the prophetic tradition in ancient Israel.

English Revised Bible (ERB)—an authorized revision of the English Bible (1885) to which the Apocrypha was added in 1898.

Enoch—the grandson of Adam who lived 365 years, walked with God, and "God took him" (i.e., like the prophet Elijah later, he did not die).

Erasmus—a Dutch humanist, scholar, theologian, and writer (ca. 1466-1536), who published the first printed edition of the Greek New Testament (March 1516).

Eschaton—the final period of history or existence, the last days (from Greek *eschatos* = "last").

Estienne, Robert (Stephanus)—published the first edition of the Greek New Testament with a critical apparatus (1550), which became the basis for the textus receptus. He introduced the modern verse divisions in the text of the Bible.

Ethiopic—stands for "Classical Ethiopic" or "Ge'ez," the language of ancient Ethiopia.

Eusebius of Caesarea—a Christian theologian and historian (ca. 263-340 CE) who became the bishop of Caesarea (ca. 315-340).

Exodus—the epic journey of the people of Israel out of slavery in Egypt under the leadership of Moses.

Ezekiel—a Hebrew prophet who ministered in Babylon during the latter part of the 7th and the first half of the sixth centuries BCE, after being taken away from Jerusalem in exile in 597 BCE. The book of Ezekiel is one of the major prophets, along with Isaiah and Jeremiah.

Ezra and **Nehemiah**—the creators of the post-exilic Jewish community in Palestine. Ezra was a Jewish scribe commissioned by the Persian king to be the religious leader in Jerusalem. Nehemiah was appointed by the Persians to be governor. The two of them led the revival of Judaism in Palestine in the 4th century BCE. The books of Ezra and Nehemiah are among the Writings in the Hebrew Bible.

Festal Scrolls or *Megilloth*—the five books which are associated with the five major festivals in Jewish tradition: Song of Songs, Ruth, Lamentations, Ecclesiastes, and Esther.

First Temple—the temple in Jerusalem which was planned by David and built by his son Solomon (10th century BCE). It was destroyed by King Nebuchadnezzar of Babylon in 587 BCE.

First Testament = Old Testament

Gallican Psalter—Jerome's translation of the Psalter into Latin, which is actually a translation of the fifth column of Origen's *Hexapla* rather than the Hebrew text.

Gemara—the section of the Talmud consisting essentially of commentary on the Mishnah.

Geneva Bible—the 1560 revision of the entire English Bible which went through 140 editions by 1644, withstanding the challenge of the Bishop's Bible (1568) and the first generation of the authorized King James Version (1611).

Gideon—one of the judges of Israel who delivered the people from the Midianites in the 11th century BCE. He was the first person whom the people of Israel asked to rule over them as king.

Gothic version—a translation of the Bible into the language of the Goths, who originated in Scandinavia migrating South and East in two branches during the early Christian centuries to settle in the Balkans and the Ukraine.

Great Bible—a revision of Matthew's Bible in 1539 published with the approval of Cromwell and Cranmer, which received its name from its great size and format.

Gregory, Caspar Rene—his publication of Tischendorf's Greek New Testament (1894) provides the main source of textual materials on which scholars still depend.

Griesbach, Johann Jakob—classified the three groups of New Testament manuscripts as Alexandrian, Western, and Byzantine.

Habakkuk—a Hebrew prophet in Judah of the latter part of the 7th and the first decade of the 6th centuries BCE who sees God's ultimate intervention in behalf of his people Israel. The book of Habakkuk is the eighth book in the Book of the Twelve (minor prophets).

Hagiographa—the term is used here to refer to an early stage in the canonical process which produced the Writings: i.e., before the addition of Daniel, Ezra-Nehemiah, Chronicles, and Esther.

Hebrew Bible (**Leeser**)—the first Jewish translation of the Hebrew Bible for American Jewry, by Isaac Leeser (1853).

Hermeneutics—the theory of interpretation of texts, which begins with determination of the original meaning of a text (exegesis) and leads to elucidation of its sense for modern readers (exposition, paraphrase, or sermon).

Hexateuch—the first six books of the Bible: the Torah plus the book of Joshua.

Hezekiah—one of the good kings in ancient Israel who was responsible for a religious reform in the eighth century BCE, in the time of the prophet Isaiah.

Higher Criticism—the study of the Bible, having as its object the establishment of such facts as authorship and date of composition.

Holy Scriptures (**1917**)—an English translation of the Hebrew Bible published by the Jewish Publication Society, which parallels the American Standard Version.

Hosea—a Hebrew prophet of the 8th century BCE who ministered primarily in the northern kingdom of Israel before and after the fall of Samaria, the capital of Israel, to the Assyrians in 722/21 BCE. The book of Hosea is the first book in the Book of the Twelve (minor prophets).

Huldah—a woman prophet in Judah in the time of Josiah, who as leader of the "men of Anathoth," was installed as the official prophet of the royal court in Jerusalem during the late 7th century BCE.

Inerrancy—the teaching within Jewish, Christian (and Muslim) tradition that the Bible (and the Koran) is free from error, which is a logical consequence of the belief that the Bible (and the Koran) is the "Word of God."

Inscriptions—information which is cut, impressed, painted, or written on stone, brick, metal, or other hard surfaces.

International Children's Bible (**ICB**)—a translation by the World Bible Translation Center (1986), which claims to be "the first translation of the Holy Scriptures prepared specifically for children."

Isaac—the second of the three major patriarchs in the book of Genesis, the son of Abraham.

Isaiah—a prophet in Jerusalem in the time of King Hezekiah (late 8th century BCE). The book of Isaiah is one of the three major prophets (along with Jeremiah and Ezekiel).

Jacob—the third of the three major patriarchs in the book of Genesis, the son of Isaac, whose name was changed to Israel.

Jephthah—another judge in ancient Israel who delivered Israel from the Ammonites in Transjordan. He is best known for the sacrifice of his daughter to fulfill a rash vow he made to Yahweh, the God of the Israelites, during a battle.

Jeremiah—a Hebrew prophet who ministered in Judah during the latter part of the 7th and the early 6th centuries BCE, primarily in Jerusalem. He died as an exile in Egypt after the fall of Jerusalem in 587 BCE. The book of Jeremiah is one of the major prophets, along with Isaiah and Ezekiel.

Jeroboam—the successor to Solomon and the first king of the northern state of Israel (as opposed to Judah), after the division of Israel into two separate political entities (late 10th century BCE).

Jerome—Christian ascetic and biblical scholar (ca. 340-420 CE) responsible for the Latin translation of the Bible (Latin Vulgate) under the auspices of Pope Damasus. His translation became the official Bible of the Roman Catholic Church.

Jerusalem Bible (JB)—an English translation (1966) adapted from the French translation (1961) by Dominican priests in Jerusalem working from the original Greek and Hebrew texts.

Jezebel—a wicked queen who was the wife of King Ahab in ancient Israel, and the adversary of the prophet Elijah.

Job—the book of Job is an example of wisdom literature in the Hebrew Bible, which is part of the Writings. Job is a foreigner in the time of Abraham who is an example of undeserved suffering.

John the Baptist—the forerunner and baptiser of Jesus (see Matt 3).

Jonah—a prophet in Israel (8th century BCE), who is best known as the one who was swallowed by a great fish and survived three days in its belly and subsequently preached in the city of Nineveh. The story appears in the book of Jonah, which is the fifth book in the Book of the Twelve (minor prophets).

Joseph—one of the twelve sons of Jacob/Israel, who was sold into slavery in Egypt and rose to high position in that country through his ability to interpret dreams (see Gen 37:1 - 47:27).

Josephus—the Jewish politician, military general, and historian who lived in the first century CE and was responsible for writings which constitute important sources of information for our understanding of biblical history and of the political history of Roman Palestine.

Joshua—the historical successor of Moses as leader of the people of ancient Israel, who led them into the Promised Land in what is often called the Conquest.

Josiah—the king of Judah in the time of the prophet Jeremiah (late 7th century BCE), who was responsible for a great religious reformation which resulted in significant canonical activity centered in the book of Deuteronomy.

***Kaige* recension**—a revision of the Greek translation of the Hebrew Bible which predates that of Aquila and Theodotion, which is labeled *Kaige* because it translates Hebrew *gam* ("also") by Greek *kaige.*

Karaite—a Jewish sect in Persia founded in the 8th century CE by Anan ben David which rejected the Talmud and the teachings of the rabbis in favor of strict adherence to the Hebrew Bible as the single authoritative source of Jewish law and practice.

King James Version—the revision of the English Bible done under the auspices of King James I (1611) which replaced the Bishop's Bible in official circles and eventually displaced the Geneva Bible in popular usage.

Kodaly Method—a method of music instruction developed by Zoltán Kodály, a noted Hungarian composer and educator, which emerged about 1940 and is now established internationally. The method uses a system of hand signs to instruct children with remarkable results.

Koran—the sacred text of Islam, believed to have been dictated to Muhammad by the angel Gabriel and regarded by Muslims as the foundation of law, religion, culture, and politics.

Lachmann, Karl—published the first eclectic text of the Greek New Testament based on the evaluation of variant readings.

Lady Wisdom—the personification of Wisdom, which is unique in the Bible. She is present with God before creation and is often described as a divine attribute, a communication of God.

Latin Vulgate—the translation of the Bible into Latin by Jerome, which became the authorized version in liturgical services of the Roman Catholic Church until modern times.

Law ... prophets—Jesus appears to be referring to the first two major parts of the canon of the First Testament: the law is the **Torah** and the prophets is what we have designated the **Former Prophets** plus the **Latter Prophets**.

Leningrad Codex—the oldest complete copy of the Hebrew Bible (1008 CE), in the tradition of the Ben Asher family of the Masoretes at Tiberias.

Living Bible (**LB**)—Kenneth Taylor's translation of the Bible (1971) in simple, everyday English.

Logos—the Greek term for "word" which became a philosophical concept for the rational principle that governs and develops the universe. The Gospel of John presents Jesus as the **logos**.

Lucianic recension— Lucian (ca. 240-312 CE), a theologian and biblical scholar in Syria, revised the Greek text of the Hebrew Bible.

Manual of Discipline—one of the manuscripts in the Dead Sea Scrolls found at Qumran which contains the rules of the monastic community which lived there.

Masoretes—a family of Jewish scholars living in Tiberias on the Sea of Galilee who were responsible for providing the already standardized text of the Hebrew Bible with vowel signs and an elaborate accentual system between the seventh and tenth centuries CE known as the Masoretic Text.

Masoretic Text—the name of the traditional Hebrew text of the Old Testament which appears to have been standardized in the first century CE. Between the 7th and the 10th centuries CE, this text was provided with vowel signs, accents, punctuation marks as well as divided into sections. The Jewish scholars who did this work were called **Masoretes**. Hence the traditional Hebrew text with its vocalization is known as the Masoretic text (abbreviated MT).

Matthew, Thomas (Matthew's Bible)—pen name of John Rogers, who published the second licensed English Bible in circulation within a year of Tyndale's execution.

Megilloth (see Festal Scrolls)

Messiah—"anointed one," in the political sphere the word refers to the kings who would continue the Davidic dynasty in Israel; in Christian usage it became a title that refers only to Jesus (Messiah = Christ).

Micah—a Hebrew prophet of the 8th century BCE who ministered primarily in the southern kingdom of Judah before and after the fall of Samaria in 722/21 BCE. The book of Micah is the sixth book in the Book of the Twelve (minor prophets).

Midrash—an early Jewish interpretation of or commentary on a biblical text, which is sometimes creative in nature in the form of a story.

Minuscules—manuscripts written in a script of smaller letters than the uncials in a cursive hand, dating from about the ninth century on.

Mishnah—the section of the Talmud which consists of the collection of oral laws edited ca. 200 CE by Rabbi Judah ha-Nasi.

Modern Language Bible (MLB)—a translation under the direction of Garrit Verkuyl (1971), which was commonly known as the Berkeley Version (1945, 1959).

Moses—the historical founder of ancient Israel who led the people out of slavery in Egypt, in what is often called the Exodus, and was their leader and lawgiver during their years of wandering in the wilderness.

Mount Horeb—another name for Mount Sinai.

Mount Nebo—a mountain peak in the ridge of Pisgah in Jordan (ancient Moab), from which Moses saw the Promised Land before he died and was buried in that same place.

Mount of Transfiguration—the mountain where Jesus was transformed in the presence of certain of his disciples, and appeared with Moses and Elijah. Peter offered to build there three booths, one each for Jesus, Moses and Elijah.

Mount Sinai—the mountain in southern Palestine where Moses received the Ten Commandments and organized the people of Israel in the story of the Exodus.

Mount Zion—refers to three different aspects of the city of Jerusalem: the ancient "city of David"; the Temple Mount complex immediately to the north (where the Dome of the Rock is located); and the hill immediately south of the southwestern corner of the present "old city." Used metaphorically, the term designates the place of God's dwelling (i.e., the "heavenly Jerusalem").

Nahum—a Hebrew prophet in Judah of the 7th century BCE who announced the fall of Nineveh, the capital of the Assyrian Empire, which took place in 612 BCE. The book of Nahum is the seventh book in the Book of the Twelve (minor prophets).

Nathan—a prophet in Judah in the time of King David (ca. 1000 BCE).

Nehemiah (see Ezra)

Nestle-Aland—a critical-eclectic Greek text of the First Testament originally published in 1898 by Eberhard Nestle, which has been continually revised with Kurt Aland as the current editor. In wording it is identical with the 3rd edition of the United Bible Societies text but differs in paragraphing, orthography, and punctuation.

New American Bible (NAB)—a Roman Catholic translation of the Bible directly from the Hebrew and Greek texts (1970) done by members of the Catholic Biblical Association of America.

New American Standard Bible (NASB)—a revision of the American Standard Version (1970), under the auspices of the Lockman Foundation.

New English Bible (NEB)—a translation of the Bible from the original languages (1970), by the Church of Scotland, which was intended to replace the King James Bible in official usage.

New International Version (NIV)—a translation of the Bible by the New York Bible Society (1978), which was done by a group of evangelical scholars and endorsed by many Protestant denominations in 1966.

New Jerusalem Bible (NJB)—a revision of the Jerusalem Bible (1985).

New Revised Standard Version (NRSV)—a revision of the Revised Standard Version (1989).

Noah—the ninth descendant from Adam, whose birth is the first recorded after Adam's death. Noah and his family are the sole human survivors of the Flood, which God used to punish human sin (Gen 6-9).

Normative—of or pertaining to a standard; the authoritative basis for behavior and beliefs.

Normative hermeneutic—the principle of interpretation of sacred texts within a given community which is authoritative, or binding, on members of that community.

Old Latin translation of the Bible—translation of the Bible from Greek into Latin in the first and second centuries CE, in various textual traditions, before the time of Jerome's Latin Vulgate.

Origen—a Christian theologian, teacher, and biblical scholar in Alexandria (ca. 185-254 CE).

Origen's Hexapla—a systematic comparison of the Greek Septuagint with the Hebrew text in six parallel columns, which includes the versions of Aquila, Symmachus, and Theodotion.

Orm—an Augustinian monk (ca. 1200) who wrote a poetic paraphrase of the Gospels and Acts in Teutonic.

Ostraca—broken pieces of pottery on which written messages were inscribed.

Papyri—the oldest existing witnesses for the text of the Second Testament are written on papyrus, a form of paper manufactured from the stalks of the papyrus plant grown in Egypt.

Passover—the annual spring festival in ancient Israel and Judaism which celebrates the story of the Exodus in which the angel of death "passed over" the people of Israel and did not kill the first-born sons as he did with the Egyptians. The festival includes the "passing over" of the waters of the Red Sea when they left Egypt, which in turn is associated with the "passing over" of the River Jordan under Joshua when the people of Israel entered the Promised Land in the Eisodus.

Peshitta—the standard Syriac version of the Bible, which was completed by the 3rd century CE.

Pharisees—a sect of especially observant and influential Jews in Palestine from the second century BCE to the first century CE who differ from the Sadducees in their strict observance of religious ritual, liberal interpretation of the Bible, adherence to oral laws and traditions, and belief in an afterlife and the coming of a Messiah.

Polyglot texts—multi-lingual printed editions of the Bible which contain the same text in several languages.

Primary History—the Torah plus the Former Prophets: i.e., the section of the Hebrew Bible which extends from Genesis through 2 Kings in the masoretic tradition.

Prophets—by **Prophets** we mean the second major section in the canon of the Hebrew Bible, which is made up of the **Former Prophets** (historical books of Joshua, Judges, Samuel, and Kings) and the **Latter Prophets** (the classical prophets: Isaiah, Jeremiah, Ezekiel, and the Book of the Twelve [minor prophets]).

Proto-Lucianic recension—a revision by unknown scholars, used by Lucian (ca. 240-312 CE), a theologian and biblical scholar in Syria, as the basis for his revision of the Greek text of the Hebrew Bible.

Psalter—the book of Psalms in the Hebrew Bible, which is part of the Writings and the longest book in the Hebrew Bible (with 150 individual psalms).

Purvey, Johny—revised Wycliffe's Bible by replacing many Latinized constructions with native English idiom and removing the preface by Jerome.

Redaction—a technical term which refers to the editorial process that produced documents which evolved over extensive periods of time in antiquity.

Revised English Bible (REB)—a revision of the New English Bible (1989) by the Churches of England.

Revised Standard Version (RSV)—a revision of the American Standard Version (1957), which subsequently became the first truly Common Bible when it was officially sanctioned by the Roman Catholic Church (1973) and the Orthodox Churches (1977).

Rheims New Testament—a Roman Catholic translation of the Second Testament into English from the Latin Vulgate (1582).

Rheims-Douay Bible—a Roman Catholic English Bible translated from the Latin Vulgate (1635).

Rheims-Douay-Challoner Bible—the second revised edition of the Roman Catholic Rheims-Douay Bible (1749-50) published by Richard Challoner.

Sadducees—a sect of Jews in Palestine from the second century BCE to the first century CE, consisting mainly of priests and aristocrats, who differ from the Pharisees chiefly in their literal interpretation of the Bible, rejection of oral laws and traditions, and denial of an afterlife and the coming of the Messiah.

Sahidic—the Coptic dialect of southern Egypt (i.e., Thebes).

Samaritan Pentateuch—the Samaritan version of the first five books of the Hebrew Bible, which constitute the entire canon for that community. It is written in archaic Hebrew script.

Saul—the first king in ancient Israel (11th century BCE) who fought against the Philistines.

Second Temple—the temple in Jerusalem, built in the time of the prophets Haggai and Zechariah and dedicated in 515 BCE, to replace the earlier Temple of Solomon which was destroyed by the Babylonian ruler Nebuchadnezzar in 587 BCE.

Second Testament = New Testament

Semler, Johann Salomo—introduced the term "recension" to describe groups of New Testament textual traditions.

Septuagint—the Greek translation of the Hebrew Bible, which is the oldest and most important of the ancient versions. According to tradition, it was done by 70 (*septuaginta* in Latin) or 72 Jewish scholars at the request of Ptolemy II in Alexandria (3rd century BCE) in 72 days [hence the abbreviation LXX = 70]. Originally the name applied to the Pentateuch only, to meet the needs of Greek-speaking Jews in Egypt. By the 2nd century CE, the name was used for the whole Greek Old Testament which was completed about the 2nd century BCE.

Shavuoth ("Weeks")—The second of three pilgrimage feasts in Judaism , coming fifty days after Passover, called The Feast of the First Fruits of Wheat Harvest; associated with the giving of the Torah to Moses.

Sixtene edition—an edition of the Latin Vulgate published by Pope Sixtus V in 1590 CE.

Sixto-Clementine edition—an edition of the Latin Vulgate published by Pope Clementine VIII in 1604 CE.

Succoth ("Booths")—the third major pilgrimage festival of Judaism. It is held in the fall and celebrates the the dedication of Solomon's Temple (1 Kings 8), the public reading of the Torah (every seven years, Deut 31:10-11), and the future ingathering of all nations to Jerusalem to worship God (Zech 14:16).

Swanson, Reuben J.—his "Variant Readings Arranged in Horizontal Line Against Codex Vaticanus" provides the student with access to the full textual evidence at a glance.

Symmachus's version—a translation of the Hebrew Bible into much more elegant Greek than either Aquila or Theodotion.

Synoptic Gospels—the Gospels of Matthew, Mark, and Luke in the Second Testament which reflect a similar perspective, a common view, in contrast to the Gospel of John.

Syro-Hexaplar—a 7th century Syriac translation of Origen's revision of the Septuagint.

Talmud—the collection of Jewish law and tradition consisting of the Mishnah and the Gemara, which was produced in two separate editions: the Palestinian (ca. 400 CE) and the larger and more important Babylonian (ca. 500 CE).

Tanakh—the Hebrew Bible, the First Testament, which is made up of the Torah plus the Prophets (Former & Latter) plus the Writings

Tanakh: The Holy Scriptures (1985)—an English translation of the Hebrew Bible by the Jewish Publication Society, sparked by the Revised Standard Version and the New English Bible.

Targums—name given to the Aramaic translations of the Hebrew Bible.

Textus receptus—"received text," a late and corrupt form of the Byzantine text type of the NT which dominated in the Western world for about three hundred years.

Theodotion's version—a somewhat less literal translation of the Hebrew Bible into Greek than that of Aquila, which was done during the reign of Marcus Aurelius (161-180 CE).

Tischendorf—discovered and published important manuscripts from St. Catherine's monastery in Sinai.

Today's English Version (TEV)—a translation by the American Bible Society (1966), which attempts to render the Bible in vernacular English.

Torah—by **Torah** we mean the first five books of the Bible, which are also known as the five books of the **Law** (i.e., the **Pentateuch**)—the five books of Moses: Genesis, Exodus, Leviticus, Numbers, and Deuteronomy.

Tyndale, William—translated the Bible into English against severe opposition which cost him his life; he was executed for heresy on October 6, 1536.

Ulfilas—"Apostle of the Goths" (311-381 CE), who translated the Bible into Gothic.

Uncial codices—codices written in a formal style of handwritten letters adapted from the Greek capitals used in inscriptions, but more rounded rather than straight and angular.

Variorum Bible—the first official revision of the New Testament of the Authorized King James Bible (1880), which prepared the way for the English Revised Bible.

Vowel points—a system of marks added to the consonantal text of the Hebrew Bible by medieval scribes known as the masoretes to indicate the vowel sounds.

Vulgate—the Latin translation of the Bible produced chiefly by St. Jerome at the end of the 4th century CE, in which the First Testament was translated directly from the original Hebrew texts as used in Palestine at that time. It became the canonical text of the Roman Catholic Church until the twentieth century.

War Scroll—also known as the *War of the Sons of Light Against the Sons of Darkness*, this scroll is an eschatological composition which concerns the final battle between Israel and the nations.

Westcott and Hort—their "genealogical theory" divided the manuscript evidence for the Greek New Testament into four types: Syrian, Western, Neutral, and Alexandrian.

Wettstein, Johann Jakob—published the first critical apparatus which identified the uncials by capital Roman letters and the miniscules by Arabic numerals.

Whittingham, William—introduced the division of the biblical text of the English New Testament into modern verses (1557), following the example of the Greek New Testament of Stephanus (1551).

Word of God—by the **Word of God** we mean what the scholars call "**revelation**"—what God chooses to disclose about Himself.

Writings—the final section of the canon of sacred Scripture in Jewish tradition, which consists of Psalms, Proverbs, Job, the five **Festal Scrolls,** Daniel, Ezra-Nehemiah, and Chronicles.

Wycliffe, John—translated the entire Bible into English for his itinerant preachers ("Lollards") from the Latin Vulgate (1380-1388 CE).

Yahweh—the personal name of God in ancient Israel; sometimes called the "tetragrammaton" (four letters, written in capitals as YHWH). The name was not pronounced.

Yom Kippur—the "Day of Atonement," a day of fasting, self-denial, and rest on which the sanctuary is cleansed of all impurities and the sins of the people are sent away on the scapegoat.

Zadok(ite)—Zadok was the other high priest whom David established in Jerusalem, and the single holder of that position after Abiathar was exiled by Solomon. His descendants, the Zadokites, continued as the established priesthood in Jerusalem until the time of Antiochus Epiphanes (mid-2nd century BCE).

Index
(computer generated)

Other Titles Available from BIBAL Press

Balla	*The Four Centuries Between the Testaments*	$7.95
Braulik	*The Theology of Deuteronomy*	18.95
Christensen	*Prophecy and War in Ancient Israel*	14.95
Christensen	*Experiencing the Exodus from Egypt*	7.95
Clements	*Wisdom for a Changing World*	7.95
Elliott	*Seven-Color Greek Verb Chart*	3.50
Gunkel	*The Stories of Genesis*	15.95
Hargrove	*Seeds of Reconciliation*	15.95
Haïk-Vantoura	*The Music of the Bible Revealed*	29.95
Hostetter	*Nations Mightier and More Numerous*	12.95
Lohfink	*The Inerrancy of Scripture and Other Essays*	13.95
Mynatt	*The Sub Loco Notes in the Torah of BHS*	18.95
Organ	*Judaism for Gentiles*	14.95
Reid	*Enoch and Daniel*	12.95
Schneck	*Isaiah in the Gospel of Mark, I-VIII*	19.95
Scott	*A Simplified Guide to BHS*	7.95
Scott	*Guia para el Uso de la BHS*	6.95
Sinclair	*Jesus Christ According to Paul*	12.95
Sinclair	*Revelation: A Book for the Rest of Us*	12.95
Sinclair	*The Road and the Truth: The Editing of John's Gospel*	12.95
St. Clair	*Prayers for People Like Me*	6.95
St. Clair	*Co-Discovery: The Theory and Practice of Experiential Theology*	12.95
Wallis	*Mark's Memory of the Future*	14.95
Wiens	*Stephen's Sermon & the Structure of Luke-Acts*	14.95

Prices subject to change

Postage & Handling: (for USA addresses)
$2.00 for first copy
plus 50¢ for each additional copy

Texas residents add 8.25% sales tax

Write for a free catalog:
BIBAL Press
P.O. Box 821653
N. Richland Hills, TX 76182